Residential Design Using AutoCAD 2014

Daniel John Stine

ISBN: 978-1-58503-793-3

Publications

Schroff Development Corporation

www.SDCpublications.com

Schroff Development Corporation
P.O. Box 1334
Mission, KS 66222
(913) 262-2664
www.SDCpublications.com

Publisher: Stephen Schroff

AutoCAD is a registered trademark of Autodesk, Inc.

Autodesk screen shots reprinted with the permission of Autodesk, Inc.

All other trademarks are trademarks of their respective holders.

Examination Copies:

Books received as examination copies are for review purposes only and may not be made available for student use. Resale of examination copies is prohibited.

Electronic Files:

Any electronic files associated with this book are licensed to the original user only. These files may not be transferred to any other party.

Foreword

To The Student:

The intent of this book is to provide the student with a well-rounded knowledge of Computer Aided Drafting (CAD) tools and techniques for use in both school and industry.

It is strongly recommended that this book is completed in lesson order. Many (pretty much all) exercises utilize drawings created in previous lessons.

This textbook starts with a basic introduction to AutoCAD 2014 and then begins a house floor plan. Using step-by-step tutorial lessons, the residential project is followed through to create elevations, sections, details, etc. Throughout the project, new AutoCAD commands are covered at the appropriate time. Focus is placed on the most essential parts of a command rather than an exhaustive review of every sub-feature of a particular command. Many instructors and students have expressed their satisfaction with the "project" approach and the feeling of actually accomplishing something at the conclusion of this textbook.

Look for the videos on the DVD with compliment the material covered in this book.

To the Instructor:

An Instructor's resource guide is available for this book. It contains:

- Answers to the questions at the end of each chapter
- Outline of tools & topics to be covered in each lessons lecture
- Suggestions for additional student work (for each lesson)

Errata:

Please check the publisher's website from time to time for any errors or typo's found in this book after it went to the printer. Simply browse to www.SDCpublications.com, and then navigate to the page for this book. Click the **View/Submit errata** link in the upper right corner of the page. If you find an error, please submit it so we can correct it in the next edition.

About the Author:

Dan Stine is a registered Architect with twenty years of experience in the architectural field. He currently works at LHB (a 200 person multidiscipline firm; www.LHBcorp.com) in Duluth Minnesota as the BIM Administrator, providing training, customization and support for two regional offices. Dan has worked in a total of four firms. While at these firms, he has participated in collaborative projects with several other firms on various projects (including Cesar Pelli, Weber Music Hall – University of Minnesota - Duluth). Dan is a member of the *Construction Specification Institute* (CSI) and the *Autodesk Developer Network* (ADN) and also teaches *AutoCAD* and *Revit Architecture* classes at Lake Superior College, for the Architectural Technology program; additionally, he is a Certified Construction Document Technician (CDT). He has presented at *Autodesk University* in Las

Vegas (http://au.autodesk.com) and the *Revit Technology Conference* in California and Georgia (http://www.revitconference.com). Mr. Stine has written the following textbooks (published by SDC Publications):

- *Residential Design Using Revit Architecture 2014*
- *Commercial Design Using Revit Architecture 2014*
- *Design Integration Using Revit 2014 (Architecture, Structure and MEP)*
- *Interior Design Using Revit Architecture 2014 (with co-author Aaron Hansen)*
- *Residential Design Using AutoCAD 2014*
- *Chapters in Architectural Drawing (with co-author Steven H. McNeill, AIA, LEED AP)*
- *Interior Design Using Hand Sketching, SketchUp and Photoshop (also with Steven H. McNeill)*
- *Google SketchUp 8 for Interior Designers; Just the Basics*

You may contact the publisher with comments or suggestions at **schroff@schroff.com**

Thanks:

I could not have written this book without support from my family; Cheri, Kayla & Carter.

Many thanks go out to Stephen Schroff and Schroff Development Corporation for making this book possible!

Table of Contents

DVD Content

Videos

Floor plan created in Chapter 4, utilizing blocks, hatching, layers, dimensions and text.

Exterior Elevation created in Chapter 5, utilizing blocks, hatching, lineweights and line types.

Introduction
Sketching Exercises::

This introduction chapter is meant to compliment the lessons learned in this book. Several hand sketching concepts and exercises are provided to help the student learn to make the most out of both digital and "analog" design techniques.

Introduction I-1:
Introduction

Hand Sketching in a Digital World

Even with the modern power of the computer and design software (which is also covered in this textbook), the designer must have the ability to sketch by hand and think three-dimensionally.

The very first thoughts of a designer, when working on a new project, involve quickly sketching those thoughts onto paper. The process involves several iterations and overlays before the first line is drawn on a computer. These sketches usually take just a few minutes each and are not typically to scale but are proportionally accurate (something that a good designer has learned to do with practice).

Hand sketching is also useful at client meetings and out in the field (where the computer is not always handy or convenient). The architect can sketch possible revisions directly on a set of blueprints (which were printed from computer generated drawings). This represents the best use of time, as all the decision makers are present (who would not want to wait for the computer to load, the project file to load, and the designer to meticulously go through all the steps required by the software to explore various solutions to the problem at hand). Once the meeting is over, the revision sketch can be brought back to the office where the drawings can be updated.

Therefore, the next several pages serve as a primer for the development of your fundamental CAD skills you will learn in this textbook. You are encouraged to work through this introductory chapter and this author believes it will indirectly aid in your thought process as it relates to learning CADD. Of course, if you have previously studied this type of material you may simply skip ahead to Chapter 1. (Hey, this is not a pass if your instructor assigned it!)

Some additional "bonus" material on Engineering Graphics has been provided in an appendix chapter at the end of this text. Make sure you take a look at the DVD for a draft version of a Roof Study Workbook provided for your use in conjunction with this textbook.

Lineweights

In this introductory section you will spend some time sketching various building forms. This will give you practice drawing various lines (i.e., weights and styles). The lines drawn will help convey the depth of the image (which is important in both hand and computer drawings; here are a few concepts to keep in mind:

- The perimeter of major building masses should have a heavy line to make it punch out from the surrounding image.
- When buildings have multiple "major elements" the lineweights should vary. Two building dormers at the same elevation should be the same lineweight, but the lines should get lighter as they step back (i.e., away from the viewer).
- The next heaviest lines should be between materials (e.g., lap siding to brick) and around elements like windows and doors. These lines will also get lighter as they step back into the image.
- The lightest lines will be the ones which represent the various building materials (e.g., shingles, siding, brick, etc.).

ROOF PLAN
VIEW

Lines get lighter as the building steps back

Lightest linework
(material patterns)

Medium linework
(around windows & doors)

Darkest linework
(closest to viewer)

EXTERIOR
ELEVATION

Tools Used for the Task…
The lineweights discussed in the sketch above are achieved by using various types of pencils. In general, the softer pencils draw heavier lines and the harder ones create lighter lines. Here is a brief description of the most common pencils and tools used for this type of free hand sketching.

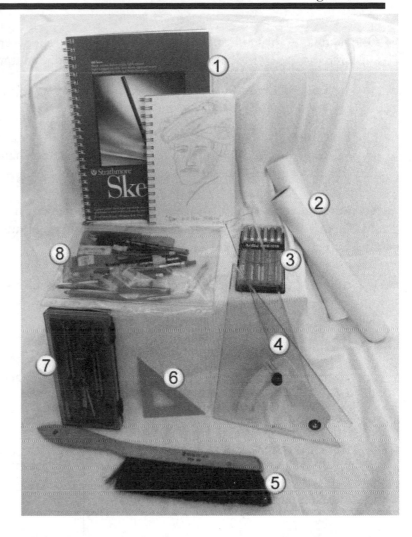

This photo shows several tools which aid in the creation of hand sketches, not everything is needed to get started but the cost is relatively cheap so it is not that difficult to obtain these items. Below is a list of the items pictured (no specific brand will be suggested):

1. *Sketch books*: come in several sizes; small ones are great for carrying around.
2. *Tracing paper (bumwad)*: lightweight and highly transparent; allows for quick overlay sketching.
3. *Ink pen set*: for crisp "final" linework.
4. *Clear plastic straight edge and adjustable triangle*: nice for setting up a few construction lines.
5. *Dusting brush*: to sweep away the eraser crumbs.
6. *Triangle*
7. *Drawing set*: for creating circles and dividing needs.
8. *Pencil sack*: see below.

The image to the left shows the basic tools required to create a decent architectural freehand sketch. Just about everything shown can be purchased in a "starter kit" at any art supply store or website. The items shown to the left (from left to right) are: Eraser, Sharpener, Blending Sticks, Tip Pointer, Mechanical Pencil, (2) Charcoal Pencils; Soft and Medium, (4) Graphite Pencils; HB, 2B, 4B, and 6B, and a Graphite Stick.

One technique this author uses to quickly distinguish between the pencils (which are lying in a cluster and are all the same color) is to add colored tape to the end of the pencils.

> *TIP: Make sure you sharpen the end opposite the hardness markings so you can tell the pencils apart after they have been sharpened a few times.*

The **blending sticks** are used to basically smudge the graphite on the paper into a solid gray/black area. This is useful when creating shades and shadows as well as transitions on curved surfaces, to name a few uses.

The **tip pointer** is basically several pieces of sandpaper on a stick. This is a convenient surface on which to rub your pencil tip back and forth to quickly sharpen the tip or create a chisel type tip for special effects.

The **mechanical pencil** can accept "lead" inserts of various types. However, it is ideal to have one mechanical pencil for each "lead" type you use. This system allows you to use more of the "lead" because the mechanical pencil can hold smaller pieces, whereas a wooden pencil becomes hard to use when it gets too small.

The **charcoal pencils** are useful for making very heavy black lines on the paper. Charcoal is very soft so the tips need to be sharpened often.

The **ink pens** are great for crisp consistent lines. However, the result is more permanent than pencil, but when using special paper (like Mylar) and special erasers, you can erase them.

The **graphite pencils** are the primary tool for architectural freehand sketching. You will typically start with the harder pencils (HB and 2B) and then embellished with the softer, darker pencils (4B and 6B).

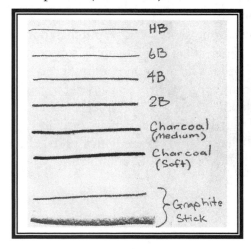

Sketch Book

The ability to sketch is one that is developed over time and with lots of practice. One way to practice is by using a sketch book. Sketch books can be purchased at any art supply store or website. They come in many shapes and sizes (make sure the paper is acid free so your sketches will last for many years). With a sketch book and a small sack of pencils, you can practice just about anywhere. Just sitting in the waiting room at the doctor's office, you can practice sketching the space, working on perspective, lineweight and detail. Your sketches do not (and should not) always be about architecture. You can practice on anything and everything. One of the examples below is a quick drawing of a BMX bike in action!

SKETCH BOOK (PENCIL)

SKETCH WITH BLENDING

CHARCOAL SKETCH

Do You Have the Time?

One of the largest obstacles to becoming a talented artist is time. Like anything in life, you have to spend a certain amount of time honing your skills, be it a sport, an instrument, or in this case, sketching. Try and spend a few minutes each day sketching something/anything. Pay attention to textures, shades and shadows and perspective. With less time than you think you will get it.

Work or Play?

Everyone should enjoy what they do for a living. Try not to approach sketching from the perspective that you have to do this to get a grade or make lots of money at work. When you focus on doing something with a 110% attitude the grade and money will likely follow. With this attitude you are more likely to retain what you are studying and be prepared to apply when needed… **so havefun**! You may, in the end, discover sketching is not for you; not all designers are great sketching artists.

Introduction I-2:
Freehand Sketching from Photos

The Grid System

The art of freehand sketching buildings is something that comes with practice. You are not expected to produce great works of art in this exercise. Rather, you should be focusing on lineweights and roof styles and forms. Therefore, to aid in sketching the buildings in this exercise, a grid system has been superimposed over each image. Directly below each image is a blank grid that is the exact same size as the image above. The student should use the blank grid as reference lines and points relative to the grid over the image above. This will aid in drawing the correct perspective and proportions for each image (again, allowing more emphasis to be placed on lineweights and observation of roof styles).

This type of exercise is meant for beginners – sketching, as stated above, to get you thinking about how lines move around relative to each other on the page. You should quickly move away from this type of sketching as it would be a crutch to reaching your full potential, and will likely create rigid, uninteresting drawings. Regardless, this is a great place to start…

Here is a sample of what you should expect to complete at a minimum. Notice the heavy points that have been added to highlight the concept of using the grid as an aid (you do not have to actually add the points in your sketches). If you have time, try sketching in some of the site context with a light pencil.

If you have a sketch book you should try sketching a few real-world buildings; the eye/hand coordination is pretty much the same as looking up at a photo on paper! Don't forget to have fun and give yourself some quality time to do a good job!

Notes:

Freehand Sketching from Photos - 1

Sketch the major forms of the building, plus the doors and windows. If you have time you can add additional detail like siding, roofing and site context.

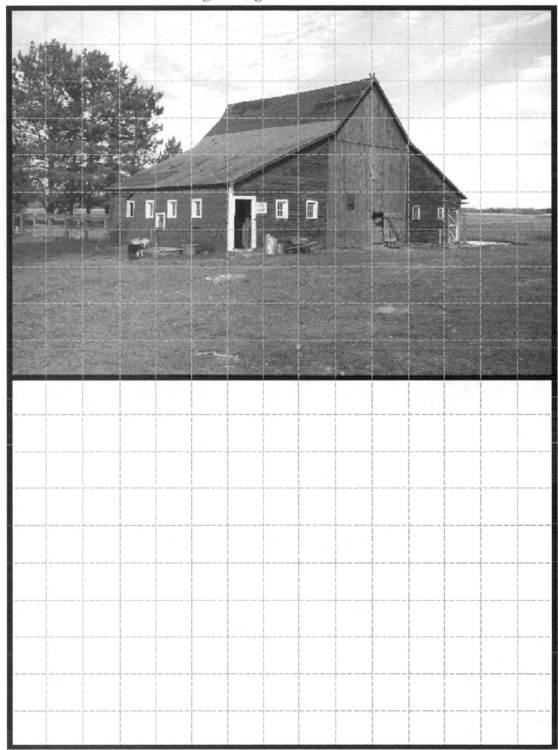

Name: _____   Date: _____

Notes:

Freehand Sketching from Photos - 2

Sketch the major forms of the building, plus the doors and windows. If you have time you can add additional detail like siding, roofing and site context.

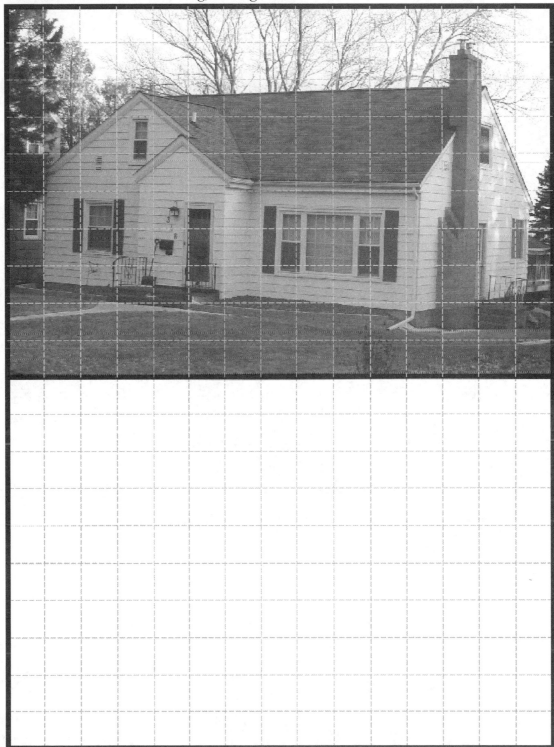

Name: _____   Date: _____

Notes:

Freehand Sketching from Photos - 3

Sketch the major forms of the building, plus the doors and windows. If you have time you can add additional detail like siding, roofing and site context.

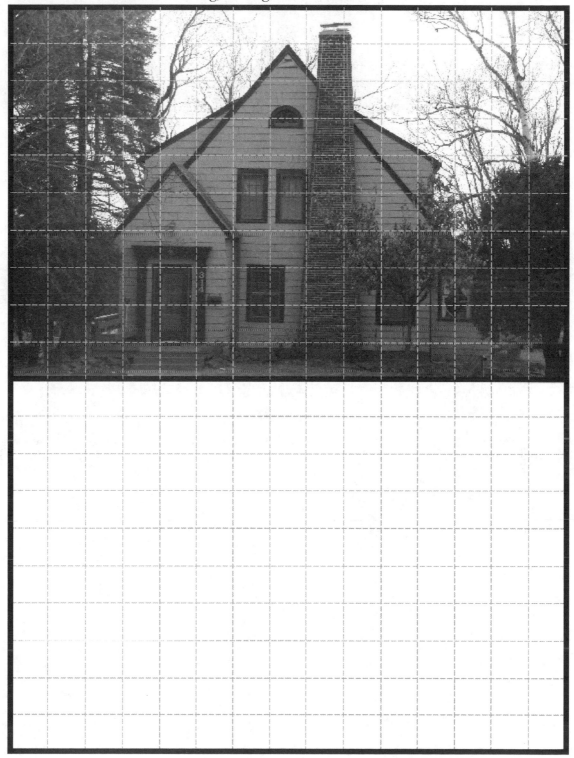

Name: _____   Date: _____

Notes:

Freehand Sketching from Photos - 4

Sketch the major forms of the building, plus the doors and windows. If you have time you can add additional detail like siding, roofing and site context.

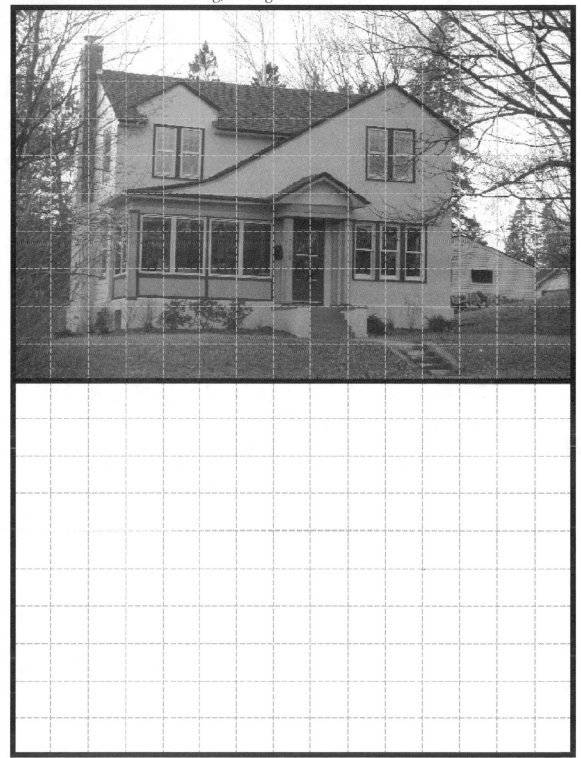

Name: _____   Date: _____

Notes:

Freehand Sketching from Photos - 5

Sketch the major forms of the building, plus the doors and windows. If you have time you can add additional detail like siding, roofing and site context.

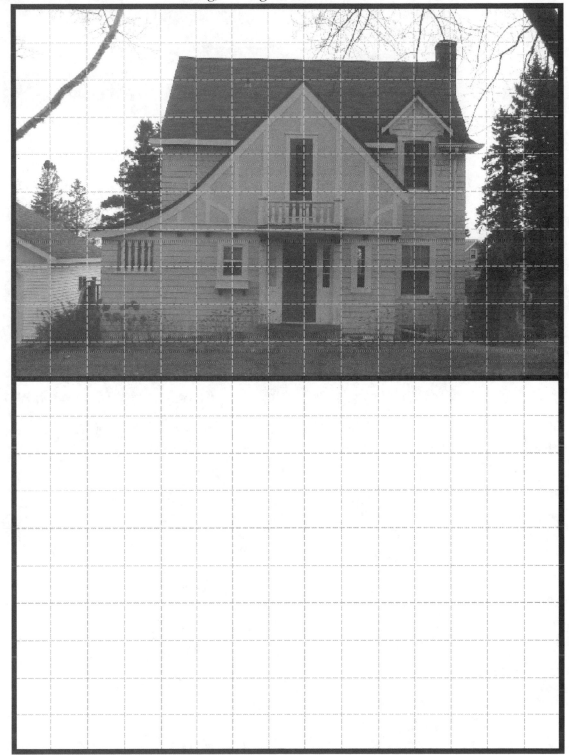

Name: _____   Date: _____

Notes:

Introduction I-3:
Surveying and Sketching Objects

Architects and designers often need to visit an existing facility, for which they have been commissioned to remodel or design an addition, and take detailed measurements and notes. There are many "tricks of the trade" involved in such an endeavor. Some are as simple as knowing the size of common building materials like ceiling tiles, floor tiles, concrete block and bricks, which allows the person surveying existing conditions to quickly get space dimensions simply by counting tiles or courses. For example, flipping ahead in this *Introduction* you will see a bench made from concrete block (pg. I-40). Knowing that the scored blocks are 8″x8″, you can count the squares and add them up. Also, another photo of a hallway (page I-44) shows 2′x2′ ceiling tile and 12″ floor tile. The hallway is three ceiling tiles wide or 6 floor tiles wide; thus, 3x2′ = 6′(using the ceiling tiles) and 6x12″ = 6′ (using the floor tiles). It is still a good idea to physically measure the walls, but this gives you a "common sense" way to double-check your numbers, which is very important (especially if the project site is hours away from your office!)

Another great tool in the toolbox for people checking existing conditions is a **laser tape measure**. This tool can aid in quick measurements and in some cases you can get distances difficult or impossible to acquire without a ladder or lift. For example, a stairwell might not have a location in which you and another person can stand next to each wall with a traditional tape measure. However, a laser tape measure can not only do this, but you can even do it by yourself (i.e., without a helper) as sketched in the image above.

In addition to sketching the building itself, you often need to take an inventory of items within each space. In some cases the items will be relocated to a new space, or you may need to know what kind of furniture or equipment is used in a space. For example, a bedroom might have a bed, night stands, dresser, etc.; or a banker's work room might have cabinets, copier, money counter, shredder, etc. These items are needed to aid in designing a space for a particular client, making sure the room is large enough, the correct proportions, has the proper electrical power supplied and the ideal heating and cooling being delivered (computers give off a lot of heat, for example).

Notes:

This page is provided for you to copy and survey the various pieces of furniture drawn in this textbook. You should not have any problem finding these at home or at a friend's/family's home. This will help you get a feel for the actual size of these objects and allow you to explore the art of sketching things in approximately the correct proportions. The sketches do not need to be to scale, but the different views should align via the grid paper (see example on previous page).

Top sketch

Isometric sketch

Front elevation sketch

Side elevation sketch

Item surveyed: _____   Overall dimensions (WxDxH): _____

Top sketch

Isometric sketch

Front elevation sketch

Side elevation sketch

Item surveyed: _____   Overall dimensions (WxDxH): _____

Name:

Date:

Notes:

Introduction I-4:
Sketching Floor Plans

When beginning to design a residence, one often sketches very rough floor plans on grid paper. This allows the designer to explore several design solutions without the time and exacting accuracy attributed to a CAD program. Such sketches are able to show adjacencies (i.e., which room is next to which room), circulation and room/building proportions.

The grid paper is used to quickly sketch to scale; you decide what one square is equal. For example, each square in the floor plan sketch on the next page is one foot square. Thus, all one has to do to determine the dimensions of a room is to count the number of squares in each direction. If the building were larger, one square might be equal to two feet or you might need to use larger grid paper. Designers with many years experience can sketch plans, elevations and details almost to scale without the aid of grid paper.

After the first few sketches, and the various spaces have been accounted for, you can use tracing paper (a.k.a., onion skin or bumwad). This highly transparent paper allows one to quickly create another design option based on another drawing (or drawings).

The image at the top of the next page shows a sheet of tracing paper with several "first thoughts" sketches quickly poured out on paper to capture the thoughts that are flowing through the designer's mind. The various portions of the sketch have been numbered and itemized below for your understanding.

Outline of items numbered in sketch on next page:

1. **Site plan:** No meaningful design can begin without understanding the context in which it will coexist. Important elements have been identified such as views ('+' means good view); buildable area per zoning; north and sun (for passive solar design consideration); existing structures and vegetation.

2. **Bubble diagrams:** The first pass at organizing spaces within a building is to think about their location relative to the site (for views, noise, etc.) and adjacencies to other spaces. The bubble diagram is just that – bubbles that abstractly represent spaces in relation to each other.

3. **Building sections:** Quick thoughts on vertical relationships; what areas are two-storied, vaulted ceilings, etc.

4. **Single line floor plans:** These are not to scale and may not even be proportionately accurate, but they capture one's early ideas so that they may be refined later with grid paper.

PRELIMINARY FLOOR PLAN
DEVELOPMENT ON TRACING PAPER

Looking at one of the bedrooms from the floor plan sketches you can see it is 13′-0″ wide (count 13 squares) by 16′-0″ (count 16 squares). Of course, from this you can also derive the square footage of the space: 13x16=**208**sf.

Once an acceptable design is developed you can then start to draw the plan in AutoCAD, using accurate dimensions as well as adding doors and windows.

TRY IT: Looking at the sketched plans on the next two pages, count the squares and write the dimensions and square footage for each room. Also add the overall building dimensions. The blank page that follows will give you the opportunity to sketch a few of your own floor plan designs!

PORTION OF FLOOR PLAN
SKETCH ON GRID PAPER

Name:

Date:

When sketching the second floor plan you should start by aligning the exterior walls. The easiest way to do this is to sketch them at the same exact location as the common walls on the first floor plan (i.e., relative location on the grid paper).

Name: Date:

Tear this page out, make copies, and create a few different floor plan designs using the same number of spaces and square footage as the floor plans on the previous two pages (which are the plans used in this text); be sure the two floors align! Remember, one square is a foot wide in each direction.

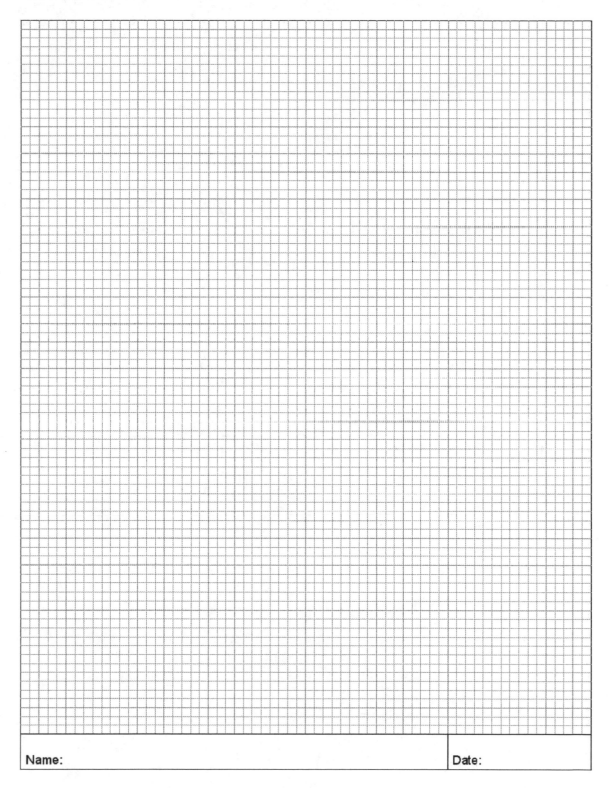

Name: Date:

Notes:

Introduction I-5:
Sketching Elevations – Two Point Perspective

Two-point perspective drawings are two-dimensional drawings that represent three-dimensional objects or scenes. As the name implies, there are two points (referred to as vanishing points or *VP*) which establish the perspective lines and which are both relative to a horizon line (*HL*). The object being depicted has three primary types of lines:

- *Perspective lines* (which always converge at the vanishing points).
- *Vertical lines* (which are always truly vertical to the page).
- *Angled lines* (which are usually drawn by 'connecting-the-dots' via linework fully developed from the previous two line types).

Two-point perspective drawings are primarily meant for rectilinear objects. For example, a uniform series of city blocks can be sketched much easier than an 'organic' shaped suburban development.

The concepts covered can be applied to more detailed embellishments, such as windows and siding, sidewalks and driveways, or fences and garages.

Below are the three primary types of perspective created by Architects and Interior Designers [*from left to right*]: one-point, two-point and three-point perspectives. You will study one and two-point perspectives in this section.

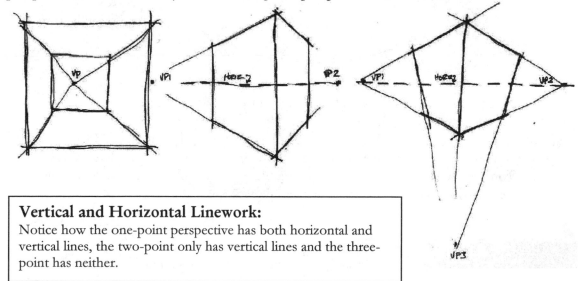

Vertical and Horizontal Linework:
Notice how the one-point perspective has both horizontal and vertical lines, the two-point only has vertical lines and the three-point has neither.

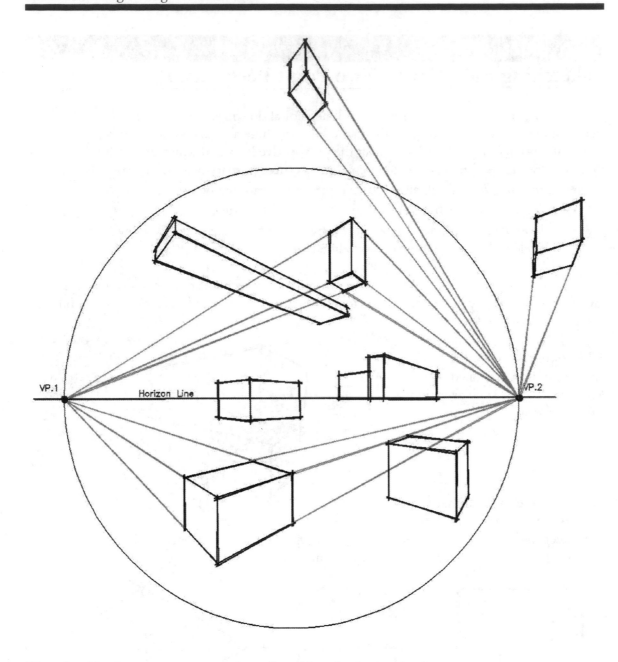

You should take a moment to notice a few things in the image above:
1) all lines are either vanishing or perfectly vertical; 2) anything drawn outside of an imaginary circle (actually shown here) is too distorted and should be avoided; 3) objects completely below the horizon are as viewed from the top and objects completely above are as viewed from below. You can quickly create rectilinear objects in any shape or size by sketching the vanishing lines and vertical lines as shown!

TRY IT: Make a few copies of the following page and try sketching some rectangular shapes similar to those shown in the image above. Try and create your own variations on this theme.

Name:_____

Date: _____

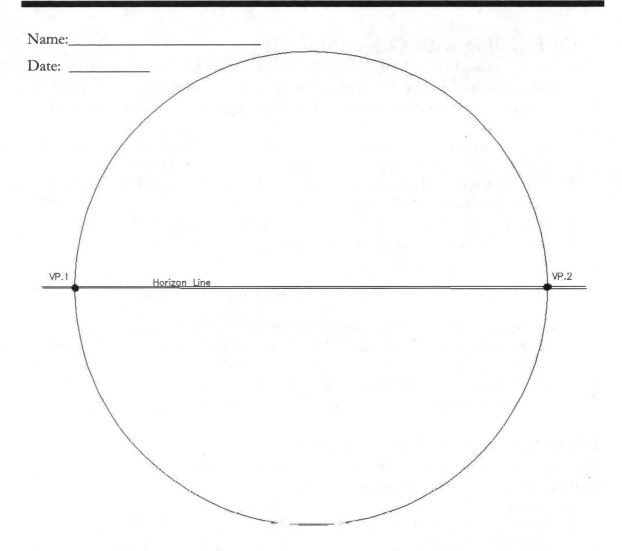

Two-Point Perspective

The following exercise will walk you through the steps required to develop a two-point perspective of the exterior of a residence. This exercise will have similar features to that of the home designed in this textbook. You are encouraged to follow along on a separate piece of paper and then sketch one or two views of the project in this book. The exact dimensions and proportions do not really matter at this time as you are focusing on the mechanics of perspective drawings. Try drawing this freehand first and then try again using a straight edge.

The steps below relate to the 'lettered' and then 'numbered' sketches on the following page:

Main Building with Gable Roof – Image A

This first step is simply sketching a basic box with a gable roof element dropped on top. You should try to make your sketch as similar as possible in terms of proportions; the vertical centerline (centered between the two vanishing points) has been added to aid in this.

1. Vertical line just to the right of the 'centerline' with equal portions above and below the *Horizon Line*. (See one vertical line, marked with a #1.)
2. Connect-the-dots: draw four lines from the *VP's* to the top and bottom of the vertical line as shown. (See the four lines marked with a #2.)
3. Draw two vertical lines to define the overall size of the main building.
4. Draw an 'X' and a vertical line at its intersection to discern the midpoint of the gable end of the building.

   NOTE: It is not the midpoint of the bottom edge of the building; confirm this with a scale.

5. Draw the ridge line of the roof: a line from VP-1 to the vertical line sketched in the previous step. (The location of this line determines the pitch of the roof; higher = steeper.)
6. Connect-the-dots: draw lines to create the gable roof edges.
7. Lightly sketch the hidden portions of the building as shown.

Bisecting the Building – Image B

Here you will learn how to find the exact middle of the building. This will help in locating the cross-gable in the next image/task.

1. Sketch an 'X' on the bottom plane of the building.
2. Draw a perspective line from VP.2 which passes through the 'X'.
3. Sketch three vertical lines as shown. (The vanishing line just drawn helps establish the starting point on the front and back face of the building.)
4. Connect-the-dots: from the intersection of the roof and three vertical lines.

   FYI: The two visible bisecting lines have an arrow at the top and bottom in this image and the next one to make them stand out... these lines will eventually be erased.

Adding Cross-Gable Entry – Image C

Next you will sketch in the "bump out" on the front of the building which is similar to the project you are working on in this book.

1. This perspective line (*from VP.1*) determines how far "out" the "bump" will be.
2. Draw two vertical lines a certain distance apart and approximately centered on the main building. (You will learn to be more precise later.)
3. Draw two perspective lines (*from VP.2*) to establish the bottom edges.
4. Draw a vertical line up to the roof edge – from the intersection of the perspective line just drawn and the bottom front edge of the main building.
5. Do the same as step3 to establish the top edges (*from VP.2*).
6. Draw this perspective line (*from VP.1*) to verify the top-front edge is correct.

All lines should be sketched very lightly and the visible lines can be made darker at the end, as well as erasing the unneeded reference lines and hidden lines.

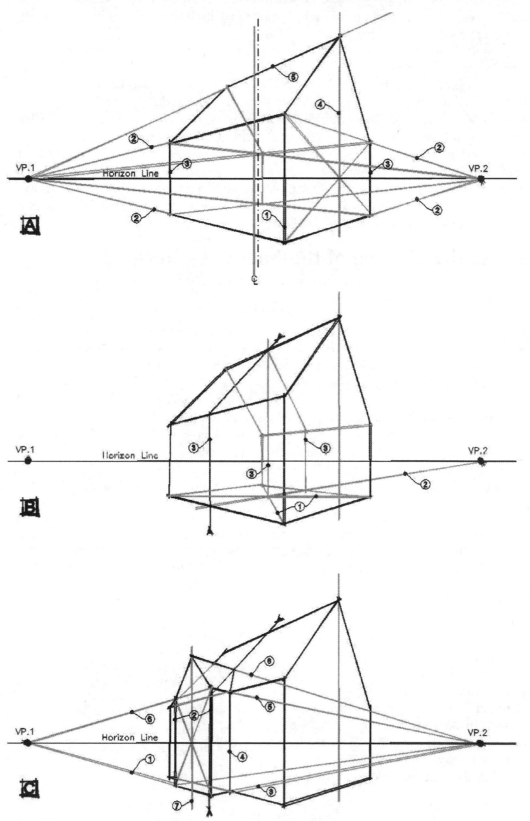

Centered and Symmetrical Addition – Image D

The following steps show you how to make an extrusion off the main building which is symmetrical. You cannot measure in from each side an equal distance because things get closer together as you approach the vanishing points.

1. The first line (*from VP.2*) will determine how large the extrusion (or addition) will be from the main mass of the residence.
2. Here you will basically extend the front and back bottom (i.e., grade) line out to the previous line drawn. (Sketch lightly as these lines will be erased.)
3. Draw an 'X' in the large, flat, rectangle just created.
4. Now you will draw a vanishing line (*from VP.2*) near the building. The intersection of this line and the 'X' lines will establish the front and back wall locations for the addition (which will be drawn in the next step).
5. Draw two lines (*from VP.1*) so that they pass through the intersection of the 'X' (from step 3) and the perspective line (from step 4), and terminate these lines at the perspective line (drawn in step 1) as shown in image D.

Completing the Massing of the Addition – Image E

Now that the footprint of the addition is sufficiently developed, you can create the remaining linework.

1. Draw four vertical lines as shown.
2. Draw a perspective line, if needed (i.e., if you erased the previous one you drew) from VP.2 to the roof edge of the main building; this assumes the roof edge of the addition will align with the main building and not be lower. (Simply swinging this perspective line down a bit would allow for this change.)
3. Draw two vanishing lines (*from VP.1*) through the line drawn in the previous step and the vertical lines at the main building (drawn in step 1).
4. Finding the middle of the gable end of the main building, you can sketch the roof slope lines. This is done in conjunction with the next step which locates the ridge line.
5. Draw the ridge line (*from VP.1*).
6. Find the middle of the gable end of the addition and finish sketching the sloped roof edges.

At this point you have developed the main masses of your structure. Now you can erase the reference lines and hidden lines, and then darken the remaining lines. Another option is to use tracing paper and a soft pencil to sketch a new image based on the 'visible' lines of your original sketch.

Again, you may use these techniques to add windows, siding, trim, chimneys, and such. Here is another good use for tracing paper (also referred to as bumwad or onionskin paper which comes on a roll and pieces are ripped off as needed): you can sketch different window and siding options on the tracing paper, thus not needing to start from scratch with the base model every time!

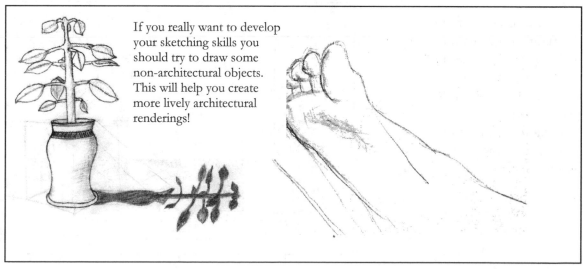

If you really want to develop your sketching skills you should try to draw some non-architectural objects. This will help you create more lively architectural renderings!

Dividing Spaces

The following technique can be used to divide a space into equal pieces. You can, of course, repeat this process to even further divide a space already divided. The graphic below pretty much speaks for itself; you start with any rectilinear face and sketch an 'X' from which you can project lines from its center point.

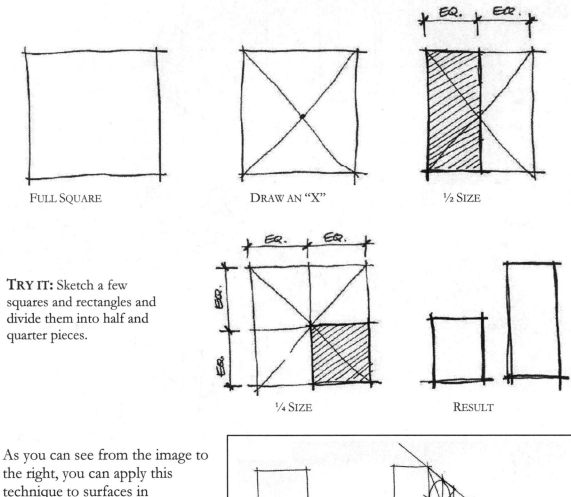

FULL SQUARE   DRAW AN "X"   ½ SIZE

TRY IT: Sketch a few squares and rectangles and divide them into half and quarter pieces.

¼ SIZE   RESULT

As you can see from the image to the right, you can apply this technique to surfaces in perspective, allowing you to develop various shapes in perspective (like this circle). Finding the center of a surface helps you to locate items, like windows, doors, etc.

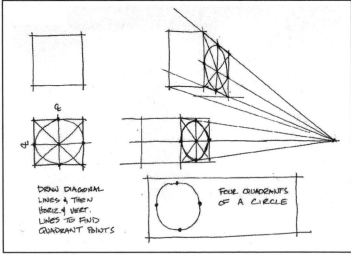

DRAW DIAGONAL LINES & THEN HORIZ. & VERT. LINES TO FIND QUADRANT POINTS

FOUR QUADRANTS OF A CIRCLE

TRY IT: Add a few circles to your boxes drawn within the large circle; remember to start with the 'X'.

Repeating Spaces in Perspective

The following steps walk through the process of repeating a shape equally as it moves towards the vanishing point. This is how you might sketch railroad tracks or a picket fence. In this example you will be applying this concept to an interior elevation of base cabinets.

Adding additional spaces of equal size:

1. Sketch an 'X' in a rectangular space (a square in this example).
2. Add a horizontal line which passes through the center of the 'X'.
3. Draw a diagonal line from the upper left, so that is passes through the intersection of the horizontal line (from the previous step) and the right edge of the square; continue this angle until you hit the bottom edge of the square. (You need to extend the top and bottom lines as shown.)
4. Sketch a new vertical line where the diagonal line meets the bottom horizontal line.
5. Repeat this process for additional segments.

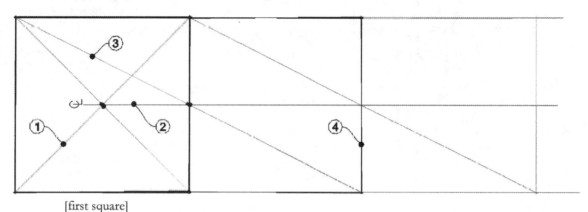

[first square]

Now you can apply this technique to surfaces that are in perspective. You can use the techniques described on the following page to finish the image which has been started for you below.

> **FYI:** *Make a few photocopies if you think you need to try it more than once. Also you can enlarge the image that way.*

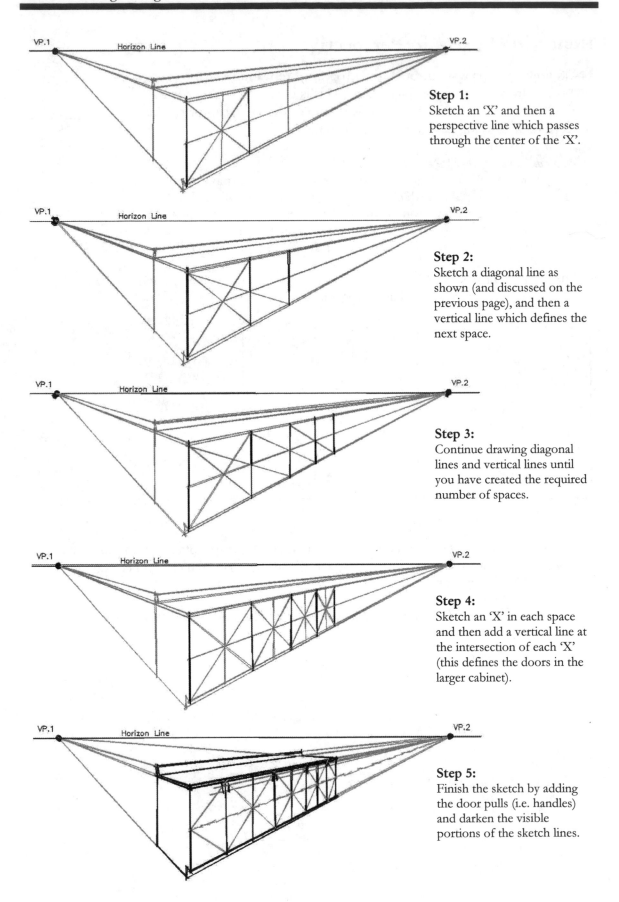

Step 1:
Sketch an 'X' and then a perspective line which passes through the center of the 'X'.

Step 2:
Sketch a diagonal line as shown (and discussed on the previous page), and then a vertical line which defines the next space.

Step 3:
Continue drawing diagonal lines and vertical lines until you have created the required number of spaces.

Step 4:
Sketch an 'X' in each space and then add a vertical line at the intersection of each 'X' (this defines the doors in the larger cabinet).

Step 5:
Finish the sketch by adding the door pulls (i.e. handles) and darken the visible portions of the sketch lines.

Sketching Two-Point Interior Perspectives

The process of creating two-point exterior perspectives can easily be applied to creating interior perspectives.

> NOTE: *The distance between the vanishing points (VP.1 and VP.2) will determine how close (or far away) and how distorted the perspective will be. Also, by making the interior perspective somewhat symmetrical about the horizon (meaning an equal portion of the drawing exists both above and below the HL) the drawing will feel like you are standing within the image and not as if you where in an airplane or as an ant!*

The perspective below is of the small portion of the floor plan shown to the right. Notice how the wall with the window does not align with the wall of the smaller room beyond. Also, the ceiling of the smaller room matches the height of the wall opening that leads into it, thus there is no line at the back side of the open/wall.

TRY IT: Create 2-point perspectives from the plans below and from this book.

Below is a photo of a bench at an inter-city bus stop made of burnished concrete block. This provides a good real world example of a three-point perspective. (Straightening the vertical lines would make it two-point.)

TRY IT: Setup a horizon line and two vanishing points on a separate piece of paper. Sketch the bench utilizing the two vanishing points and vertical lines. You will have to lightly sketch a few hidden lines to locate certain points. You should also utilize the techniques just covered to create equally spaced blocks as they move back towards the horizon.

This sketch shows how you can use the technique of creating additional, equally sized spaces, as previously covered. This method is not limited to only one direction. Notice how one space is skipped to create a void. Compare this sketch to the top portion of the bench directly above.

Introduction I-6:
Sketching Elevations – One Point Perspective

Now that you have taken a look at sketching two-point perspectives, you will now shift your attention to developing one-point perspectives. A number of concepts covered in the development study of two-point perspectives also apply to one-point, so it would be helpful if you have previously studied that section of this *Introduction* chapter.

The sketch below shows a simple example of a one-point perspective. The partial floor plan sketch below the perspective is the basis of the sketch. Using this technique, you can quickly create a sketch that helps you to visualize the space three-dimensionally. From here you might adjust the floor plan or add color and present it to your client for their approval.

Floor Plan

The Basic Components of a One-Point Perspective

The process of creating a one-point perspective is prescribed on the following page. The mechanics are very simple and do not take much time to master (like anything it just takes practice).

Establishing Depth in Your Perspective

The page after the next shows how to develop a three-dimensional grid which can be used to more accurately sketch items in perspective (in terms of depth from the viewer). This is a very rigid process and often only used for more formal presentation drawings.

> **NOTE:** *The location of the Diagonal Point (DP) will establish the depth of the view; when positioned correctly, the view will have the proper feeling of scale and proportions.*

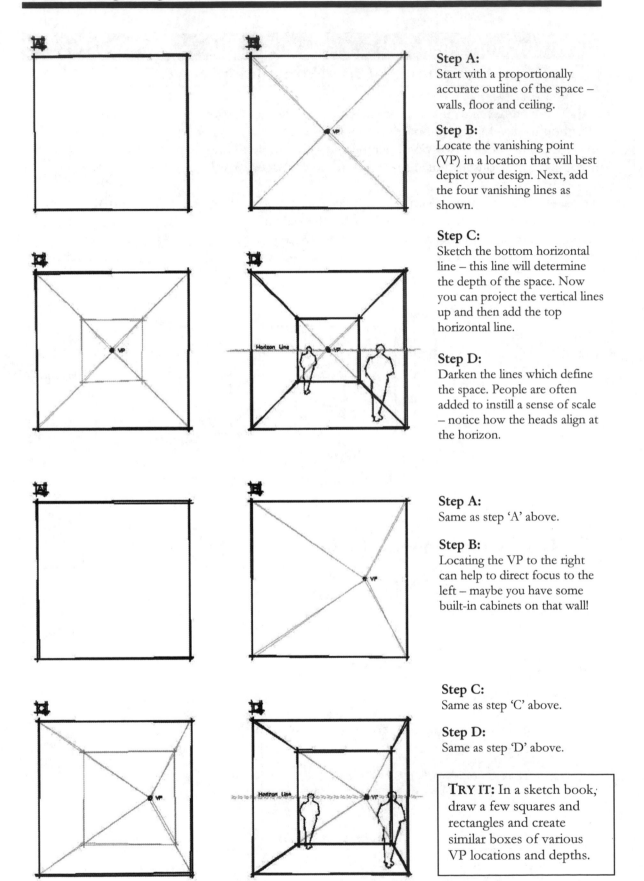

Step A:
Start with a proportionally accurate outline of the space – walls, floor and ceiling.

Step B:
Locate the vanishing point (VP) in a location that will best depict your design. Next, add the four vanishing lines as shown.

Step C
Sketch the bottom horizontal line – this line will determine the depth of the space. Now you can project the vertical lines up and then add the top horizontal line.

Step D:
Darken the lines which define the space. People are often added to instill a sense of scale – notice how the heads align at the horizon.

Step A:
Same as step 'A' above.

Step B:
Locating the VP to the right can help to direct focus to the left – maybe you have some built-in cabinets on that wall!

Step C:
Same as step 'C' above.

Step D:
Same as step 'D' above.

TRY IT: In a sketch book, draw a few squares and rectangles and create similar boxes of various VP locations and depths.

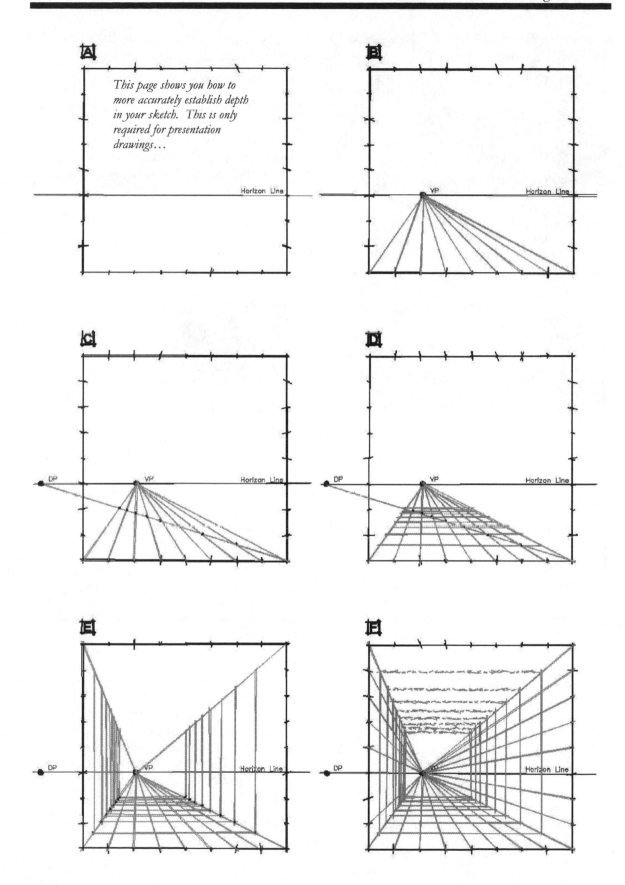

A

This page shows you how to more accurately establish depth in your sketch. This is only required for presentation drawings...

Horizon Line

B

VP   Horizon Line

C

DP   VP   Horizon Line

D

DP   VP   Horizon Line

E

DP   VP   Horizon Line

F

DP   VP   Horizon Line

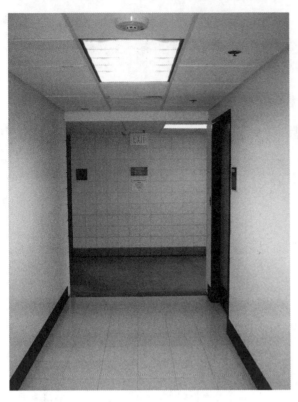

The photo to the left shows a hallway which should help you see how a one point perspective relates to the real world.

TRY IT: Try sketching this image in a sketch book or on some scrap paper. Establish a vanishing point and add the various perspective lines, the horizontal lines and the vertical lines. Notice the pattern in the flooring, the ceiling and the wall at the end of the hallway.

Vanishing point lines
derived from a
photo...

Equally Dividing a Line...

Here is a tip for equally dividing a line: Say you need eight equal spaces like the third line below. If you start at one end and try working your way to the other end you will almost never end up with equally spaced segments (it is too hard to judge how big the segments should be). The trick is to divide and conquer. Start with one tick in the middle (it may not be perfect but you will get very close). Next, you can divide each half in half (see the second line below). You continue this process until you have the desired number of segments; *this only works for even numbered segments.*

> **TRY IT:** Try sketching several lines and then divide them into even numbered segments. Just focus on eyeing the center point for each segment about to be divided. Sketch light lines in case you need to make adjustments.

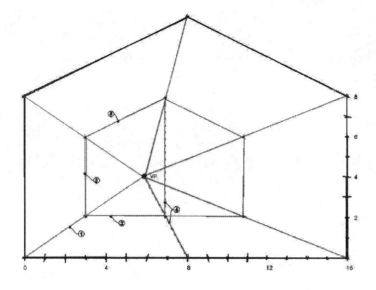

Developing a One-Point Perspective

Read though the following steps and then try them with the "starter" image that follows:

1. Sketch the five perspective lines from VP to corners.
2. Add the horizontal line; its location will define the depth of the space.
3. Sketch two vertical lines.
4. Locate the center of the back wall with a perspective line, and then add a vertical line up to the ridge line.
5. Connect-the-dots: add the last two sloped lines at the back edge of the roof.

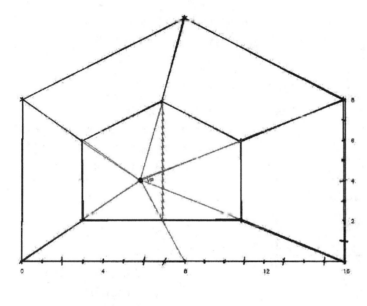

1. [See floor plan below.] Sketch perspective lines to define door width and location.
2. Locate height on adjacent wall.
3. Then project over onto back wall.
4. Add vertical lines as shown.

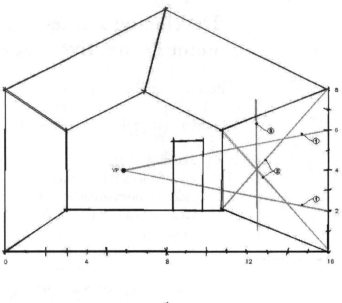

Now you will add a pair of windows to the east wall:

1. Add the two perspective lines to determine the window head and sill locations.
2. Sketch an 'X' to find the center of the wall.
3. Add a vertical line at the center of the wall.

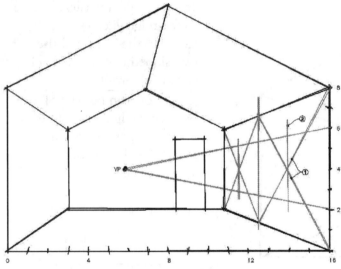

You know the window is 4´ wide and the wall in this view is 8´ wide (see plan view on previous page), thus you can divide the spaces as previously covered:

1. Sketch 'X's in the two spaces.
2. Add a vertical line of the intersection of each 'X'.
3. You now have the extents of the window defined and can be darkened for clarity.

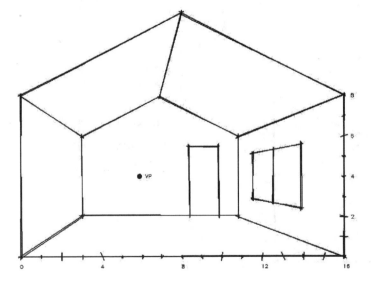

Next you will try this yourself as well as add a few more items and use a different vanishing point to better see the difference.

Name:_____

Date: _____

TRY IT: Use the image above as a starting point to create the same perspective as covered on the previous pages. Don't forget to make a few copies if you think you might need a few practice runs. Also, follow the following comments:

1. Add a vanishing point (*VP*) more to the right to create a unique view.

2. Add the door and window per the examples above and the floor plan.

3. Also add the following items:
    a. 2'x4' skylight
    b. Add 3 cabinets to the left wall (2'-0"x2'-0"x3'-0" high).
    c. Sketch a 4'x8' rug centered on the room.

    TIP: You can print out your CAD building sections and turn them into one point perspectives quickly for client meetings!

Notes:

Introduction I-7:
Sketching Plans – One Point Perspective

Once you have learned to create one-point interior elevations you can easily apply that technique to creating one-point floor plans. This type of perspective drawing allows you to quickly think about the design of an entire room, rather than just one corner (i.e., two walls).

Your CAD files can be used to help create the one-point perspective or they may be created after the perspective depending on the designers preferred workflow...

Simply sketch the footprint of the room, pick a vanishing point (*VP*) and then project the walls up and add features. See the next page for examples on various *VP* locations and how it affects the resultant perspective.

Plan or Elevation and VP Location...

You need to think about the information you want to convey in your one-point perspective before you start drawing. You could find you have wasted a lot of time if you get started too quickly, without thinking through to your desired result. If you want to highlight a lot of detail on the wall, then you should do a perspective from an elevation vantage point; or, if you want to show overall relationships and circulation, you should create a plan-type perspective.

In the example below, you see a rough sketch of a kitchen floor plan (on the left) and (3) plan-type and (3) elevation-type one-point perspectives. Notice the various vanishing point (*VP*) locations and what they show and don't show.

TRY IT: Using the kitchen room layout in the CAD section of this textbook, add cabinets and appliances similar to those shown in the sketched plan above. Create one floor plan perspective and one elevation type perspective. Try to find the best vanishing points for each view that best portray the kitchen design.

Below is an example of the melding of a digital CAD drawing and a hand sketch. Simply print out a floor plan or building section, lay a piece of tracing paper over it, and begin producing a one-point perspective. Picking the vanishing point is very important; you want to make sure no major features are hidden. Once the vanishing point has been established you can then project lines from the *VP* through the various corners within the floor plans. The first line you draw to represent the top-of-wall will dictate all others via the "connect-the-dots" process.

This concept even works for 3D programs like Revit Architecture. You can print out an exterior perspective of the building and then hand sketch various siding and window options quickly without having to meticulously layout each in an exacting BIM program.

TRY IT: When you get to the point in the textbook where you have finished developing the floor plans, you can print either the first or second floor out on a printer and try sketching a one-point perspective over the top of it.

Notes:

Lesson 1
Getting Started with AutoCAD 2014:

This chapter will introduce you to AutoCAD 2014. You will study the User Interface (UI); you will also learn how to open and exit a drawing and adjust the view of the drawing on the screen. It is recommended that the student spend an ample amount of time learning this material, as it will greatly enhance your ability to progress smoothly through subsequent lessons.

Exercise 1-1:
Overview of AutoCAD 2014User Interface

What is AutoCAD 2014?
AutoCAD 2014 is the world's standard 2D Computer Aided Design (CAD) software. AutoCAD 2014 is a product of Autodesk, which also makes Revit, AutoCAD Architecture and 3DS Max to name a few. The Autodesk company web site (www.autodesk.com) claims more than 8 million users in over 100 countries. Autodesk's thousands of employees create products available in many languages.

What is AutoCAD 2014used for?
AutoCAD 2014 is used by virtually every industry that creates technical drawings.

Just a small sampling of AutoCAD users include industries like:

Construction (Architects, Manufacturers and Contractors)	Automotive
	Ship Design
Aviation	Facilities
Management	Media and Entertainment

Why use AutoCAD 2014?
Many people ask the question, why use AutoCAD 2014 versus other programs? The answer can certainly vary depending on the situation and particular needs of an individual/organization.

Generally speaking, this is why most companies use AutoCAD:
- Many designers and drafters are using AutoCAD to create highly accurate drawings that can be easily modified.
- As the "standard" CAD software among many industries, transferring drawings (i.e., sharing) is very simple.
- AutoCAD's large set of features and ability to handle very large, complex drawing projects.
- Many people are trained to use AutoCAD,whether at a previous job or in school. An employer is more likely to find an employee trained in the use of AutoCAD than any other CAD program.

Many universities and colleges teach AutoCAD. Many companies require potential employees to know how to use AutoCAD.

Architecture and AutoCAD?

The Architectural profession heavily uses AutoCAD, or AutoCAD Architecture, to create drawings, schedules and presentation materials. A seasoned AutoCAD user can quickly generate several design options of a reception area, for example, and then even create a photo-realistic 3D rendering to show the client.

What about the Architectural Programs?

Many architectural firms still use AutoCAD even though there are several software packages that are specifically designed for architecture. The general reason has to do with design tools needed, cost, and staff knowledge of the software.

The architectural programs, like Autodesk Revit Architecture(RAC) and AutoCAD Architecture (ACA), cost quite a bit more than AutoCAD, and for good reason. For example, ACA is built on top of AutoCAD. That means that ACA has everything AutoCAD has plus many additional features geared specifically towards architecture; it stands to reason that ACA would be equal to the cost of AutoCAD plus something for the additional features.

In any case, students are typically first trained using AutoCAD and then they are exposed to the more advanced programs (either in school or industry). This is similar to other programs such as Computer Science, where the student first learns a popular/industry standard program (to focus on the basics) and then, later in the program, tackles advanced languages such as Microsoft .Net.

32 bit versus 64 bit?

Starting in the 2009 version of AutoCAD, a 64 bit version of the software is available. This allows the software to take full advantage of hardware that, for the most part, has been 64bit for a few years now. One of the biggest advantages is access to more than 3GB of RAM. Many CAD stations have 8GB of RAM to handle large projects. It should be pointed out that most computers come with a 32 bit operating system (e.g., Windows XP, Vista or Windows 7); however both have 64bit versions which cost a little more.

New features?

Every version of AutoCAD is usually packed with new features. The goal of this text is to teach you the basics and if those fundamental tools have changed you will then be learning something unique to this version of the software. But this book is not going to cover a new feature just because it is new – many new features are often intermediate to advanced tools such as the recently added "organic" 3D modeling tools. A new user needs to focus on the basics before jumping in the deep end!

Exercise 1-2:
Overview of AutoCAD 2014 User Interface

AutoCAD is a powerful and sophisticated program. Because of its powerful feature set, it has a measurable learning curve. However, when broken down into smaller pieces, you can easily learn to harness the power of AutoCAD; that is the goal of this book.

This exercise will walk through the different sections of the User Interface (UI). Understanding the user interface is the key to using any program's features.

*NOTE: Make sure the Workspace feature is set to **Drafting & Annotation** (see pg. 1-10); this will help ensure your screen matches the book images.*

APPLICATION MENU (THE LARGE LETTER A)

QUICK ACCESS TOOLBAR

WORKSPACE LIST

CURRENT DRAWING NAME (IN TITLEBAR)

EXCHANGE CENTER

RIBBON TABS

OPEN DRAWING TABS

RIBBON PANEL

VIEWCUBE

DRAWING WINDOW

CURSOR (CROSSHAIRS)

NAVIGATION BAR

PALETTE

USER COORDINATE SYSTEM (UCS) ICON

COMMAND WINDOW

DRAFTING & DISPLAY TOOLS

STATUS BAR

FIGURE 1-2.1
AutoCAD User Interface

The AutoCAD User Interface (the details):

Application Menu: Clicking the large, red "A" shaped letter reveals several menus and tools. AutoCAD has a series of menus on the left. Click on each of the menus to explore their contents.

FYI: The circled numbers indicate the steps required to access the feature used to print a drawing.

The *Open, Save and Close* commands will be covered in the next exercise.

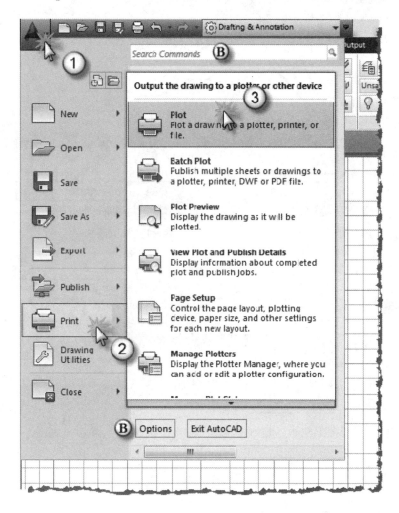

Item A:
The *Search* box, highlighted by the letter A, allows you to type in a word to find related commands. For example, try typing "arc" (no need to press Enter) and you will see several items appear. Click the "X" to the right of the search box to clear the search.

Item B:
The *Options* button opens a dialog with a plethora of settings; the new user would do well to avoid changing settings here.

Next you will explore the *Ribbon* and how the various *Tabs* control the tools displayed there. Again, if your screen does not have these kinds of graphics, you need to make sure the "Workspace" is set to **Drafting & Annotation** (see pg. 1-10 for more information).

> ***FYI:*** *You should know that some of the graphics you see in this textbook for the User Interface are new to this version of AutoCAD, so if you are using an older version of the program you will not have access to the same graphics. (You should use the version of this textbook that matches the version of your software.)*

Next you will just look at a few of the *Panels* on the Home tab.

Home → **Draw**:

The *Draw* panel, on the *Home* tab, contains commands which allow you to draw basic 2D lines and shapes as well as hatching (hatching is a type of object that fills an area with a pattern).

Expanding panels

Many *Panels* have additional, but less used tools, available in a fly-out portion of the *Panel;* you can tell if a *Panel* can be expanded by the little down-arrow (triangle) next to the panel name (see upper example to the left). Clicking anywhere in the bottom "titlebar" will expand the *Panel* as shown to the left. Once you click away from the *Panel* the extended portion will close – unless you click the "pin" icon in the lower right, which will keep the *Panel* expanded until you un-pin it. The remaining example images in this section will only be shown expanded (if available) to save space in this book.

Home → **Modify**:

This *Panel* contains commands that modify objects in your drawings: Move, Mirror, Array, Stretch, Copy, Offset, Rotate and Erase.

This book spends a significant amount of time helping you develop a solid understanding of how these tools work; you use these commands throughout the book – practice makes perfect!

Home → **Layers**:
This *Panel* contains tools to create and manage drawing *Layers*.

FYI: *Layers allow you to manage the display and the organization of drawing entities; more on this later.*

TIP: *When nothing is selected, the Layer drop-down list displays the current layer; when something is selected, it displays which layer the selected entity is on. (If objects on multiple layers are selected the display is blank.)*

Layer Drop-Down List

View control icons:

When you are ready to print a drawing you create a *Layout View*. Each *Layout View*, represented by the thumbnails after the Model thumbnail, contains various settings such as paper size and drawing scale. The icons on the *Status Bar* allow you to switch between these views quickly.

Overview of numbers in image below:
1.) Model Space/Paper Space Toggle
2.) Show/Hide Layout thumbnails
3.) Show/Hide Open drawings thumbnails
4.) Toolbar for Layout thumbnail mode shown by clicking on item #2

MODEL THUMBNAIL

LAYOUT VIEW THUMBNAILS

A feature of your operating system,**Windows 7**: you can also hover over the AutoCAD button on the taskbar to see a preview of any open drawings (see image to the right).

Command Window:

The *Command Window* allows you to type in commands; suggested commands will be listed as you type (Auto Complete). AutoCAD displays options and prompts for specific input for a command. When the main line says "*Type a command*", as in the image below, you know there are not any commands active or running. Command history is displayed above the *Command Window*.

TIP: If you accidentally close the Command Window, you can restore it by pressing **Ctrl + 9** *(i.e., press both keys at the same time) on the keyboard.*

Drafting & Display:

This area indicates the status of various settings plus the coordinates of the cursor (cross-hairs) on the screen. It also displays the length and angle of a line while it's being created. The icons are buttons which toggle whether that feature is on or not. You can also right click on the buttons to adjust the settings associated with each tool. You may wish to click the **Grid Display** icon to toggle it off as it is not needed now.

TIP: When you hover over an icon, a tooltip will appear telling you the name of the icon; this is handy until you learn what the icon for each tool looks like

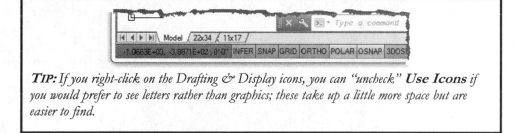

TIP: If you right-click on the Drafting & Display icons, you can "uncheck" **Use Icons** *if you would prefer to see letters rather than graphics; these take up a little more space but are easier to find.*

Title Bar:

The *Title Bar* lists the program name, when space permits, and then the name of the drawing that is active. The *Quick AccessToolbar*, on the left, gives you convenient access to often used commands: New, Open, and Save drawing, plus Print, Undo and Redo. The area on the right provides quick access to search the *Help System* and log into *Autodesk 360*; more on both of them later in this chapter.

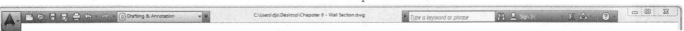

UCS Icon:

This symbol helps to keep track of your drawing's orientation relative to the X, Y, Z coordinate system. It also serves as a visual indicator of the current display mode: 2D view, 3D view, perspective, or shade mode, for example.

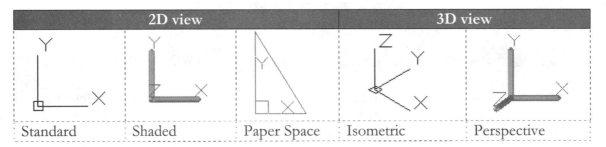

2D view			3D view	
Standard	Shaded	Paper Space	Isometric	Perspective

Welcome Screen:

The Welcome Screen is the first screen you see when AutoCAD is started. This interface gives you access to relevant information from Autodeskand access to add-ins, which can extend the capabilities of AutoCAD. Some add-ins are free, while others require payment. The checkbox in the lower left corner allows you to prevent this from appearing each time AutoCAD is launched.You may reopen it at any time by typing "welcome" and then pressing *Enter*.

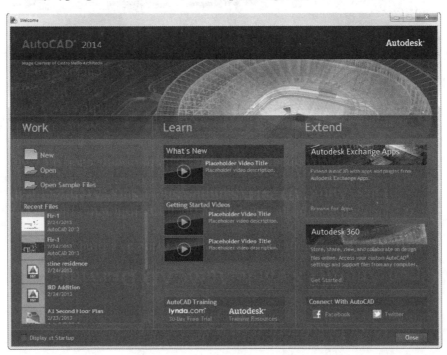

Quick Properties:

When the *Quick Properties* tool icon is toggled on the *Status Bar* (see image at bottom of this page), AutoCAD will automatically display a small *Properties* palette near any selected item. When multiple items are selected it will list the quantity selected and any common properties that would normally be displayed by *Quick Properties*. When you press **Esc** to deselect everything, the *Quick Properties* palette goes away.

The example below shows a *Block* (i.e., symbol – of a toilet in this case) selected. You need to open the main *Properties* palette to see all properties (via Ctrl+1).

TOILET SELECTED

TIP:
Press **Esc** *to unselect*

Drawing Tabs:

Each open drawing file is represented by a tab just below the *Ribbon* (see image below). This allows you to quickly switch between drawings. You can click the "X" to the right of the drawing name to close the file; if the drawing has unsaved changes (indicated by an asterisk next to the name), you will be prompted to save them. The plus icon to the right of the last tab allows you to quickly start a new drawing. A right-click presents several options. Finally, hovering your cursor over a tab shows the model/paper space previous similar to the status bar option.

Resetting the User Interface:

If the *User Interface* shown in Figure 1-2.1 does not match your computer's display, you can reset it. You, or someone who uses your workstation, may have customized some settings (although settings should be saved by user login). The next steps will describe how to reset the screen configuration.

> *NOTE: This step is not necessary to work through this book. It is simply offered for individuals that may have an extremely customized display and want to reset it to make comparing the images in the textbook easier.*

1. **Open AutoCAD** (see Exercise 1-3 for instruction on this).

2. Locate the **Workspace Switching** icon as shown in Figure 1-2.2.

> *NOTE: The* Workspace Switching *icon is located on the* Quick Access Toolbar *in the upperleft corner of the screen.*

FIGURE 1-2.2 Workspace switching menu – menu shows after clicking down-arrow

3. Click the down arrow and select **Drafting & Annotation** from the pop-up menu.

> *FYI: Another option is* **3D Modeling** *which reorganizes the screen to make the 3D commands readily available (not used in this book). You can try switching to another Workspace to see what it does, just switch back to Drafting & Annotation before moving on.*

Your screen should look similar to Figure 1-2.2. You can reset this anytime to get back to a clean slate.

If you are still having problems, you can try Resetting the program to its default settings. This will remove any customization that has been applies to the user interface. The tool to reset AutoCAD is found in the *Windows* **Start** menu, not AutoCAD. With AutoCAD closed, click Start → Autodesk → AutoCAD 2014 – English →**Reset Settings to Default**. This command can be seen in the image on the next page.

This concludes our brief overview of the AutoCAD user interface.

Exercise 1-3:
Open, Save and Close an Existing Drawing

Open AutoCAD 2014:

AutoCAD
2014 -
English

Start → *All Programs* → *Autodesk* → *AutoCAD 2014 - English* → *AutoCAD 2014 - English* (*Figure 1-3.1*) *– see notes below.* Or *double-click the AutoCAD icon from your desktop.*

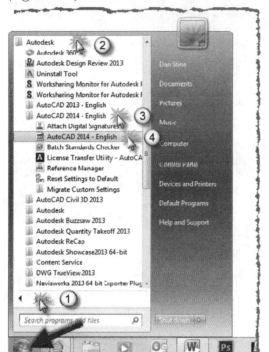

FIGURE 1-3.1 Start Menu (Windows 7 shown)

Notes on starting AutoCAD:

- Click the items in the order shown; the first click area says *All Programs* until you click on it.

- You may also simply type "autocad" in the search box located just below click#1. A link to start AutoCAD 2014 will appear at the top of the list.

- You may also start the program by double-clicking on a file via your file browser (i.e., My Computer, Windows Explorer, Computer).

Open an AutoCAD Drawing:

By default, AutoCAD will open a new blank drawing. The first thing we will do is close this drawing.

1. Select **Application Menu** → **Close**; if you are prompted to save the drawing, click the **No** button (see Figure 1-3.2).

You can also click the "X" in the *Drawing Tab*, just below the *Ribbon* as shown in the image below.

FIGURE 1-3.2 Closing the current drawing

2. Click the **Open** icon on the *Quick Access Toolbar (QAT).* (See Figure 1-3.3).

TIP: You may also open drawings by going to the Application Menu, *click* Open *and then selecting* Drawing. *Many users prefer using keyboard shortcuts; you can select a drawing to open by pressing Ctrl + O at the same time on the keyboard.*

FIGURE 1-3.3 Open icon on the QAT

3. Browse to the following folder: **C:\Program Files\Autodesk\AutoCAD 2014\Sample\Sheet Sets\Architectural\Res** (see Figure 1-3.4A).

4. Select the file named **Exterior Elevations.dwg** and click **Open** (Figure 1-3.4B).

The *Exterior Elevations.dwg* file is now open, and the last saved view is displayed in the *Drawing* window.

FIGURE 1-3.4A Finding the "C" drive

The *Open Documents* listed via the ***Application* Menu** are the drawings currently open on your computer.

5. Click the *Application* menu and then select the **Open Documents** icon (Figure 1-3.5).

FIGURE 1-3.4B Selecting a file to open

Notice that *Exterior Elevations.dwg* is listed. You can quickly toggle between opened drawings from this menu, as you will see in the next steps.

FIGURE 1-3.5 Open Documents list – one file shown to be open

> *FYI: You can also see a list of the open drawings from the View tab, in the Windows panel, by clicking on the Switch Windows icon… all located on the Ribbon. Also, try clicking on the* **Quick View Drawings** *icon on the Status Bar for thumbnail views!*

Open Another Sample AutoCAD Drawing:

AutoCAD lets you open more than one drawing at a time.

6. Using the steps just described, open the following file: **C:\Program Files\AutoCAD 2014\Sample\Sheet Sets\Architectural\A-03.dwg**.

   a. If the Sheet Set Manager palette opens, click the "X" to close it.

Notice that *A-03.dwg* is now listed in the *Open Documents* list (see Figure 1-3.6). Try toggling between drawings by clicking on *Exterior Elevations.dwg*.

> *TIP: Press* **Ctrl + Tab** *to cycle through open drawings quickly without opening the Application Menu. Also, if open, click the "X" in the floating palette (Sheet Sets) to close it as it is not needed at the moment.*

FIGURE 1-3.6 Open Documents list – two files shown to be open

Close an AutoCAD Drawing:

7. Select **Application Menu →Close**. Do <u>not</u> save if asked.

This will close the current drawing. If more than one drawing is open, only the current drawing will close unless you selected *Close → All Drawings*. Also, if you right-click on a *Drawing Tab*, below the *Ribbon*, you can select **Close All Except This Tab** from the pop-up menu. Finally, see the "Closing AutoCAD" section below for yet another way to close a file.

8. Repeat the previous step to close the other open drawing file.

Whenever you try to close a drawing, if you have not saved your drawing, you will be prompted to do so before AutoCAD closes the drawing. **Do not save at this time**. Just know that if you forget to *Save* before closing a drawing the software will remind you to save first.

Saving an AutoCAD Drawing:
At this time you will <u>not</u> actually save a drawing.

To save a drawing, click the **Save** icon (looks like a floppy disk) from the *Quick Access* toolbar (see image to right). The next exercise shows you how to save your files to the *Cloud*; This is a safe and secure way to back up your files and access them from anywhere.

FIGURE 1-3.7 Save icon

You should get in the habit of saving often to avoid losing work due to a power outage or program crash.

> *FYI: The program does perform automatic saves that are available only if AutoCAD closes abnormally. See HELP for more information on this (type 'savetime' to set auto-save time interval).*

Closing the AutoCAD Program:

Finally, from the *Application Menu*, select **Exit AutoCAD**. This will close any open drawings and shut AutoCAD down. Again you will be prompted to save (if needed) before AutoCAD closes any open drawings. Do not save at this time.

> *TIP: To close AutoCAD, you can also click the X in the <u>upper</u> right corner of the AutoCAD window (see image to the right); clicking the <u>lower</u> "X" closes the current drawing file.*

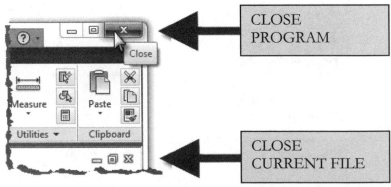

CLOSE PROGRAM

CLOSE CURRENT FILE

FIGURE 1-3.8 CLOSE icons

Exercise 1-4:
Creating a New Drawing

Creating a New Drawing File:

The steps required to set up a new AutoCAD drawing file are very simple. As mentioned earlier, simply opening the AutoCAD program starts you in a new unnamed drawing file. The important thing to remember is to start with the correct template file, as this will save you lots of work!

To manually create a new drawing (maybe you just finished working on a previous assignment and want to start the next one):

1. Select **Application Menu → New → Drawing**. (See Figure 1-4.1.)

Now you are in the *Select Template* dialog box (Figure 1-4.2).

FIGURE 1-4.1 New Drawing command

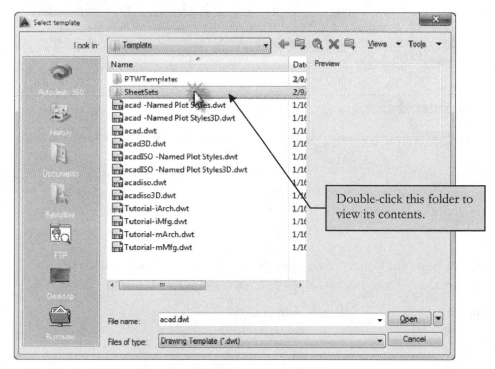

FIGURE 1-4.2 Select Template dialog box

The *Select Template* dialog box lets you specify the template file you want to use; the template file is explained below.

2. Double-click on the **Sheet Sets** folder to view its contents.

3. Select the **Architectural Imperial.dwt** *template file*.

    FYI: *You may need to scroll to the right to see the file details.*

    IMPORTANT: *This is the file you will use to start all drawings created in this book. The* Sheet Sets *feature will be covered later in this book.*

4. Click **Open**. You now have a new "unnamed" drawing file.

To name an unnamed drawing file, you simply save it. The first time an unnamed drawing file is saved, you will be prompted to specify the name and location for the drawing file.

5. Select the **Save** icon from the *Quick Access* toolbar. (You do not have to actually save your drawing at this time.)

6. Specify a **name** and **location** for your new drawing file.
    Your instructor may specify a location or folder for your files if you are in a classroom setting.

    TIP: *You can also select the New Drawing icon on the Quick Access Toolbar (Figure 1-4.3).*

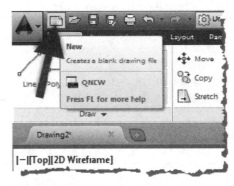

FIGURE 1-4.3 New drawing icon (QAT)

What is a Template File?

A template file allows you to start your drawing with certain settings preset the way you like or need them.

For example, you can have the units set to Imperial or Metric. You can have things like dimension and text styles preloaded, etc. You can also have your company's title block and standard *Layers* preloaded.

A custom template is a must for design firms using AutoCAD and will prove useful to the student as he or she becomes more proficient with the program.

> ***BE AWARE:*** *It will be assumed from this point forward that the reader understands how to create, open and save drawing files. Please refer back to this section as needed. If you still need further assistance, ask your instructor for help or search the AutoCAD Help system (more on how to do this at the end of the chapter).*

Exercise 1-5:
Using Zoom & Pan to View Your Drawings

Learning to *Pan* and *Zoom* in and out of a drawing is essential to accurate and efficient drafting and visualization. You will review these commands now so you are ready to use them with the first drawing exercise.

Open AutoCAD 2014:

You will select a sample file provided on the DVD that came with the book.

1. Select **Open** on the *Quick Access* toolbar.

2. Browse to the following folder on your DVD:
   D:\Sample Files\Residence (assumes your DVD drive is "D")

3. Select the file named **A1 - First Floor Plan.dwg** and click **Open**; your *Drawing* window should look similar to Figure 1-5.1.

   FYI: If they are open, you may close the Tool Palette, Design Feed and Sheet Set Manager for now; just click the "X" in that palette's titlebar.

FIGURE 1-5.1 A1 - First Floor Plan.dwg drawing

Switching to Model Space:

The *Layout* tab(s) to the right of the *Model* tab is primarily used for printing sheets with drawings, details and title blocks composed on them.

The *Model* tab (i.e., *Model Space*) is really where all the drawing is done. Then the drawings are arranged in *Layout Views* on sheets (e.g., 8 ½" x 11" or 24" x 36") for printing.

The *A1 - First Floor Plan* drawing should have opened with the *Layout1* tab current.

> *NOTE:* Layout Views *can be named (or renamed) to anything you want; simply right-click on the tab and select* Rename.
> *(EXCEPTION: You cannot rename the* Model *tab.)*

Next you will switch to the *Model Space* where you will learn to *Zoom* and *Pan* in a drawing.

4. Click on the *Model* tab directly below the *Drawing Window* (Figure 1-5.2); you are now in a *Model Space* (Figure 1-5.1).

Layout tabs below the Drawing Window

Using Zoom and Pan Tools:

You can access the zoom tools from the *Navigate 2D* panel on the *View* tab, the *Navigation Bar* and the *scroll wheel* on your mouse (the latter being the most used).

The icons have a label next to them which aptly describes what each icon is programmed to do (see Figure 1-5.3). The most used tools are **Zoom Window**, **Zoom Previous** and **Zoom Extents**. You will look at each of these plus the **Pan** tool located just above the **Zoom** icon.

FIGURE 1-5.3 *Zoom* tools on the *Navigate 2D* panel (left) and the Navigation Bar (right)

Zoom In:

5. Select the Zoom **Window** tool by clicking on its icon (Figure 1-5.3).

6. Select a window over your floor plan. The dashed-line rectangle has been added to Figure 1-5.4 to describe where you should click.

    TIP: Click and release the mouse button; do not "drag".

FIGURE 1-5.4 Zoom Window area

You should now be zoomed in to the specified area (Figure 1-5.5). Depending on the proportions of the rectangular area selected (and compared to the proportions of your monitor), the "zoomed in" area may be slightly larger in one direction.

FIGURE 1-5.5 Zoom Window results

Zoom Previous: Previous

7. Select the **Zoom Previous** tool by clicking on its icon in the *Navigate* panel on the *View* tab (Figure 1-5.3).

You should now be back where you started.

> *FYI: AutoCAD generates a smooth transition between zoom operations. This helps you keep track of where you are in the current drawing.*

Zoom Extents: Extents

This tool allows you to quickly get to a view where you see everything in the current drawing; this is more useful if you are in a floor plan drawing rather than a drawing of all the utilities for an entire city (as you may essentially be zoomed too far out). If you have "garbage" lines way off to one side of your drawing, the main drawing area will not fill the screen (keep it clean!)

8. Select the **Zoom Extents** tool by clicking on its icon (Figure 1-5.3).

9. Take a minute and try the other zoom tools to see how they work. When finished, click **Zoom Extents** before moving on.

FYI: Whenever this book refers to clicking the mouse button, it is always referring to the left button. Any other variation will be specifically instructed. For example: Right-click on the OSNAP icon on the Status Bar.

Pan: 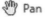 Pan

The **Pan** tool allows you to slide the viewing area, in <u>real-time</u>, to a different part of a "zoomed in" drawing (floor plan, elevation, detail, etc.).

Panning is similar to using the horizontal and vertical scroll bars next to the drawing window (these are turned off by default), except you drag the mouse on the screen and are able to go in both directions at the same time (i.e., at an angle).

Realtime means that you see the drawing "smoothly" slide across the screen as you move the mouse. On older versions you would pick two points and then AutoCAD would move the drawing instantly from point A to point B with no "smooth" transition between.

10. Click the **Pan** icon; this icon is located in the *Navigation* panel on the *View* tab (Figure 1-5.3); it is also on the *Navigation Bar*.

You should now notice a **Hand Symbol** in place of the typical Arrow Pointer (or cursor). You can think of this hand as grabbing *Model Space* (when you hold down the mouse button) and "moving" it within the *Drawing* window.

11. Try panning around in the *A1 - First Floor Plan* drawing currently open on your computer; hold the mouse button down, drag the mouse, release the mouse button; drag again if you wish.

    BE AWARE: *You are not moving the drawing. You are just changing what part of the drawing you see in the drawing window.*

12. When you are done *Panning*, right-click anywhere in the *Drawing* window, and then select **Exit** from the pop-up menu (Figure 1-5.6), or press the *Esc* key.

Notice the other options you have in the pop-up menu shown in Figure 1-5.6. You can quickly toggle from **Pan** to **Zoom**, or **Zoom Window, Original** or **Extents**.

13. **Close** the *A1 - First Floor Plan* drawing <u>without</u> saving.

FIGURE 1-5.6 Pan right-click pop-up menu

Using the Scroll Wheel on the Mouse:

Using a mouse with a scroll wheel is highly recommended for AutoCAD users. You can seamlessly perform most of the commands covered in this exercise without typing a command or clicking on any icons. Learning to use the wheel is so straight forward and intuitive that the following paragraph should be all that is required for you to start using the wheel productively!

Scroll Wheel

The scroll wheel on the mouse is one of the best improvements to the computer in recent years. In AutoCAD you can Pan and Zoom without even clicking a zoom icon. You simply **scroll the wheel to Zoom** and **hold the wheel button down to Pan**. This can be done while in another command (e.g., while drawing lines). Another nice feature is that the drawing zooms into the area near your cursor, rather than zooming only at the center of the drawing window like the **Zoom In** tool does. Finally, if you double-click on the wheel, AutoCAD zooms the extents of the drawing.

FIGURE 1-5.7 Microsoft's Optical IntelliMouse shown

The sample floor plan drawing used in this exercise is based on the residential project used in the author's textbook *Residential Design Using Autodesk Revit Architecture 2014*. The image below shows a rendering of the exterior of the building, similar to one created in that book.

RENDERING OF RESIDENTIAL PROJECT;
RESIDENTIAL DESIGN USING AUTODESK REVIT ARCHITECTURE 2014

Exercise 1-6:
Using the AutoCAD Help System

The AutoCAD Help system can be very useful when you understand how it works. This exercise will walk you through the Help system user interface.

This is a "project based" book; you will end up with a cohesive project, rather than a hundred drawings that have nothing to do with each other. Furthermore, only the commands necessary to complete a task are covered in depth.

Many commands, such as the **Arc** command, have several sub-commands. Rather than study every feature of a command, you will only study the essential parts so as not to overwhelm you with too much information. The book will occasionally make reference to the **Help** system so you can review a command more thoroughly if you are having problems.

This section (and book) will help you find answers to questions on your own. And with AutoCAD (as with architecture) there is so much to know, it's often better to know how to find the information than it is to remember ALL the information.

Open AutoCAD 2014:

1. Select the **Help** icon (question mark) from the upper right corner of the program window (Figure 1-6.1).

    TIP: Click directly on the question mark; the small down-arrow reveals additional Help related items.

FIGURE 1-6.1 Help access icon

You should now be in AutoCAD's *Help* system window (Figure 1-6.2). The next section walks you through its various features. Note that the *Help* window is a local website that you may leave open and return to AutoCAD and work while the *Help* window remains open. However, when you close AutoCAD the *Help* window will be closed as well. Finally, you may close the *Help* window at any time by clicking the "X" at the upper right.

Keyboard Shortcuts:

Many commands in AutoCAD have a keyboard shortcut, which means you can press a key(s) on the keyboard instead of clicking an icon or the application menu. **For example**: to start the **Line** command (and you are not currently in another command), you can type the letter **L** and then *Enter*. The Help system can be accessed by pressing **F1** on the keyboard.

Most advanced users employ a combination of keyboard and icon use.

Exploring the Help System User Interface:

AutoCAD contains an extensive set of documentation on your computer's hard drive. This is basically your owner's manual; from this window you can research the "ins" and "outs" of the program. Notice that this is part of the *Autodesk Exchange* screen seen when first starting the program.

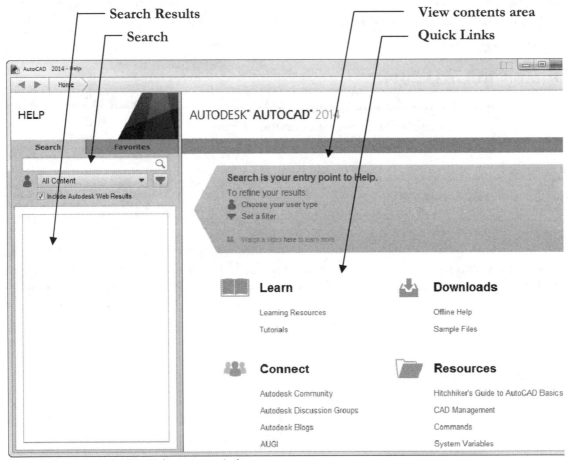

FIGURE 1-6.2 AutoCAD's Help system window

Help System in Action:

You will learn how to find information in the *Help System* on drawing *Circles*.

2. Click in the *Search* text box and enter **draw circle** (Figure 1-6.3).

    a. Notice the option to include web results. This will maximize the search results.

    b. Leave the filter set to *All Content*.

FIGURE 1-6.3 Searching help

3. Press **Enter**.

You should see the results shown in Figure 1-6.4. Notice the other "All Content" drop-down in the image above. This list allows you to narrow down the results.

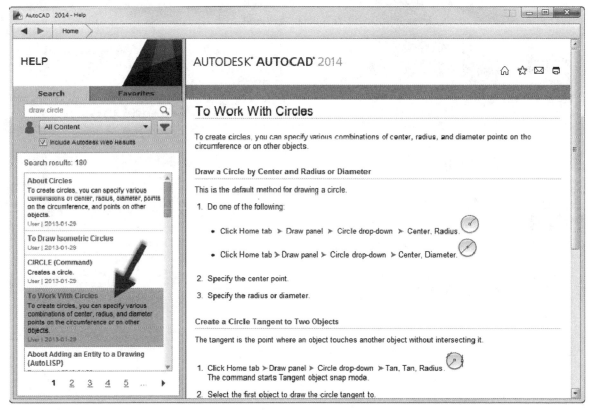

FIGURE 1-6.4 Search results

4. Click the link **To Work With Circles** (see Figure 1-6.4).

You will see specific instructions on drawing a circle in AutoCAD. Notice the various links near the bottom of the view contents window: Related Tasks, Related References, Related Concepts. These are all bits of information closely related to the main topic.

5. Click the **Home** link at the very top of the *Autodesk Help* screen to get back to the main *Help* interface (Figure 1-6.5).

Next you will narrow the search to just items related to end users rather than developers or system administrators.

FIGURE 1-6.5 Help system: Home option

6. Change the *Search* filter to **User** in the upper left corner (Figure 1-6.6).

7. Search for **zoom**.

You now have several options to choose from related to zooming in AutoCAD.

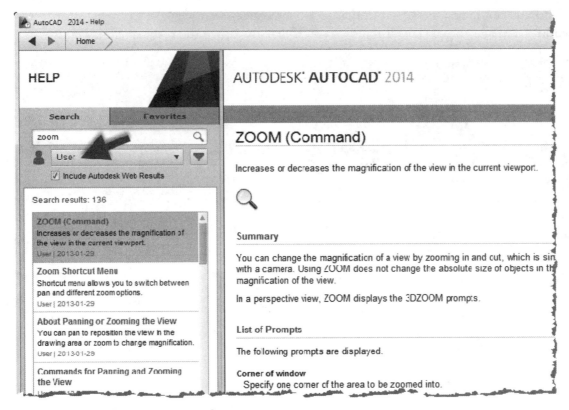

FIGURE 1-6.6 Help system: zoom reference

Discussion Groups:

You can also post questions in a user-to-user forum at Autodesk's website; http://forums.autodesk.com/. Here, other users can respond to your question. Sometimes you will get three ways to do the same thing. You choose which is best for you. However, beware, as not all replies will help and some may create more problems.

That concludes the brief overview of the *Help System* in AutoCAD. If you are having trouble or would like a little more information about a specific command, be sure to use the *Help System*.

Exercise 1-7:
Introduction to Autodesk 360

We will finish this chapter with a look at Autodesk 360, which is "ground zero" for all of Autodesk's **Cloud Services**. It is important that the student read this information in order to follow along in the book when specific steps related to using these cloud services are covered. The reader does not necessarily need to use Autodesk's cloud services to successfully complete this book.

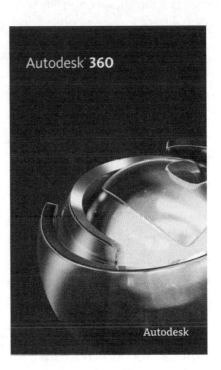

The main features employed in the book are:

- Saving your work to *Autodesk 360* so you can access the data anywhere and know that the files are in a secure, backed up location. This feature is free to anyone, with some limitations to be discussed later.
- Sending your photorealistic rendering project to the *Cloud* to dramatically reduce the overall processing time. This feature is free to students and a free trail is available to everyone else.

Here is how Autodesk describes *Autodesk 360* on their website:

> The Autodesk® 360 cloud-based framework provides tools and services to extend design beyond the desktop. Streamline your workflows, effectively collaborate, and quickly access and share your work anytime, from anywhere. With virtually infinite computing power in the cloud, Autodesk 360 scales up or down to meet business needs without the infrastructure or upfront investment required for traditional desktop software.

Before we discuss *Autodesk 360* with more specificity, let's define what the *Cloud* is. **The Cloud is a service, or collection of services, which exists partially or completely online.** This is different from the *Internet*, which mostly involves downloading static information, in that you are creating and manipulating data. Most of this happens outside of your laptop or desktop computer. This gives the average user access to massive amounts of storage space, computing power and software they could not otherwise afford if they had to actually own, install and maintain these resources in their office, school or home. In one sense, this is similar to a *Tool Rental Center*, in that the average person could not afford, nor would it be cost-effective to own, a jackhammer. However, for a fraction of the cost of ownership and maintenance, we can rent it for a few hours. In this case, everyone wins!

Creating a Free Autodesk 360 Account

The first thing an individual needs to do in order to gain access to *Autodesk 360* is create a free account at https://360.autodesk.com (students: see tip below); the specific steps will be covered later in this section, so you don't need to do this now. This account is for an individual person, not a computer, not an installation of Revit or AutoCAD, nor does it come from your employer or school. Each person who wishes to access *Autodesk 360* services must create account, which will give them a unique username and password.

> *TIP:* Students should first create an account at http://students.autodesk.com. This is the same place you go to download free Autodesk software. Be sure to use your school email address as this is what identifies you as a qualifying student. Once you create an account there, you can use this same user name and password to access *Autodesk 360*. Following these steps will give you access to more storage space and unlimited cloud rendering!

Generally speaking, there are three ways you can access *Autodesk 360* cloud services:
- Autodesk 360 website
- Within Revit or AutoCAD; local computer
- Mobile device; smart phone or tablet

Autodesk 360 Website

When you have documents stored in the *Cloud* you may access them via your web browser. Here you can manage your files, view them without the full application (some file formats not supported) and share them. These features use some advanced browser technology, so you need to make sure your browser is up to date; specifically:

To view most 2D documents, use these browsers:

- Mozilla® Firefox® 10 and later

- Google Chrome™ 16 and later

- Microsoft® Internet Explorer® 8 and later

- Apple® Safari® 5.1 and later

To view both 2D and 3D documents, use these browsers:

- Mozilla® Firefox® 10 and later

- Google Chrome™ 16 and later

Important: Depending on your browser, the Adobe® Flash® Player may be required to upload files and view video.

Using the website, you can upload files from your computer to store in the *Cloud*. To do this, you switch to the **Folders and Categories** section and click the **Upload** option (Figure 1-7.1). **Tip:** If using Firefox or Chrome, you can drag and drop documents into the *Upload Documents* window. This is a great way to create a secure backup of your documents.

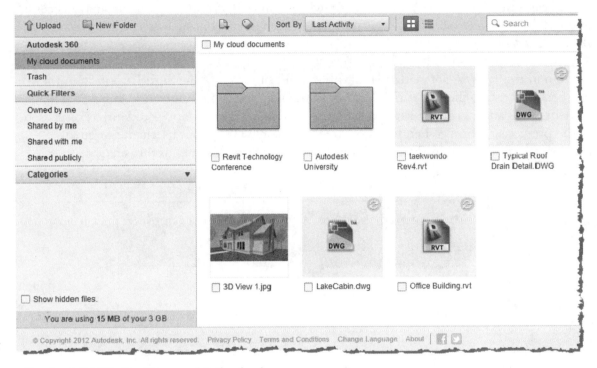

FIGURE 1-7.1 Viewing files stored in the cloud

You can share files stored in the *Cloud* with others. <u>Private sharing</u> with others who have an *Autodesk 360* account is very easy. Another option is <u>public sharing</u>, which allows you to send someone a link and they can access the file, even if they don't have a 360 account. Simply right-click on a file within *Autodesk 360* to see the sharing options (Figure 1-7.2).

FIGURE 1-7.2 Sharing files stored in the cloud

Autodesk 360 within Revit or AutoCAD; local computer

Another way in which you can access you data, stored in the cloud, is from with-in your Autodesk application; for example, Revit or AutoCAD. This is typically the most convenient as you can open, view and modify your drawings. Once logged in, you will also have access to any *Cloud Services* available to you from within the application, such as rendering or *Green Building Studio*.

To sign in to *Autodesk 360* within your application, simply click the **Sign In** option in the notification area; in the upper right corner of the window. You will need to enter your student email address and password (or personal email if you are not a student) as discussed in the previous section. When properly logged in, you will see your username or email address listed as shown in Figure 1-7.3 below. You will try this later in this section.

FIGURE 1-7.3 Example of user logged into Autodesk 360

Once you are logged in, and if *Autodesk 360* is installed on your computer, you will also see an *Autodesk 360* option in the drop-down list of the *Open* dialog box, as shown in Figure 1-7.4.

FIGURE 1-7.4 Autodesk 360 accessed from the open dialog

Keep in mind that ALL files stored in Autodesk 360 are saved on the hard drive of ANY computer you are using; this is ONLY true if you log into *Autodesk 360*. The files are not easy to find manually, but a search could reveal them rather quickly. The files are NOT deleted off of the local computer when you log out either. This should not be a problem for working through this book, but you will want to be careful when working with design files from your firm or office (if you work in one).

When you are logged into *Autodesk 360* from within your application, you can also view your files using *Windows Explorer*. Notice in the image below (Figure 1-7.5), that *Autodesk 360* is listed as a *Favorite*. When you click the Autodesk 360 link, your files and folders are shown to the right. Using this view, you can more easily add folders and copy files.

FIGURE 1-7.5 Autodesk 360 files accessed from windows explorer

Using Revit or AutoCAD on your computer, it is possible to work on files directly in the cloud – kind of. You actually work on the local version of your files, which are automatically synced with the online version anytime they change. Keep in mind this does not work for the multi-user environment, called work-sharing, which Revit is capable of.

When *Autodesk 360* is installed on your local computer system, you will have an icon for it in the *Windows* system tray as shown in Figure 1-7.6. If you right-click on this icon you will be presented with a few options. Such as, open the local folder, open the website view, Sync now, pause sync and preferences.

Clicking preferences presents the dialog box shown in Figure 1-7.7. Here you can see how much space you have available, enable automatic log-in upon system start up and what to do with linked files. You can also force a *Sign Out* to manually break the connection to the *Cloud*. Your local version of the files will still be on your computer, but the Autodesk 360 links will not reveal them.

FIGURE 1-7.6
Autodesk 360 in the system tray

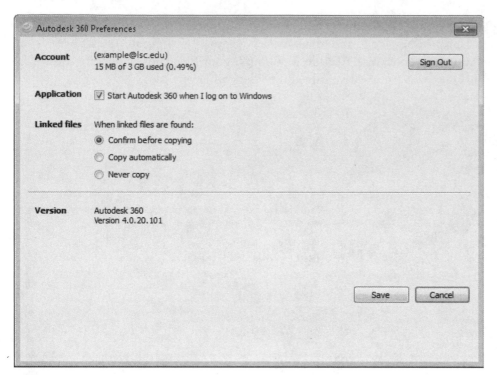

FIGURE 1-7.7 Autodesk 360 preferences for your computer

When using the **Render in Cloud** feature, you must be logged into *Autodesk 360* within the application. This is how the *Cloud Service* validates your job request. You either need to be a student, have an account associated with Autodesk Subscription, or have pre-paid for Autodesk Cloud credits.

Render Render
in Cloud Gallery

On the **Autodesk 360** tab (Figure 1-7.8) you have several tools and settings related to *Autodesk 360* close services. One option is to backup any customization you have made to your AutoCAD software. These setting will then follow you to each computer you work on, as long as you are logged into Autodesk 360. You should not need to do this while working through this book. You can also share a document; this might be an option for turning in your assignments for class.

FIGURE 1-7.8 Cloud-based tool within the application

The first time you log into Autodesk 360 you are presented with a dialog box to set a few initial options related to syncing data (Figure 1-7.9). One option is to automatically copy all your drawings you work on to the *Cloud*. You may want to enable this feature as a way to back up your files automatically. In any case, you should at least be manually saving your files to Autodesk 360 for back up and remote access.

The second option is to sync your customization setting in AutoCAD. As previously mentioned, you may not want to do this until you are more experienced; if you mess something up, you don't want those settings following you to another computer.

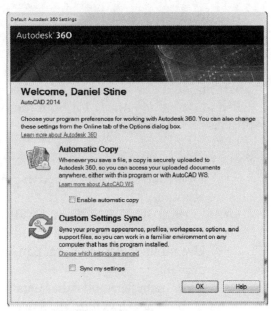

FIGURE 1-7.9 Initial settings dialog

You can access these settings later by typing **Options** in the *Command Window*. On the *Online* tab you will see these options, plus additional information (Figure 1-7.10). Notice the amount of *Cloud Storage* space is listed.

FIGURE 1-7.10 Online settings via AutoCAD options dialog

Autodesk 360 Mobile

Once you have your files stored in the *Cloud* via Autodesk 360, you will also be able to access them on your tablet or smart phone if you have one. Autodesk has a free app called *Autodesk 360 Mobile* for both the Apple or Android phones and tablets.

Some of the mobile features include:
- Open and view files stored in your Autodesk 360 account
- 2D and 3D DWG™ and DWF™ files
- Revit® and Navisworks® files
- Use multi-touch to zoom, pan, and rotate drawings
- View meta data and other details about elements within your drawing
- Find tools that help you communicate changes with your collaborators

The Android app is installed via *Google Play* and the Apple app comes from *iTunes*.

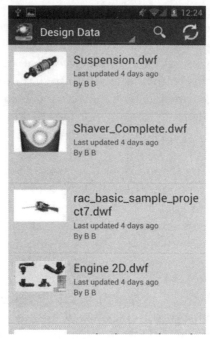

FIGURE 1-7.11
Viewing files on smart phone

Setting up your Autodesk 360 account

The next few steps will walk you through the process of setting up your free online account at *Autodesk 360*. These steps are not absolutely critical to completing this book, so if you have any reservations about creating an *Autodesk 360* account – don't do it.

1. To create a free Autodesk 360 account, do one of the following:

   a. If you are a **student**; create an account at http://students.autodesk.com.

   b. If you work for a company who has their Autodesk software on **subscription**; ask your *Contract Administrator* (this is a person in your office) to create an account for you and send you an invitation via http://subscription.autodesk.com.

   c. **Everyone else**; create an account at: https://360.autodesk.com

   FYI: The "s" at the end of "http" in the *Autodesk 360* URL means this is a secure website.

2. Open your application; AutoCAD or Revit.

3. Click the **Sign In** option in the upper-right corner of the application window (Figure 1-7.12).

FIGURE 1-7.12 Signing in to Autodesk 360

It is recommended, as you work though this book, that you save all of your work in the *Cloud*, via Autodesk 360, so you will have a safe and secure location for your files. These files can then be accessed from several locations via the three methods discussed here. It is still important to maintain a separate copy of your files on a flash drive, portable hard drive or in another *Cloud*-type location such as *Dropbox*. This will be important if your main files ever become corrupt. You should manually backup your files to your backup location so a corrupt file does not automatically corrupt your backup files.

TIP: If you have a file that will not open try one of the following:

*   In AutoCAD: Open AutoCAD and then, from the *Application Menu*, select Drawing Utilities → Recover → Recover. Then browse to your file and open it. AutoCAD will try and recover the drawing file. This may require some things to be deleted, but is better than losing the entire file.

*   In Revit: Open Revit and then, from the *Application Menu*, select Open, browse to your file, select it. Click the Audit check box, and then click Open. Revit will attempt to repair any problems with the project database. Some elements may need to be deleted, but this is better than losing the entire file.

Be sure to check out the Autodesk website to learn more about Autodesk 360 and the growing number of cloud services Autodesk is offering.

Self-Exam:

The following questions can be used as a way to check your knowledge of this lesson. The answers can be found at the bottom of the next page.

1. The *Modify* panel allows you to save your drawing file. (T/F)

2. You can zoom in and out using the wheel on a wheel mouse. (T/F)

3. AutoCAD is made specifically for architectural design. (T/F)

4. A _____ file allows you to start your drawing with certain settings preset the way you like or need them.

5. In the AutoCAD user interface, the _____ _____ displays prompts for specific user input.

Review Questions:

The following questions may be assigned by your instructor as a way to assess your knowledge of this section. Your instructor has the answers to the review questions.

1. Many commands have a keyboard shortcut. (T/F)

2. AutoCAD does not provide much in the way of online documentation. (T/F)

3. The drawings listed in the *Open Documents* menu allow you to see which drawings are currently open. (T/F)

4. When you use the **Pan** tool you are actually moving the drawing, not just changing what part of the drawing you can see on the screen. (T/F)

5. To *close* AutoCAD you simply click the X in the upper right. (T/F)

6. The icon with the floppy disk image (⊞) allows you to _____ a drawing file.

7. A *Ribbon* "panel" with a small black down-arrow to the right of the label has additional tools in an extended panel fly-out. (T/F)

8. Use the _____ _____ tool to switch the view back to the one just prior to your last zoom command.

9. Holding the Scroll Wheel down initiates the _____ command.

10. The **Model** tab (aka Model Space) is where most of the actual drafting and design is done. (T/F)

Lesson 2
Crash Course Introduction (the Basics)::

This lesson is meant to give you a brief introduction to a few of the most used commands. You will be walked through each drawing in this lesson, step-by-step. The intent is for the user to get some of the basic concepts in mind before going through subsequent chapters.

Exercise 2-1:
Lines and Shapes

Drawing Lines:

The number one command in AutoCAD is the **Line** command. Lines in AutoCAD are extremely precise drawing elements. This means you can create very accurate drawings. Lines, or any drawn object, can be as precise as eight decimal places (i.e., 24.999999999) or 1/256.

AutoCAD is a vector based program. That means each drawn object is stored in a numerical database. For example, a line is stored in the drawing's database as the X,Y, Z coordinates for its starting point and the X,Y,Z, coordinates for its endpoint. These coordinates are all relative to the drawing's 0,0,0 position, called the **Origin**.

When a line needs to be displayed on the screen, AutoCAD reads the line's coordinates from the drawing database and displays a line between those two points on the screen. This means that the line will be very accurate at any scale or zoom magnification.

A raster based program, in contrast to vector based, is comprised of dots that infill a grid. The grid can vary in density, and is typically referred to by its resolution (e.g., 600x800, 1600x1200, etc.). This file type is used by graphics programs that typically deal with photographs, such as Adobe Photoshop. There are two reasons this type of file is not appropriate for CAD programs:

1. A raster based line is composed of many dots on a grid (which also represents the line's width). When you zoom in (or magnify) the line, it becomes pixilated and you actually start to see each dot in the grid. In a vector file you can "infinitely" zoom in on a line and it will never become pixilated because the program recalculates the line each time you zoom in.

2. A CAD program, such as AutoCAD, only needs to store the starting point and end point coordinates for each line; the dots needed to draw the line are calculated on the fly for the current screen resolution. Whereas a raster file has to store each dot that represents the full length and width of the line. This can vary from a few hundred dots to several thousand dots, depending on the resolution, for the same line.

The following graphic illustrates this point:

<u>Vector vs. Raster lines</u>

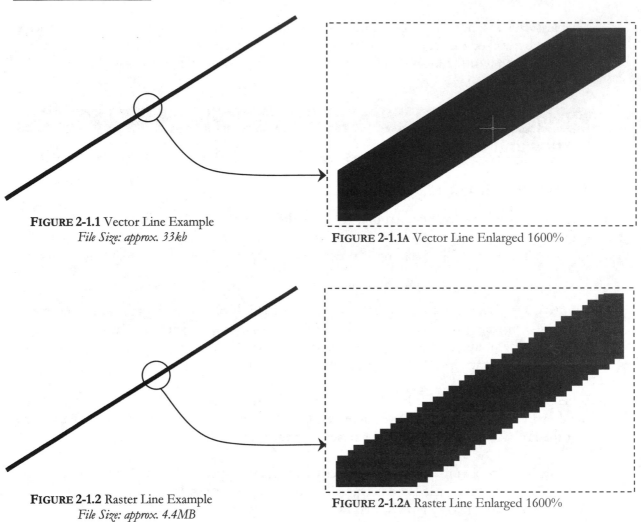

FIGURE 2-1.1 Vector Line Example
File Size: approx. 33kb

FIGURE 2-1.1A Vector Line Enlarged 1600%

FIGURE 2-1.2 Raster Line Example
File Size: approx. 4.4MB

FIGURE 2-1.2A Raster Line Enlarged 1600%

The Line Command:

You will now study the **Line** command.

3. **Open** AutoCAD; maximize the application window so it fills the screen.

4. **Close** the empty drawing automatically opened by AutoCAD.

   WARNING: *The empty startup drawing that is opened by default when you start AutoCAD does not have the various variables preset for architectural CAD use. So you should make sure you start with the correct template file whenever instructed to start a new drawing file in this book.*

5. Select **New** from the *Application* menu *(large red abstract "A" symbol).*

6. Use the following *template* file to start your new drawing from: **Architectural Imperial.dwt** *(in the SheetSets sub-folder).*

7. Click on the ***Model*** tab to switch to *Model Space* (which is where all the drawing is done as previously mentioned); see Figure 2-1.3.

   a. Turn off the *Grid Display* toggle if it is on (via the *Status Bar*).

   NOTE: *Your* Drawing Window *background should be black – the images in the book have it set to white for clarity in printing.*

FIGURE **2-1.3** Switching to Model space

8. Select the **Line** tool (*Home* tab, *Draw* panel).
   Line

9. **Draw a line** from the lower left corner of the screen to the upper right corner of the screen (by simply clicking two points on the screen); see **Figure 2-1.4**.

   TIP: *When clicking the second point, do not click on, or over, the ViewCube in the upper right. See Figure 1-2.1.*

   NOTE: *Do not drag/ hold your mouse button down; just click.*

FIGURE 2-1.4 Your first line!

After clicking your second point, you should notice by looking at the *Command Window*, that the **Line** command is still active. You could continue to draw lines, with the last point picked becoming the first point for the next line segment. In this case you will end the **Line** command per the following instructions.

10. After clicking your second point (i.e., the endpoint), **right-click** anywhere on the screen and select **Enter** from the pop-up menu (Figure 2-1.5).

This constitutes your first line! However, as you are probably aware, it is not a very accurate line as far as length and angle are concerned.

> *FYI: Your line length and proportions may vary slightly from the image above and the following few steps based on your screen size and resolution. This will not negatively affect your ability to complete this section. In any case, you should maximize the AutoCAD program so you see the largest drawing window possible.*

FIGURE 2-1.5
Right-click Menu;
Line command active

The Properties Palette:

Typically you need to provide information such as length and angle when drawing a line; you rarely pick arbitrary points on the screen like you did in the previous steps. Most of the time you also need to accurately pick your starting point (for example, how far one line is from another or picking the exact middle point on another line).

DID YOU MAKE A MISTAKE? LOCATION: *QUICK ACCESS TOOLBAR*

Whenever you make a mistake in AutoCAD you can use the **UNDO** command to revert to a previous drawing state. You can perform multiple UNDOs all the way to your previous *Save* (and then some).

Similarly, if you press **Undo** a few too many times, you can use **REDO**.

Having said that, however, the line you just drew still has precise numbers associated with its length and angle. In the next step you will use the *Properties* palette to view the line's length and angle.

11. Select the **Properties** icon (**View** tab, *Palettes* panel) or press Ctrl + 1.

Properties

You now have the *Properties* palette open on your screen. Notice that the textbox at the top says "*No selection*"; this is because no objects are selected yet (Figure 2-1.6).

> *TIP: If the* Properties *palette is too narrow on the screen, some information may not be completely visible. You can easily resize any palette by dragging one of the three sides (opposite the palette title bar).*

Now that the *Properties* palette is open, you can select the line to display its properties.

12. **Select the Line**; hover the cursor over the line and click on it.

> *FYI: Notice the line highlights before you select it. This helps to select the correct line the first time.*

FIGURE 2-1.6 Properties Palette; No objects selected

You should now see the line's properties. Notice the textbox at the top now indicates what type of object is selected (Figure 2-1.7).

Are Your Units and Drawing Window Size Correct?

If the properties on your computer are displaying the line's data in decimals instead of feet and inches (as shown in Figure 2-1.7), that means you did not start using the correct template file.

Similarly, if your *Drawing Window* is not approximately 5'-6" x 3'-0" then you either started with the wrong template or your template file has been altered; if the latter is the case, which is less likely, zoom in (or out) to "correct" the screen display for this exercise.

If you started with the wrong template you should close the drawing and start this lesson over.

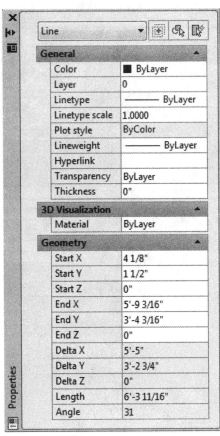

Notice the information displayed for the selected line:

- o The X, Y and Z coordinates are listed, relative to the drawing's origin (0,0,0), for both the start and end points.

- o The line's Length and Angle are listed.

- o Delta X and Delta Y; the Delta X is the horizontal distance between the start point and the end point.

The white areas are editable and the grey areas are not. You cannot edit the length, for example, because AutoCAD needs more info, like what direction to make the line longer.

FIGURE 2-1.7
Properties palette; Line selected

You should make one final observation about the line's properties and the current view: the Delta X and Delta Y represent the horizontal and vertical distances between the line's start and end points. This tells us that the drawing area, currently visible on the screen, is about 5'-5" across (horizontally) and 3'-2" up and down (vertically). That means that the largest item we can draw (and still see what we are doing) is something that is 5'-5" wide x 3'-2" tall. (See Figure 2-1.8.)

> **RECAP:** *At any given time you could draw a diagonal line, from one corner of the Drawing window to the other, list that line's Properties, observe the Delta X and Delta Y values, and infer from that information the current drawing area that you are zoomed into.*

FIGURE 2-1.8 Visible area of current drawing

Everything is DrawnFull-Scale:

Even though your current view is showing a relatively small area, *Model Space* (where you do all your drafting and design) is actually an infinite drawing board.

In architectural CAD drafting, everything is drawn "real-world" size (or full-scale). ALWAYS! If you are drawing a building, you might draw a line for the exterior wall that is 600'-0" long. If you are drawing a window detail, you might draw a line that is ⅛" long. In either case you are entering that line's actual length.

You could, of course, have a ⅛" line and a 600'-0" line in the same drawing. Either line would be difficult to see at the current drawing magnification (i.e.,approx. 5'-5"x3'-2" area). So you would have to zoom in to see the ⅛" line and zoom out to see the 600'-0" line. You will try this next:

Draw a ⅛" Line:

13. For now, **Close** the *Properties* palette by clicking the **X** in the upper corner of the palette.

The next steps will walk you through drawing a ⅛" horizontal line. AutoCAD provides more than one way to do this. You will try one of them now.

You should understand that it is virtually impossible to draw a perfectly horizontal or vertical (or any precise angle) line by visually picking points on the screen. You need AutoCAD's help!

14. On the *Status Bar*, make sure **Polar Tracking** is turned on. (Figure 2-1.9). *It should have a bluish background.*

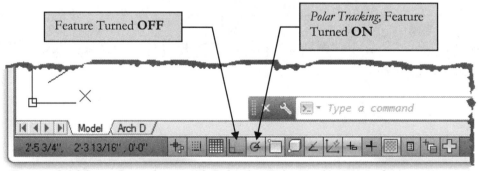

FIGURE 2-1.9 Status Bar – shown with Polar (i.e., Polar Tracking) turned on.

TIP: You can adjust the Polar *settings by right-clicking on the button and selecting* Settings.

Polar Tracking:

This drawing aid feature allows you to draw lines at precise angles. When you are in the process of drawing a line, *Polar Tracking* will "snap" to certain angles in the *Drawing* window whenever your cursor comes close to that angle.

A dashed line will appear on the screen giving you a visual tip that the line is "snapped" to one of the predefined angles set within the *Polar Tracking* settings. In addition to the dashed line, the tooltip (near your cursor) displays the word *Polar* and the locked angle.

Clicking the mouse or entering a length, while the dashed line is visible, ensures the line's proper angle.

15. Using the **Line** command, pick a point somewhere in the upper left corner of the *Drawing* window.

16. Start moving the mouse towards the right, and generally horizontal until you see a dashed reference line (extending off the screen in the direction you want to draw the line) appear on the screen as in Figure 2-1.10.

FIGURE 2-1.10 Drawing a line with the help of Polar Tracking

TIP: *In order to see the on-screen dimension and the tooltip you need to make sure the* ***Dynamic Input*** *icon is toggled on (on the Status Bar).*

17. With the dashed line and *tooltip* visible on the screen, take your hand off the mouse (so you don't accidentally move it), type **1/8** and then press **Enter**; finish the **Line** command. **Right-click** and select **Enter** to finish the line command.

> ***TIP:*** *Notice you did not have to type the inch symbol; AutoCAD always assumes you mean inches unless you specify otherwise. A future lesson will review the input options in a little more detail.*

You have just drawn a line with a precise length and angle!

18. Use the ***Properties*** palette to verify it was drawn correctly (similar to Steps 11 and 12); check the *length* and *angle* values.

19. Use the **Zoom Window** tool to enlarge the view of the ⅛″ line (or – *better* – use your wheel mouse).

20. Now use the **Zoom Extents** tool so that both lines are visible again (or double-click on the wheel button).

Draw a 600′ line:

21. Select the **Line** icon and pick a point in the lower right corner of the *Drawing* window.

> ***FYI:*** *Selecting a tool cancels any active commands.*

22. Move the crosshairs (i.e., mouse) straight up from your first point so that *Polar Tracking* activates (Figure 2-1.11).

23. With the dashed line and tooltip visible on the screen, take your hand off the mouse (so you don't accidentally move it), and type**600′** and then press **Enter**.

FIGURE 2-1.11 Drawing another line with the help of Polar Tracking

> ***TIP:*** *Notice this time you had to type the foot symbol (′) or AutoCAD would have assumed you meant 600 inches, which is only 50′.*

24. End the **Line** command *(right-click and select Enter).*

Because the visible portion of the drawing area is only 3'-2" tall (Figure 2-1.8), you obviously would not expect to see a 600' line. You need to change the drawing's magnification (i.e., zoom out) to see it.

25. Use **Zoom Extents** to see the entire drawing (Figure 2-1.12) – *View* tab, *Navigate* panel *(or double-click the center wheel mouse button).*

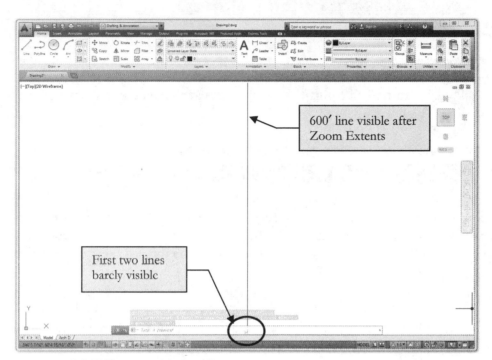

FIGURE 2-1.12 Drawing with three lines

Drawing Shapes:

AutoCAD gives you the commands to draw common shapes like square/rectangles, circles, ellipses, polygons. These commands can be found in the *Draw* panel on the *Home* tab. You will take a look at the **Rectangle** and **Circle** commands now.

SETTING YOUR WORKSPACE: AutoCAD has two very different looking User Interfaces: the newer one used throughout this textbook and a "classic" one which mimics previous versions of AutoCAD. So, if your screen does not look similar to the screen shots in this book, click on the small gear icon in the lower right corner of the screen and select Drafting and Annotation from the popup list that appears; this can also be changed on the Quick Access Toolbar in the upper left corner.

Drawing a Rectangle:

26. Use **Zoom Previous** (or **Zoom Window**) to get back to the original view.

27. Select the **Rectangle** tool from the *Draw* panel.

    Notice the *dynamic tooltip* prompt near your cursor:

    > *TIP: Pay attention to these prompts while you are learning AutoCAD; they tell you what information is expected/requested. Similar prompts are also displayed in the Command Window.*

28. Pick your "**first corner point**" somewhere near the middle-bottom of the *Drawing* window (Figure 2-1.13).

    Notice the *dynamic tooltip* prompt near your cursor:

At this point you can pick a point on the screen, type an X,Y,Z coordinate, or enter the dimensions on-screen via the dynamic tooltip feature near your cursor; you will use the latter method as it is easiest (*Dynamic Input* must be toggled "on" down on the *Options Bar*).

29. While being prompted for the "other corner", simply start typing (AutoCAD defaults to the *Width* tooltip for dynamic input). Type **6.5** (this equals 6½″) and then press the **Tab** key on the keyboard; do not press Enter.

Pressing **Tab** toggles you over to the *Height* tooltip for dynamic input (see prompt image at the top of the next page).

Notice the *Width* just entered has a padlock symbol next to it, which means that value is locked in. So, even though you will enter a numeric value for the *Height*, you could pick a point on the screen and no matter where you picked the *Width* would be 6.5″.

> *TIP: When drawing a rectangle, typing negative values allows you to dictate in which direction the rectangle is drawn (relative to your first pick point). When both numbers are positive, as in the previous example, the rectangle is drawn up and to the right of your first pick point.*

    Notice the current on-screen prompt:

30. Type **14** and then press **Enter** (this equals 1′-2″).

FIGURE 2-1.13 Drawing with Rectangle added

Drawing a Circle:

31. Select the **Circle** tool from the *Draw* panel.

Circle

32. You are now prompted to pick the center point for the circle; pick a point approximately as shown in Figure 2-1.13.

    You should now see the following on-screen prompt:

Tooltip menus:

Whenever you see a down-arrow icon within the on-screen tooltip (like the one above), you can press the down-arrow key on the keyboard to see a list of options pop up below the tooltip (see example to right). The options relate to the active command (the active command being the Circle command in this example).

Right-click menus:

Another option is to right-click the mouse to see the same options as above plus a few standard options; this is called the context menu. If you clicked Diameter, the context menu goes away and AutoCAD expects you to enter the diameter rather than the radius.

Move your mouse around to see that you could arbitrarily pick a point on the screen to create a quick circle if needed, then proceed to the next step where you will draw a circle with a radius of 6⅝″.

33. Type **6-5/8** and then press **Enter** (this equals 6⅝″). (See Figure 2-1.14 on the next page.)

34. View the properties for both the Circle and Rectangle.

   NOTE: *See Figure 2-1.15 for the Circle's properties; you can actually modify the Circle by entering a new Circumference or Area.*

35. **Save** your drawing as **ex2-1.dwg**.

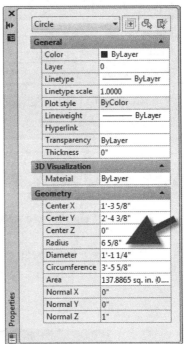

FIGURE 2-1.15 Properties for circle

FIGURE 2-1.14 Drawing with Circle added

Where Should I Save My Files?

You should save your files to your Autodesk 360 storage space if you have set that up. Refer back to chapter one for more information on how to setup Cloud Storage.

You can also create a folder in which to save your AutoCAD files, typically a sub-folder in the My Documents folder. Your instructor may specify a location for your files if you are using this textbook in a classroom setting.

Thus far you have learned how to draw accurate orthogonal lines (i.e., horizontal and vertical) and verify their accuracy using the *Properties* palette. You can also accurately draw rectangles and circles. You have also employed *Dynamic Input* and *Polar Tracking*.

Everything drawn so far has been separate, isolated items. More often than not you will want to draw lines that connect to each other, and as previously mentioned, it is virtually impossible to simply visually pick a point on the screen and have it be perfectly accurate. So when you want to draw a new line in relation to a previously drawn one you have to use a special feature known as *Object Snaps* when drawing and modifying objects in AutoCAD. You will learn about this feature next.

Exercise 2-2:
Object Snaps

Introduction

Object Snap is a tool that allows you to accurately pick a point on an object. For example, when drawing a line you can use *Object Snap* (*OSNAP*) to select as the start-point, the endpoint or midpoint of another line.

This feature is absolutely critical to drawing accurate technical drawings. Using this feature allows you to be confident you are creating perfect intersections, corners, etc. (Figure 2-2.1).

Object Snaps Options:

You can use *Object Snaps* in one of two ways:

o   Using the *Running OSNAP* mode
o   On an individual pick-point basis

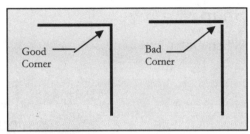

FIGURE 2-2.1 Typical problem when Object Snap is not used

Running OSNAP mode is a feature that, when turned on, constantly scans the area near your cursor when AutoCAD is looking for user input. You can configure which types of points to look for.

Using an *Object Snap* for individual pick-points allows you to quickly select a particular point on an object. This option will also override the *Running OSNAP* setting, which means you tell AutoCAD to just look for the endpoint on an object (for the next pick-point only) rather than the three or four types being scanned for by the *Running OSNAP* feature.

Enabling Running Object Snaps:

To toggle *Running Object Snap* on and off you click the **Object Snap** button on the *Status Bar*.

FIGURE 2-2.2 Status Bar – shown with OSNAP (Object Snap) turned on

Snap Symbols:

When *Object Snap* is turned on, AutoCAD displays symbols as you move your cursor about the *Drawing* window (while you are in a command like **Line** and AutoCAD is awaiting your input or pick-point).

If you hold your cursor still for a moment, while a snap symbol is displayed, a tooltip will appear on the screen. However, when you become familiar with the snap symbols you can pick sooner, rather than waiting for the tooltip to display.

Symbol	Position	Keyboard Shortcut
✕	Intersection	INT
▢	Endpoint	END
△	Midpoint	MID
◇	Quadrant	QUA
○	Center	CEN
⊠	Nearest	NEA
⌊	Perpendicular	PER
○	Tangent	TAN

FIGURE 2-2.3 OSNAP symbols that are displayed on the screen when selecting a point.

The **Tab** key cycles through the available snaps near your cursor.

The keyboard shortcut turns off the other snaps for one pick. For example, if you type *END* on the keyboard while in the **Line** command, AutoCAD will only look for an *Endpoint* for the next pick.

Finally, if you need a particular snap for just one pick, you can hold the ***Shift* key and right-click** for the *OSNAP* context menu (see image to left). If you pick **Center**, AutoCAD will only look for a Center to snap to for the next pick and then revert back to the previous settings.

Setting Object Snaps:

You can set AutoCAD to have just one or all *Object Snaps* running at the same time. Let's say you have *Endpoint* and *Midpoint* set to be running. While using the **Line** command, move your cursor near an existing line. When the cursor is near the end of the line, you will see the *Endpoint* symbol show up. When you move the cursor towards the middle of the line, you will see the *Midpoint* symbol show up.

The next step shows you how to tell AutoCAD which *Object Snaps* you want it to look for.

First you need to **Open** the drawing from the DVD.

1. **Open** drawing **ex2-1 Osnap.dwg** from the DVD.

2. Next, do a **Save-As** and save to your hard drive.

3. Right-click on the *OSNAP* button on the *Status Bar* and select **Settings** from the pop-up menu (Figure 2-2.4).

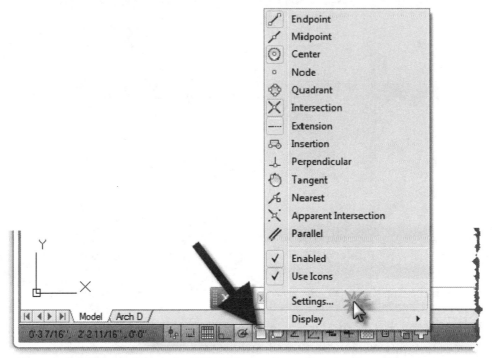

FIGURE 2-2.4 Right-click on the OSNAP button located on the *Status Bar*

You are now in the **Drafting Settings** dialog box on the *Object Snaps* tab; compare to **Figure 2-2.5.**

4. Make sure only the following *Object Snaps* are checked:
   a. Endpoint
   b. Midpoint
   c. Center
   d. Intersection
   e. Perpendicular

5. Click **OK** to close the *Drafting Settings* dialog box.

   FOR MORE INFORMATION: For more on using Object Snaps, search AutoCAD's Help system for **Drafting Settings.** *Then click the* **Drafting Settings Dialog Box** *and select the* **Object Snap** *link within the article.*

   FYI: The Running Object Snaps *shown in Figure 2-2.5 are for AutoCAD in general, not just the current drawing. This is convenient; you don't have to adjust to your favorite settings for each drawing (existing or new).*

FIGURE 2-2.5 Object Snap tab on Drafting Settings dialog

Now that you have the *Running Object Snaps* set, you will give this feature a try.

6. On the *Home* tab, in the *Draw* panel, pick the **Line** command, move your cursor to the lower-left portion of the diagonal line (Figure 2-2.6).

Line

7. Hover the cursor over the line's endpoint (without picking), when you see the *Endpoint* symbol you can click to select that point.

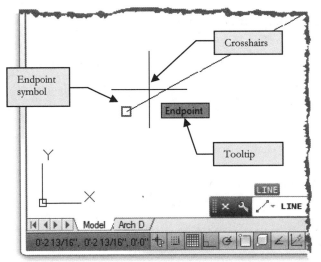

FIGURE 2-2.6 Endpoint OSNAP symbol visible

JUST SO YOU KNOW...

It is important that you see the *OSNAP* symbol before clicking. Also, once you see the symbol you should be careful not to move the mouse too much.

These steps will help to ensure accurate corners.

While still in the Line command, you will draw additional lines using *OSNAP* to accurately select the line's *start point* and *endpoint*.

8.   Draw the additional lines shown in **Figure 2-2.7** using the appropriate *Object Snap* (changing the *Running Snap* as required to select the required point).

> ***TIP #1:*** *When using the Line command you can draw several line segments without the need to terminate the Line command and then restart it for the next line segment. After picking the start and end points for a line, the end point automatically becomes the first point for the next line segment; this continues until your finish the Line command (i.e., right-click and select Enter).*

> ***TIP #2:*** *At any point, while the Line command is active, you can right-click on the OSNAP button (on the Status Bar) and adjust its settings, or press Shift+Right-click; the Line command will not cancel.*

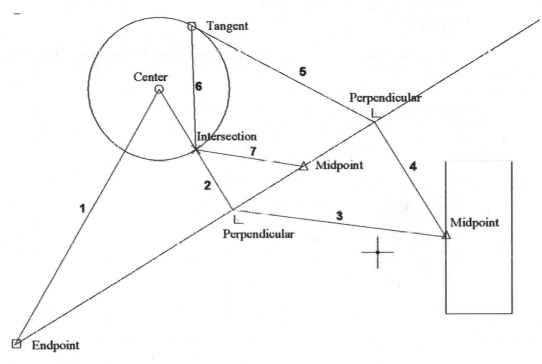

FIGURE 2-2.7 Several lines added using running OSNAPs.
The numbers indicate the order in which the lines are to be drawn.

9.   **Save** your drawing as ex2-2.dwg.

This is an Architectural Example?

OK, this is not really an architectural example yet. However, the point here is to focus on the fundamental concepts and not architecture just yet.

Exercise 2-3:
Modify Tools

The *Modify* tools are the most used group of tools in AutoCAD. Much time is spent tweaking designs and making code related revisions.

Example: Use the *Draw* tools (e.g., Lines, Circles, Rectangles) to initially draw the walls, doors, windows and furniture. Then use the *Modify* tools to *Stretch* a room so it is larger, *Mirror* a door so it swings in the direction of egress, and *Move* the furniture per the owner's instructions.

The ability to instantly modify drawings is why CAD is so useful to architects and designers. Compared to the days of hand drawings, erasing and redrawing, CAD is a significant productivity booster.

You will access the various *Modify* tools from the *Modify* panel on the *Home* tab as introduced in Lesson 1.

This textbook focuses on the parts of a command needed to complete a specific task. If you are interested in a further investigation of a specific feature or command, you may use the *Help* system; the image below (Figure 2-3.1) shows the *Select Objects* section selected.

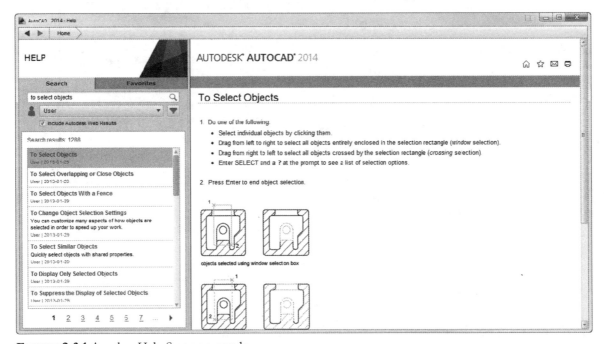

FIGURE 2-3.1 Another Help System example

In this exercise you will get a brief overview of a few of the *Modify* tools, manipulating the tangled web of lines you have previously drawn.

1. **Open** drawing **ex2-2.dwg** from the previous lesson.

2. **Save-Asex2-3.dwg**.

> *FYI: You will notice in this book that instructions or commands that have already been covered will have fewer "step-by-step" instructions.*

Erase Command:

It is no surprise that the **Erase** tool is a necessity, things change and mistakes are made. You can erase one entity at a time or several. Erasing entities is very easy; you select the **Erase** icon, pick the objects to erase and then right-click (which equals pressing *Enter* on the keyboard). You will try this on two lines in your drawing.

3. Select **Erase** (*Modify* panel, *Home* tab).

4. [Notice the *Command* line is prompting: **Select objects:**]
   Use the mouse to select the lines identified in **Figure 2-3.2**.

   > *TIP: See the section on Selecting Entities on the next page.*

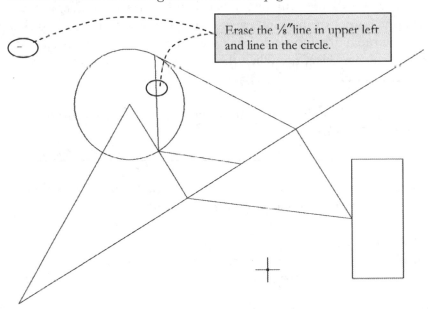

Erase the ⅛″line in upper left and line in the circle.

FIGURE 2-3.2 Lines to be erased

5. **Right-click** to complete the task.

Selecting Entities:

At this time we will digress and take a quick look at the various techniques for selecting entities in AutoCAD. Most commands work the same when it comes to selecting entities. As mentioned before, you need to keep your eye on the *prompts* so you know when AutoCAD is ready for you to select entities or provide other user input.

When selecting entities, you have two primary ways to select them:
- o   Individually select entities one at a time
- o   Select several entities at a time with a window

You can use one, or a combination of both, methods to select entities (when using the Copy command for example).

Individual Selections:

When prompted to select entities (to copy or erase, for example), simply move the cursor over the object and click. With most commands you repeat this process until you have selected all the entities you need (selections are cumulative), then you typically press **Enter** or right-click to tell AutoCAD you are done selecting. Holding the *Shift* key while selecting will remove items from the current selection set. Pressing the *Esc* key (1-3 times) will unselect everything and cancel the current command.

Window Selections:

Similarly, when prompted to select entities, you can pick a Window around several entities to select them all at once. To select a window, rather than selecting an object as previously described, you select one corner of the window you wish to select (that is, you pick a point in "space"). Now as you move the mouse you will see a rectangle on the screen that represents the window you are selecting. When the window encompasses the entities you wish to select, click the mouse.

You actually have two types of windows you can select. One is called a **Window** and the other is called a **Crossing Window**.

Window:
This option allows you to select only the entities that are completely within the *Window*. Any lines that extend out of the *Window* are not selected.

Crossing Window:
This option allows you to select all the entities that are completely within the *Window* and any that extend outside the *Window*.

Using Window versus Crossing Window:
To select a *Window* you simply pick your two points from left to right (Figure 2-3.3a).

Conversely, to select a *Crossing Window*, you pick the two diagonal points of the window from right to left (Figure 2-3.3b).

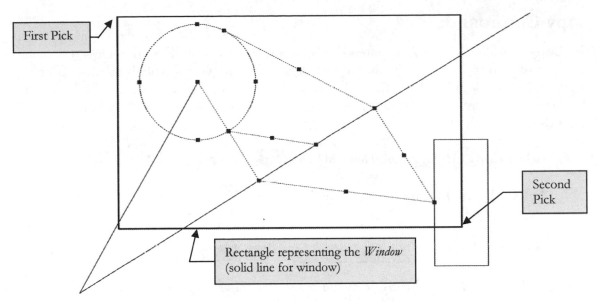

FIGURE 2-3.3A Lines selected using a *Window*, only the lines within the window are selected.

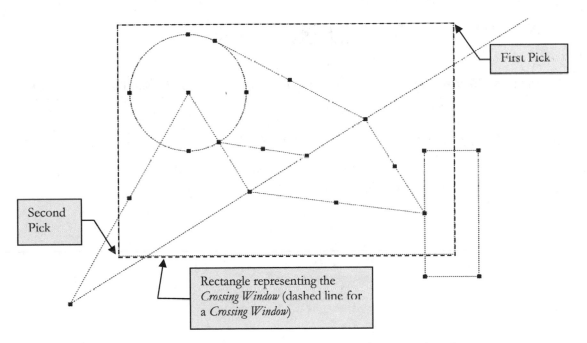

FIGURE 2-3.3B Lines selected using a *Crossing Window;* all lines are selected.

Copy Command:

The **Copy** tool allows you to accurately duplicate an entity(s). You select the items you want to copy and then pick two points that represent an imaginary vector (which provides both length and angle) defining the path used to copy the entity to; you can also type in the length and angle if there are no convenient points to pick in the drawing. You will try both methods next.

6.   Select **Copy** (*Modify* panel, *Home* tab).

7.   **Select the circle** and then **right-click**. *This tells AutoCAD that you are done selecting entities to copy.*

    Notice the prompt:

8.   Pick the ***Center*** of the **circle** as the base point (Figure 2-3.4).

    FYI: *You actually have three different OSNAPs you can use here: Center, Endpoint and Intersection. All occur at the exact same point.*

    Notice the prompt: Specify second point or ▣ 2'-1 1/8" < 265°

9.   Pick the ***Endpoint*** of the angled line in the lower left corner. (See Figures 2-3.4 and 2-3.5.)

    FYI: *At this point you could continue copying the circle all over your drawing; AutoCAD will remain in copy mode until you press Esc or Enter.*

10. Press **Enter** to finish the command.

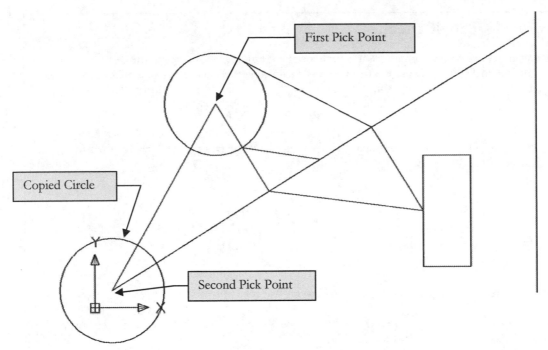

FIGURE 2-3.4 Copied circle; also indicates points selected

TIP: You may need to zoom out to see the entire circle just copied.

11. Select **Copy** again.

12. **Select the rectangle** and then **right-click**.

13. Pick an arbitrary point on the screen and then start moving your cursor up and to the right; your line cannot be "snapped" to the horizontal. *(In this scenario, it makes no difference where you pick; you will see why in a moment.)*

At this point you will type in the displacement data (i.e., distance and angle), rather than picking a second point on the screen.

14. *The following will be entered via the on-screen Dynamic Input:* Type **18**, press **Tab** then type **45** and press **Enter**. (See Figure 2-3.5 and on-screen prompts below.) Finally, press **Enter** to finish the command.

What does 18 Tab 45 mean?

When you need to *Move* or *Copy* something to a very specific location, you can type in the distance and angle from the original entity (i.e., use the first point as displacement). This is very useful when you do not have any entities drawn that represent this distance and angle (e.g., as per the steps when you copied the circle, Figure 2-3.4).

The **18** represents the distance, in this case 18 inches. Remember, if you do not specify feet or inches <u>AutoCAD assumes inches</u>. So in this example you would not have to press the extra key for the inch symbol; although 18″ would work.

Here are some other valid distances:

1′4	equals	1′-4″		16	equals	1′-4″
3′	equals	3′-0″		36	equals	3′-0″
0-3/4	equals	¾″		.75	equals	¾″
3-5/8	equals	3⅝″		1′3-5/8″	equals	1′-3⅝″

Tab toggles over to the angle parameter (a second *Tab* gets you back to length).

The **45** represents the angle (or direction) the entities will be Moved or Copied; the angle is based off of the positive x-axis in a counter-clockwise direction.

Here are some angles and a graphical representation of their direction:

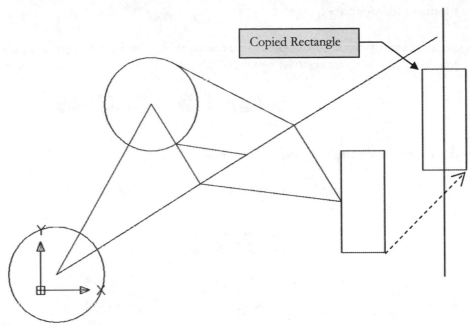

FIGURE 2-3.5 Copied rectangle. Dashed line represents the distance and angle of displacement.

> *NOTE: Your drawing may look a little different than this one because your drawing is not to scale.*

Move Command:

The **Move** command works exactly like the **Copy** command except, of course, you move the entities rather than copy them. Given the similarity to the previous command covered, the **Move** command will not be covered here. You are encouraged to try it yourself. Use the **Undo** command to get back to the drawing shown in Figure 2-3.5 before proceeding if you decide to try the **Move** command.

Rotate Command:

With the **Rotate** command, you can arbitrarily or accurately rotate one or more entities in your drawing. When you need to rotate accurately, you can pick points that define the angle (assuming points exist in the drawing to pick) or you can type a specific angle. The architectural template you are using in this book has the degrees "type" set to decimal. Other types are available such as Deg/Min/Sec and Radians, but architects typically use decimal angles unless drawing a site plan from a surveyor's drawing that has angles listed in another format.

15. Select **Rotate** (*Modify* panel, *Home* tab). Rotate

16. **Select the rectangle** you just copied (i.e., the new one) and then **right-click**; *this tells AutoCAD that you are done selecting entities to rotate.*

    You are now prompted: Specify base point: | 6'-3 3/8" | 2'-2 9/16" |

This is the point about which the rotation will occur.

17. Pick the *Midpoint* of the vertical line on the left side of the rectangle (Figure 2-3.6).

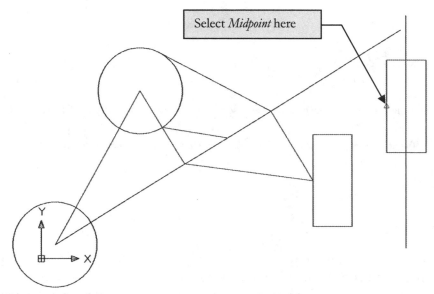

Select *Midpoint* here

FIGURE 2-3.6 Rotate command. First Step - Select *Midpoint* of left vertical line.

    You are now prompted: Specify rotation angle or ⊞ | 90 |

18. Type **90** and then press **Enter**.

Similar to the rotation angle examples recently discussed, the previous step just rotated the rectangle 90 degrees counter-clockwise (Figure 2-3.7).

19. Select the **Undo** command.

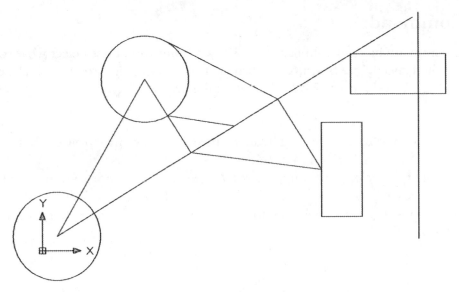

FIGURE 2-3.7 Rotate command – Rectangle rotated

Now you will do the same thing, except with a different angle. A negative angle rotates the entities in a clockwise direction.

20. After selecting **Undo** in the previous step, use the **Rotate** command, **select the rectangle** and then **pick the same *Midpoint*** as in Step 17.

21. This time, for the *Rotation Angle,* type **-45** and **Enter**.

Notice, now, that the rectangle rotated 45 degrees in the clockwise direction (Figure 2-3.8).

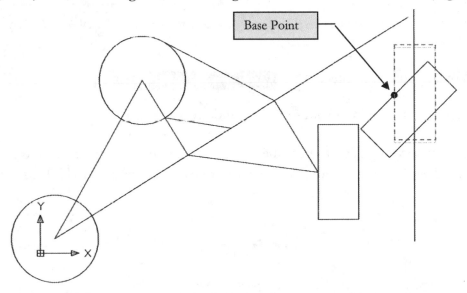

FIGURE 2-3.8 Rectangle rotated. Dashed rectangle represents original position.

Scale Command:

The **Scale** command has steps similar to the **Rotate** command. First, select what you want to scale and then specify the base point. Then, instead of entering a rotation angle, enter a scale factor (e.g., 2 or .5; where 2 would be twice the original size and .5 would be half the original size).

Next you will use the **Scale** command to adjust the size of the circle near the bottom.

Before you scale the circle, you should use the ***Properties*** dialog box to note the **radius** of the circle. After scaling the circle, you will refer back to the *Properties* palette to note the change. This step is meant to teach you how to verify the accuracy and dimensions of entities in AutoCAD.

> *TIP: You can double-click on most objects to view theirquick properties.*

22. Select **Scale** (*Modify* panel, *Home* tab).

23. **Select the circle** (the one at the bottom) and then **right-click**. *(Again, this tells AutoCAD you are done selecting items to scale.)*

    You are now prompted:

    > *TIP: The numbers shown in the prompt above are X and Y values from the Origin; you will pick a point, not type values.*

The *Base Point* is the point about which the entity (or entities) will be scaled; see the examples on the next page.

24. Pick the center of the circle. *(In this case you can use one of three OSNAPs: Center, Endpoint or Intersection.)*

    You are now prompted: Specify scale factor or ⬆ .5

25. Type **.5** (as shown in previous prompt) and press **Enter**.

Now use the ***Properties*** palette to note the change in the size of the circle, from 6⅝″ to 3⁵/₁₆″ radius. A *Scale Factor* of .5 reduces the entities to half their original scale (Figure 2-3.9).

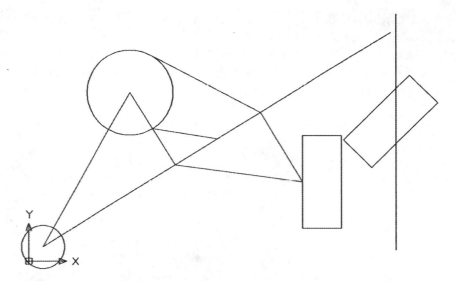

FIGURE 2-3.9 Scaled circle. Notice it is half the size of the other circle.

Selecting the Correct Base Point:

To get the desired results, you need to select the appropriate base point, for both the *Scale* and *Rotate* commands. A few examples are shown in Figure 2-3.10. The dashed line indicates the original position of the entity being modified. The black dot indicates the base point selected.

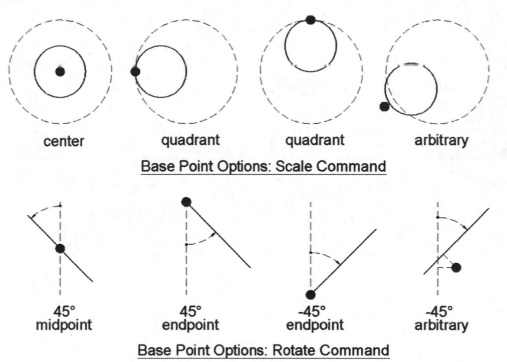

FIGURE 2-3.10 Base Point Options. The various results when different base points are selected.

This will conclude the brief tour of the *Modify* panel.

As you surely noticed, the *Modify* panel has a few other icons that have not been investigated yet. Most of these will be covered later in this book.

26. **Save** your drawing. (Your drawing should already be named: **ex2-3.dwg** per step number 2 of this exercise.)

Carter Residence

Images courtesy of LHB
www.LHBcorp.com

Exercise 2-4:
Annotations

Annotations (text; notes) allow designers and drafters to accurately describe the drawing. You will take a quick look at this feature now.

Annotations:

Adding annotations to a drawing can be as essential as the drawing itself. Often the notes (i.e., annotations) describe something about a part of the drawing that would be difficult to discern from the drawing alone.

For example, a wall section drawing showing a bolt may not indicate, graphically, how many bolts are needed or at what spacing (because the spacing of the bolts is perpendicular to the view). The note might say *"5/8″ anchor bolt at 24″ O.C."* (O.C. = on center)

Next you will add text to your drawing.

1. **Open** drawing **ex2-3.dwg** from the previous lesson.

2. **Save-As ex2-4.dwg**.

3. **Zoom** out, if required; your screen should look like Figure 2-4.2.

4. Select the **Multiline Text** - referred to as **Mtext** (*Annotation* panel, *Home* tab). Click *OK* to any prompts about selecting an *Annotation Scale*.

    a. Just click the top part of the split button to start the **Multiline Text** command.

Notice the current *Command* prompt; you are prompted to **"Specify first corner"**. Basically you are specifying a window (or box) that will contain the text, which is easily adjusted later as well (Figure 2-4.1).

FIGURE 2-4.1 Command prompt for Mtext command

5. Pick your first point and then your second point to define a box as shown in **Figure 2-4.2**.

   TIP: You rarely click and drag your mouse button in AutoCAD; mostly you click and release the mouse button, position the cursor at the second location, and then click again.

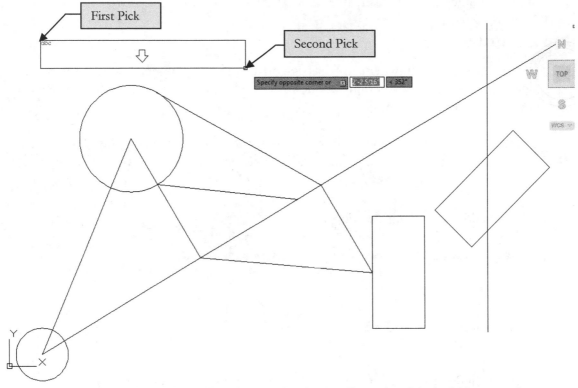

FIGURE 2-4.2 Mtext; defining the window that contains the text (first point picked; picking second)

When picking the *Mtext* window, the width is all that really matters. The width of the selected window is what controls the text wrapping feature. AutoCAD will never hide text; so as you type, if the line of text becomes longer than the width of the *Mtext* window you specified, the text will return to the next line (just like a word processor). AutoCAD will create as many lines as are required to show all the text you typed, regardless of the initial height of the *Mtext* window.

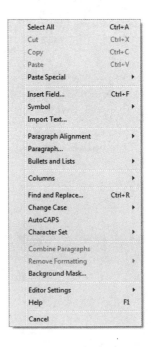

   TIP: In the Mtext editor you can right-click to see a pop-up menu that gives you access to several tools like Select All, Change Case (which is an easy way to make previously typed text all upper case) and Find and Replace. See image to the right for an example.

You can now enter text in the *Mtext* window. This window will not be visible when you are done typing. The *Mtext* tool is similar to text editors like MS Word or WordPerfect; you can make text bold, italic, centered, underlined, etc.

Next you will enter some text.

6. In the *Mtext Editor* you will type the following text (Figure 2-4.3):

    a. Set the height to 1″. (You will have to type it in.)

    b. Type: **Learning AutoCAD is fun!**

    FYI: Do not add the second line (i.e., your name) yet.

FIGURE 2-4.3 Mtext; text typed in text editor window; Text Formatting ribbon displayed

7. When finished typing text, click the **Close Text Editor** button on the *Ribbon* shown in Figure 2-4.3 above; notice the *Ribbon* changes while in text edit mode.

    TIP: If you ever want to cancel the Text Editor window without typing text, you can simply press the Escape (Esc) key on the keyboard.

Your text should look similar to Figure 2-4.4. Text can be Moved and Rotated with the tools on the *Modify* toolbar.

TIP: Whenever you select an Mtext object, AutoCAD displays a grip in each corner to represent the Mtext window. A grip can be moved to increase or decrease the width of the window. The height will automatically adjust accordingly. Try it.

Whenever you want to edit text, you double-click on it.

8. Double-click on the text, position the cursor at the end of the sentence, press **Enter** (to start a new line) and then type *your* name (not the author's).

9. **Save** your drawing.

FIGURE 2-4.4 Mtext; final results of text entered

When modifying previously typed text (i.e., bold, underline, text height, etc.) you must select the text within the text edit window. To do this you drag the cursor over the desired text until it is highlighted.

> ***TIP:*** *With the* Mtext Editor *open (Figure 2-4.3), you can Copy/Paste text in from other programs such as MS Word. Most of the formatting (e.g., font, bold, underline, etc.) will be preserved.*

Exercise 2-5:
Printing

The final exercise in this lesson will cover another essential feature in CAD, which is printing. Printing takes some time to fully understand. It will be covered more, later in this book (Lesson 10).

Print Room in a large architectural firm   *Image courtesy of BWBR Architects*
www.bwbr.com

In this exercise you will print to an 8 ½″ x 11″ piece of paper with the drawing filling the paper (i.e., not to scale).

1. Open drawing **ex2-4.dwg**.

2. Use the **Zoom** tools if required to display the portion of drawing shown in Figure 2-4.4.

3. Select the **Plot** icon from the *Quick Access* toolbar (called *print* in other programs).

    a. You can also select *Print* → *Plot* from the *Application Menu*

You are now in the *Plot* dialog box. This is where you tell AutoCAD what printer or plotter to use, what scale and what size paper, to name a few examples (Figure 2-5.1).

FIGURE 2-5.1 Plot Dialog Box; basic options

4. Make the following adjustments (Figure 2-5.1):

    a. Select a **Printer** you have access to.

    b. Paper size: **Letter (8.5 x 11 in.)**

    c. What to plot: **Display**

    d. **Center the plot**: *checked*

    e. Plot scale: **Fit to paper** *checked*

    FYI: *The Display option (item 4c above) will only plot what is visible on screen; that is why you need to zoom in or out per Step 2.*

Additional settings are available, but are hidden because they are not used as often. You will take a quick look at this before plotting.

5. Click the "more options" arrow in the lower right corner of the *Plot* dialog box (Figure 2-5.1).

6. The only setting you need to verify is that *Drawing Orientation* is set to **Landscape**.

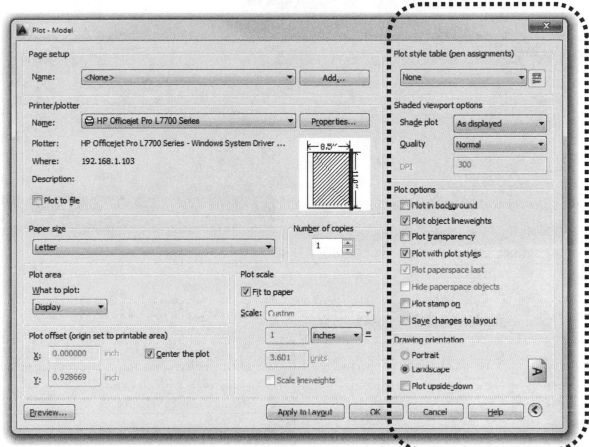

FIGURE 2-5.2 Plot Dialog Box; basic + more options shown

AutoCAD can print to any printer/plotter installed on your computer.

A <u>Printer</u> is an output device that uses smaller paper (e.g., 8 ½″x11″ or 11″x17″). A <u>Plotter</u> is an output device that uses larger paper; plotters typically have one or more rolls of paper ranging in size from 18″ wide to 36″ wide. A roll feed plotter has a built-in cutter that can, for example, cut paper from a 36″ wide roll to make 24″x36″ sheets.

Plotter with three paper rolls

Color **printer** / copier

7.   Click **OK** to send the plot (print).

Using PREVIEW...

Before you click **OK**, it is a good idea to click the **Preview** button first. This will show how your drawing will look on the size paper selected.

Doing a *Preview* first will save time and paper.

Lesson 2 Recap:

In this lesson, *Crash Course Introduction (the Basics)*, you learned how to draw accurate lines and circles, use the *Object Snap* feature for precise pick points, use a handful of *Modify* tools (e.g., Copy, Move, Rotate and Scale). You also had a brief introduction to creating text and plotting. You should have a well-balanced amount of base knowledge to begin creating more meaningful objects, which is what you will do in the next lesson!

Self-Exam:

The following questions can be used as a way to check your knowledge of this lesson. The answers can be found at the bottom of this page.

1. AutoCAD is only accurate to 3 decimal places. (T/F)

2. The diamond shaped *OSNAP* symbol represents the *Midpoint* snap. (T/F)

3. "Full Preview" in the *Plot* dialog WILL save you time and paper. (T/F)

4. Use the _____ command to duplicate objects.

5. When selecting entities, use the _____ _____ to select all the entities in the selection window and all entities that extend through it.

Review Questions:

The following questions may be assigned by your instructor as a way to assess your knowledge of this section. Your instructor has the answers to the review questions.

1. AutoCAD is a raster based program. (T/F)

2. The Base Point you select for Rotate and Scale is not important. (T/F)

3. Entering 16 for a distance, actually means 16'-0″ to AutoCAD. (T/F)

4. Use the _____ command to create squares.

5. You can change the height of the text while in the *Mtext* editor. (T/F)

6. Selecting this icon () ws you to _____ one or more entities in a drawing.

7. What is the name of the *template* file you are to use when creating a new drawing in this book? _____

8. With the **Rotate** command, typing 45 for the degrees prompt, rotates the entities in the _____ direction; whereas -45 rotates the entities in the _____ direction.

9. List all the *OSNAP* points available on a circle (ex. Line: endpoint, midpoint, nearest) _____.

10. The **OSNAP** button on the *Status Bar* must be "pushed in" (i.e., on) to automatically and accurately select snap points while drawing. (T/F)

Notes:

Lesson 3
Drawing Architectural Objects (Draw & Modify)::

This lesson is meant to give you practice drawing in AutoCAD. While doing so, you will become familiar with the various shapes and sizes of the more common symbols used in a residential set of drawings.

Each drawing will be created in its own drawing file. The drawings (i.e., symbols) will be used later to automate drafting.

For some of the symbols to be drawn, you will have step-by-step instruction and/or a study on a particular command that would be useful in the creation of that object. Other symbols to be drawn are for practice by way of repetition and do not provide step-by-step instruction.

Do NOT draw the dimensions; they are for reference only.

For extra practice, work on Chapter 12 on the DVD directly after this chapter!

Exercise 3-1:
Rectilinear Objects

Overview:

All the objects you will draw in this exercise consist entirely of straight lines, either orthogonal (i.e.,horizontal or vertical) or angular.

As previously mentioned, all the objects MUST BE drawn in SEPERATE drawing files. Each object will have a specific name provided, which is to be used to name the drawing file. All files should be saved in your personal folder created for this course.

Each object drawn will have the lower left corner located at the origin (0,0,0). This will be discussed further in a moment.

Each new drawing created for this course should be done using the **Architectural Imperial.dwt** template file (*Sheet Sets* sub-folder).

ALL entities drawn in Exercises 1 and 2 should be drawn on the default layer, that is, *Layer 0* (zero). So just make sure the *Layers* panel displays *Layer 0* similar to the *Layers* panel shown on page 1-6.

filename: **Bookcase.dwg**

This is a simple rectangle that represents the size of a bookcase.

Drawing origin (0,0,0)

1. **Open** a new drawing.

2. Switch to *Model Space*.

3. Select the **Rectangle** command.

4. For the first point, enter **0,0** *(include the comma)*.

   NOTE: *When entering an X,Y,Z coordinate, AutoCAD assumes Z equals 0 if you only enter X and Y values.*

5. At the **Specify Other Corner** prompt, type **3′** and then press the **Tab** key (this is for the *Width*, or the "X" value). See tip below if you have any problems.

6. Enter **1′** and **Enter** (this is for the *Height*, or the "Y" value).

   TIP: Dynamic Input must be toggled on for the previous steps to work properly (as instructed).

7. **Save** your drawing per the name listed above (bookcase.dwg).

filename: **Coffee Table.dwg**

8. Similar to the steps listed above, plus the suggestions mentioned below, create the coffee table shown to the left.

Entering fractions: The 3′-10½″ can be entered in one of three ways.

- o 3′10.5
  Notice there is no space between the feet and inches.
- o 3′10-1/2
  Note the dash location; it separates the inches: whole–fraction.
- o 46.5
  This is all in inches; that is 3′- 10½″ = 46.5″

filename: **Desk-1.dwg**

9. Draw the *Desk* in its own file, similar to the steps outlined above.

10. **Save.** After completing *desk-1.dwg*, select **Save-As** from the *Application* menu *(the large red "A")*.

11. Enter **Night Table.dwg** for the name and then click **Save.**

You are now in a new file and *desk-1* is closed.

filename: **Night Table.dwg**

Obviously you could draw this quickly per the previous examples. However, you will take a look at the **Stretch** command now.

You will use the **Stretch** command to stretch the 3'-0″ wide desk down to a 1'-6″ wide night table; you don't want to move the lower left corner which aligns with the *Origin*.

12. Select **Stretch** from the *Modify* panel.

13. Select a ***Crossing Window*** as shown in **Figure 3-1.1**.

   TIP: *Pick your window from right to left; refer back to page 2-23 for more on Crossing Windows.*

14. Press **Enter** and then pick any point on the screen.

15. Make sure ***Polar Tracking*** is turned on *(**TIP:** Status Bar)*. Move your cursor to the left, with the *Polar Tracking* locking into the horizontal position, as shown in Figure 3-1.2.

16. Type **1'6** *(dash and inch symbol are not required)* and press **Enter**.

17. **Save** your drawing.

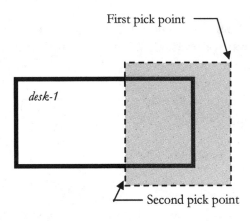

First pick point

desk-1

Second pick point

FIGURE 3-1.1 Stretch command –
Crossing Window selection shown

Which Objects Get Stretched and Which Objects Don't?

When you select a portion of a drawing to be stretched, like the example to the left, some entities are stretched while others are moved.

Notice in the example to the left (Figure 3-1.1), the two horizontal lines are stretched, whereas the vertical line simply moves 1'-6" to the left.

You can think of it this way:
Any lines that pass through the *Crossing Window* are stretched. Any lines that are completely within the *Crossing Window* are moved.

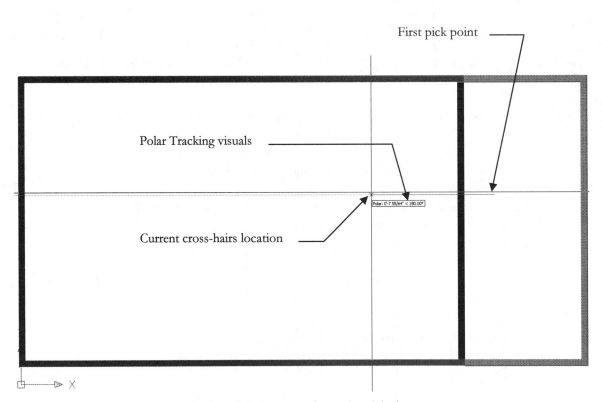

First pick point

Polar Tracking visuals

Polar: 0'-7 55/64" < 180.00°

Current cross-hairs location

FIGURE 3-1.2 Stretch Command – Stretch in progress; first point picked

filename: **Dresser-1.dwg**

18. Draw the dresser using the following *TIP*.

   TIP: *Simply draw two rectangles. Make sure the large rectangle is at the Origin. Move the smaller rectangle into place using the Move command and OSNAPs.*

filename: **Dresser-2.dwg**

19. Draw this smaller dresser.

filename: **Desk-2.dwg**

20. Draw this desk in the same way you drew dresser-1 (i.e., two rectangles). Make sure the lower left is at the *Origin*!

filename: **File Cabinet.dwg**

1'-3"

2'-3"

21. Draw this file cabinet.

filename: **Chair-1.dwg**

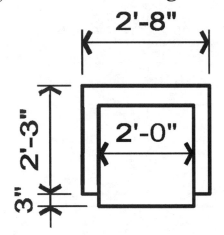

2'-8"

2'-3"

2'-0"

3"

22. Draw this chair per the following *TIP*.

TIP: *Draw the 2'x2' square first, and then draw three (temporary) rectangles as shown to the right. If necessary, move them into place with Move and OSNAPs. Next, draw a line for the arms and backrest and then delete the three temporary rectangles.*

filename: **Sofa.dwg**

6'-2"

2'-3"

5'-6"

3"

23. Do a **Save-As** from the chair-1 file and **Stretch** to create the sofa.

filename: **Bed-Double.dwg**

24. Draw the following **three** beds using lines and rectangles; the exact size of items not dimensioned is not important. Use **Stretch** to create the two larger beds.

filename: **Bed-Queen.dwg**

Image courtesy of
Stanius Johnson Architects
Daniel's Construction, Amery WI.
Photo by Robert Aho
www.staniusjohnson.com

filename: **Bed-King.dwg**

FIGURE 3-1.3 Floor Plan example using similar furniture to those drawn in this exercise.

Image courtesy of Stanius Johnson Architects
www.staniusjohnson.com

Exercise 3-2:
Objects with Curves

Similar to the previous exercise, you will draw several shapes; this time the shapes will have curves in them. You will look at the various commands that allow you to create curves, like Arc, Circle and Fillet.

Again, you will not draw the dimensions as they are for reference only. Each drawing should be drawn in its own drawing file; save the drawing with the filename provided.

One more thing about *Layers*: they all occupy the same space. *Layers* are similar to a stack of transparencies in that you can slip one out of the stack (i.e., turn a layer *off*).However, in AutoCAD, all the transparencies in the stack would occupy the space as if there were only one and not a stack. Everything in this exercise should also be drawn on *Layer* zero (i.e., *Layer0*).

Finally, the black dot on each of the drawings is for reference only. This dot represents the location of the *Drawing Origin* (0,0).

filename: **Laundry-Sink.dwg**

2'-0"

1'-6"

Drawing
origin (0,0,0)

This is a simple rectangle that represents the size of a laundry sink, with a circle that represents the drain.

1. **Open** a new drawing.

2. Select the **Rectangle** command.

3. Enter the *dimensions* shown.

4. Use the **Move** command to position the rectangle relative to the *Origin*. Pick the **Move** icon, select the rectangle, <u>pick the midpoint of the top horizontal line</u> for the first point, and then type **0,0** for the second point, and then press **Enter** (*Dynamic Input* must be toggled off per the *TIP* below).

> ***TIP:** Turn off Dynamic Input, on the Status Bar, so AutoCAD will move the rectangle to the drawing's Origin and not just relative to your first point, which is to not move it at all (i.e., 0,0 would mean 0x and 0y displacement).*

Next you will draw a circle for the drain. The drain needs to be centered left and right, and 5″ from the top edge. The following steps will show you one way in which to do this.

5. Toggle *Dynamic Input* back on, and then pick the **Circle** tool.

6. Type **0,0** to locate the center point of the circle. *(This is the midpoint of the top edge of your rectangle.)*

7. Type **1** for the radius and press **Enter**. *(This creates a 2″ diameter circle.)*

FIGURE 3-2.1 Creating a circle and moving it into place.

Next you will use the Move command to reposition the circle.

8. Select the **Move** icon.

9. Pick the circle. *(Press **Enter** to tell AutoCAD you are done selecting entities to move.)*

10. For your **First point of displacement**, pick anywhere in the *Drawing* window; in this example the first point is irrelevant.

11. For your **Second point of displacement**, move the cursor in the direction you want the circle moved (*downward on the screen*) until *Polar Tracking* locks in, and then enter **5**.

12. If you haven't already done so, press **Enter** to complete the **Move** operation (Figure 3-2.1).

13. **Save** the file per the name listed above.

    REMEMBER: *The black dot shown on the previous page represents the drawing's* Origin *and is not to be drawn. This may be a little confusing on the* Laundry Sink *example because you drew a circle at that same location. But, if you recall, you* Moved *the circle (as opposed to* Copying *it). So the circle should not be there anymore.*

filename: **Dryer.dwg**

Here you will draw a dryer with rounded front corners. This, like all the other symbols in this lesson, is a plan view symbol (i.e., as viewed from the top).

14. Draw a 30″x26″rectangle.

15. **Move** the rectangle into place as described in the previous drawing (*Laundry Sink*).

Next you will draw the line that is 2½″ from the back of the dryer.

16. Make sure the following features are enabled on the *Status Bar*. **Polar Tracking**, **Object Snap**, **Object Snap Tracking** and **Dynamic Input**.

17. Select the **Line** icon.

18. Hover the cursor over the upper left corner and then, without clicking, move the cursor straight down; type **2.5** and then press **Enter**. *TIP: Nearest OSNAP must be off.*

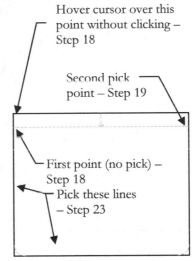

FIGURE 3-2.2 Drawing a line

You should have seen a small "x" snapped to the vertical line as you moved the cursor down. Typing 2.5 and pressing Enter tells AutoCAD the first pick point is to be 2½″ over from the reference point (i.e., the point you paused the cursor over). You may have to try this a few times to get the hang of it; if you are having problems, make sure you are not creating short vertical lines. Remember you do not actually click the first point of the line, only the second point.

19. Move the cursor to the right and use the *Perpendicular* snap on the right-hand vertical line; this is the endpoint of the new horizontal line.

Notice that you did not have to tell AutoCAD (by entering a number) how long the line needed to be. Instead, you picked two points that you knew were 30″ apart.

Next you will round-off the front corners of the dryer.

20. Select the **Fillet** icon from the *Modify* panel.

21. Type **R** and then **Enter**. *(This runs the sub-command **Radius**.)*

Notice the prompt in the *Command Window* (Figure 3-2.3). The default *Radius* is set to zero; you will need to change that to 2″.

FIGURE 3-2.3 Fillet command – *Command Window* prompts after initiating the command

22. Type **2** and then **Enter**.

Next you will select the two lines, whose intersection you want filleted.

23. Select the vertical line on the left and then select the horizontal line on the bottom (front). See Figure 3-2.2.

    a. Notice as you hover your cursor over the second line, a preview of the fillet is shown. This allows you to see what the fillet is going to look like before committing to it. If it is too big or too small, you can type "R" again and change the radius before finalizing the change. Do not change the radius at this time.

24. Repeat the previous step to **Fillet** the other "front" corner.

25. **Save** your drawing.

filename: **Washer.dwg**

This drawing is identical to the dryer except for the door added to the top. You can open the dryer drawing and do a *Save-As* to get a jump start on this drawing.

To draw the door you will use the **Offset** command on the *Modify* panel, found on the *Home* tab.

The **Offset** command is easy to use. To use it you…

- o   Enter the distance you want to offset a line.
- o   Select the line you want to offset.
- o   Pick which side of the line you want to offset to.

26. Select the **Offset** icon on the *Modify* panel, *Home* tab.

27. Type **4** and then press **Enter**.

28. Select the rectangle (that represents the perimeter of the washer) as the line you wish to offset.

29. Pick anywhere inside the rectangle.

FIGURE 3-2.4 Outer rectangle offset inward 4″. Note that the dashed lines are the location of the "door" after it is stretched in Step 31.

Picking within the rectangle caused the rectangle to offset towards the inside. You are encouraged to **Undo** at this point and see what happens when you click on theoutside of the rectangle. Obviously the rectangle will offset to the outside of the existing rectangle. When finished experimenting with the **Offset** command, make sure to restore the proper rectangle per Step 29 above.

Next you will stretch the rectangle to adjust its width.

30. Use the **Stretch** techniques previously covered to stretch the right side of the inner rectangle **2″** to the left (Figure 3-2.4).

31. Repeat the previous steps to **Stretch** the left side **2″** to the right (Figure 3-2.4).

You should now have a properly sized door (1′-6″ x 1′-6″).

You should occasionally double check your dimensions; it is easy to accidentally type the wrong distance. Next you will verify the door is the correct size using the **Distance** tool (there are other ways to do this, but this is the best one for this task).

32. Use the **Distance** command (*Home* tab, *Utilities* panel) from the *Ribbon* and pick two points shown (i.e., dimensioned) for the washer drawing on page 3-13.

    TIP: Make sure you use the OSNAPs to accurately pick the points to which you are dimensioning.

33. Note the distance listed in the *Command Window*.

    a. The distance will also show up next to your cursor if you have *Dynamic Input* turned on.

    b. Notice the additional information shown in the *Command Window*. The Delta X and Delta Y values tell you the relative change in the X and Y directions for a diagonal measurement. This would give you the overall size of a rectangle with one measurement.

Next you will **Fillet** the corners of the door. AutoCAD provides a sub-command for Fillet that will round all the corners at once. You will try this option now.

    *NOTE: This option only works on polylines, which is what the **Rectangle** command creates. If you simply drew the rectangle with individual lines, you would have to fillet each corner separately.*

34. Select the **Fillet** icon and set the radius to **1″**.

35. Type **P** (for **Polyline**) and press **Enter** (refer back to Figure3-2.3).

36. Select the washer door [i.e., the rectangle].

All four corners should now be rounded off. The image below shows the various results when using the **Polyline** sub-command for Fillet. Try it!

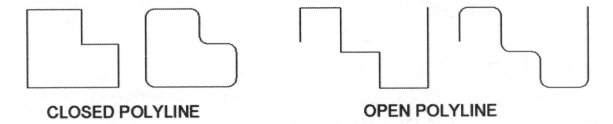

CLOSED POLYLINE   **OPEN POLYLINE**

37. Draw a small 4″x1″ rectangle to represent the door handle; draw it anywhere. Using *OSNAPs*, move it to the midpoint of the bottom door edge, and then move the handle 2″ up.

38. **Save** your drawing (make sure the name is *Washer*).

filename: **Range.dwg**

Now you will draw a Kitchen Range with four circles that represent the burners.

In this exercise you will have to draw temporary lines (called construction lines) to create reference points needed to accurately locate the circles. Once the circles have been drawn, the construction lines can be erased.

39. Draw the *Range* with a 2″ control panel at the back. Refer to the steps described to draw the *Dryer*, if necessary.

40. Draw the four construction lines shown in Figure 3-2.5. (They do not need to be dashed lines.)

FIGURE 3-2.5
Range with four temporary construction lines (shown dashed)

41. Draw two **9½″** circles and two **7½″** circles using the intersection of the construction lines to locate the centers of the circles (Figure 3-2.5).

42. **Erase** the four construction lines.

43. **Save** your drawing.

filename: **Chair-2.dwg**

Process Snapshot

Now you will draw another chair. You will use the Line and Offset commands as well as the Arc command.

First you will draw the three straight lines at the perimeter.

LINES   ARC   OFFSET

44. First draw the **2'-6"** line across the bottom. Use one of the following methods to accurately position the line relative to the drawing *Origin* (0,0); your options are:

    a. Drawing the line, type **0,0** for your first point and then type **2'-6"** (with *Polar Tracking* on; to the right). Finally, move the line **1'-3"** to the left. (This will position the line such that your 2'-6" line's midpoint is at the *Origin.*)

    b. Anywhere in the drawing, draw a horizontal line **2'-6"** long. Now use the **Move** command. Pick the *Midpoint* of the line for the first point and type **0,0** for the second point (*Dynamic Input* off).

45. Using *Polar Tracking* (or *Ortho*) draw two vertical lines **1'-3"** long (Figure 3-2.6).

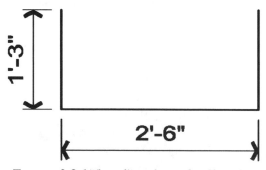

FIGURE 3-2.6 Three lines drawn for Chair-2

Next you will draw an arc to complete the chair's perimeter.

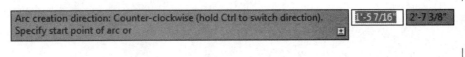

46. Select the **Arc** tool named **Start, End, Direction** from the *Draw* panel, via the down-arrow.

    Notice you are prompted to **Specify start point of arc**.

    > Arc creation direction: Counter-clockwise (hold Ctrl to switch direction). Specify start point of arc or   1'-5 7/16"   2'-7 3/8"

    > *TIP: If you press the down arrow on the keyboard, you get access to the Center/End options that you see listed in the Command Window.*

47. Pick the upper *Endpoint* of the vertical line on the right. (See Figure 3-2.7A.)

You are now prompted in the *Command Window* **Specify end point of arc:**

The on-screen prompt says: Specify end point of arc: 0'-6 1/8"   < 42°

48. Pick the upper *Endpoint* of the vertical line on the left for the arc's endpoint (Figure 3-2.7A).

Second pick point ⎯⎯⎯⎯

First pick point

1'-3"

2'-6"

FIGURE 3-2.7A Pick points for **Arc** command

49. Move your cursor straight up with *Polar Tracking* snapped to the vertical plane (Figure 3-2.7B).

50. Once snapped to the vertical plane, click to create the circle.

You have now completed the perimeter of the chair. If the arc is in the wrong position you may have picked your points in the wrong order.

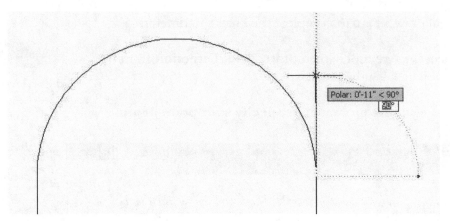

FIGURE 3-2.7B Picking direction for arc command

51. Use the **Offset** command to offset the arc and two vertical lines the required distance.

Notice that because you drew the perimeter with individual lines, the entire outline did not offset like the rectangle did. This would work if you turned these lines into polylines (which will be covered later).

52. **Save** your drawing.

filename: **Love-Seat.dwg**

Process Snapshot

You should be able to draw this *Love Seat* without any further instruction. You can do so using a combination of the following commands:

- o Line
- o Fillet
- o Offset
- o Move

TIP: When starting the Love Seat *drawing above, you might initially get the idea to draw a 2'-6" line from the* Origin *to the right and then another 2'-6" line from the* Origin *to the left. This would give the appearance of a 5'-0" line with the center at 0,0. Typically that should be avoided. Anything that looks like one line should actually be only one line in AutoCAD. It is considered sloppy drafting when you have several smaller lines make up one line, or to have several overlapping lines.*

filename: **Tub.dwg**

Process Snapshot

Now you will draw a bath *Tub*. You will use several commands previously covered. You will also be introduced to another command called **Explode**; this command allows you to turn a polyline (e.g., rectangle) into individual lines.

53. **Draw** the rectangle.

54. **Offset** the rectangle inward **4"**.

Next you will use the **Explode** command to change the smaller rectangle from a *polyline* to *individual lines* so you can edit them separately.

55. Select the **Explode** icon on the *Modify* panel.

56. **Pick** the smaller rectangle and then **Enter.**

Select one of the lines to see that only one line is selected, rather than the entire rectangle (i.e., all four lines). Press **Escape** to unselect the line and proceed to the next step.

57. **Erase** the vertical line on the left (Figure 3-2.8).

58. **Stretch** the two horizontal lines 1'-0" to the right (Figure 3-2.8).

FIGURE 3-2.8 Horizontal Lines stretched 1'-0" to the right

59. Draw an **Arc** with a **1'-0"** radius (refer back to *Chair-2* if you need help with this step).

60. **Fillet** the two corners to have a **4"** radius.

61. **Save.**

You can start to see how the small handful of commands you have learned thus far can be used to draw many different things!

filename: **Lav-1.dwg**

Draw this *Lavatory* per the following specifications:

o Larger arcs shown shall have a 2½" radius.
o Smaller arcs shown shall have a 1" radius.
o Sides and Front of sink to have 1½" space (offset).
o Back to have 4" space (offset).
o Small rectangle to be 4½" x 1" and 1½" away from the back.
o 2" Dia. Drain, 8" from Origin.

filename: **Lav-2.dwg**

Process Snapshot

ELLIPSE   OFFSET   MOVE   COPY/PASTE

1'-10"

Next you will draw another lavatory. This time you will use the **Ellipse** command.

62. Open a new drawing.

63. Select the **Ellipse** tool **Axis, End** in the *Draw* panel on the *Home* tab via the down-arrow (see image below).

First you will specify the vertical axis for the ellipse.

64. Type **0,0** for the axis endpoint.

65. With ***Polar Tracking*** (or *Ortho*) turned on, point the cursor straight down (i.e., vertical in the negative direction) and then type **1'7**; press **Enter**.

Now you need to specify the horizontal axis of the ellipse.

66. Again, with ***Polar Tracking*** on, position the cursor towards the right until it snaps to the horizontal plane and type **11** and then **Enter**.

   NOTE: *11" is half the width, 1'-10".*

That's all it takes to draw an ellipse!

67. **Offset** the ellipse inward **2½″** (Figure 3-2.9).

68. **Move** the inner ellipse downward (towards the front of the sink) **1″**.

FIGURE 3-2.9
Ellipse offset inward 2½″

Next you need to draw the faucet and drain. As it turns out, the faucet and drain for *Lav-1.dwg* are in the same position relative to the *Origin*. So to save time you will Copy/Paste these items from the *Lav-1.dwg* drawing into the *Lav-2.dwg* drawing.

69. **Open Lav-1.dwg**.

The command you will use next is <u>not</u> located on the *Ribbon* so you have to type it in the *Command Window*. The command allows you to specify the insertion point before copying entities to the *Windows Clipboard*, allowing you to more accurately place the geometry when pasted in later. If you were to just use the *Copy Clip* icon on the *Home* tab, the insertion point would just be the lower left corner of the extents of the geometry in the clipboard.

70. Click in the *Command Window* and type **copybase** (with no spaces) and then press **Enter**.

71. Type **0,0** and then **Enter**.

72. Select the faucet (i.e., the small rectangle) and the 2″ drain; then press **Enter**.

73. **Close** the **Lav-1.dwg**.

74. In the **Lav-2.dwg** drawing, select **Paste to Original Coordinates** from the *Clipboard* panel on the *Home* tab *(see image to the right)*.

You should now have the faucet and drain correctly positioned in your *Lav-2.dwg* drawing.

75. **Save** your drawing.

filename: **Sink-1.dwg**

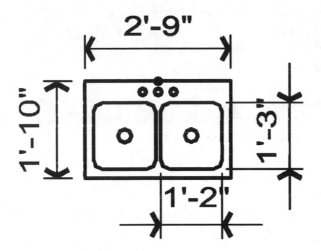

Draw this lavatory per the following specifications:

- o 2″ space (i.e., offset) at sides and front.
- o 3″ Dia. Circles centered in sinks.
- o 2″ rad. for Fillets.
- o 1½″ Dia. at faucet spacing 3½″ apart.

filename: **Water-Closet.dwg**

You should be able to draw this symbol without any help.

TIP: Draw a construction line from the Origin straight down 11″ (2′4″ – 1′-5″ = 11″). This will give you a point to pick when drawing the ellipse.

*NOTE: You could also start the **Ellipse** command and type 0,-11 for the first point. These are coordinates relative to the Origin.*

filename: **Tree.dwg**

76. Draw one large circle and then copy it similar to this drawing.

77. Draw one small circle (1″Dia.) with the center at the *Origin*.

78. **Save** to Tree.dwg.

filename: **Door-36.dwg**

This symbol is used to show a door in a floor plan. The arc represents the path of the door as it opens and shuts. The hinges are at the origin in this example.

A symbol like this, 90 degrees open, helps to avoid the door conflicting with something in the house (e.g., cabinets or toilet)

79. Draw a **2″ x 3′-0″ rectangle**.

FYI: The rectangle represents a 2″ thick x 3′-0″ wide door.

80. Draw an **Arc** (using **Start, End, Radius**) with a 3′-0″ radius. Instead of picking points, enter the following coordinates: <u>start point</u> at **3′,0** and <u>endpoint</u> at **0,3′**.

REMEMBER: These points are relative to 0,0; also Dynamic Input needs to be toggled off for this to work.

filename: **Door-30.dwg**

Using the previous two steps as an example, draw this smaller door.

NOTE: A door's thickness does not usually change, so leave it at 2″.

AutoCAD has a feature called <u>Dynamic Blocks</u>. They are advanced symbols that allow visual edits via grip-like controls. One example would be to have a door block where you can flip/mirror to change the door swing or adjust the door size, all via special on-screen grips.

filename: **Door2-36.dwg**

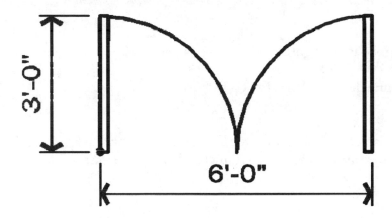

Here you will use a previous drawing and the Mirror command to quickly create this drawing showing a pair of doors in a single opening.

81. **Open** drawing **Door-36.dwg**.

82. **Save-As** to drawing **Door2-36.dwg**.

Next you will mirror both the rectangle and the arc.

83. Pick the **Mirror** icon from the *Modify* panel, *Home* tab.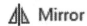

84. Select the rectangle and arc, and then press **Enter**.

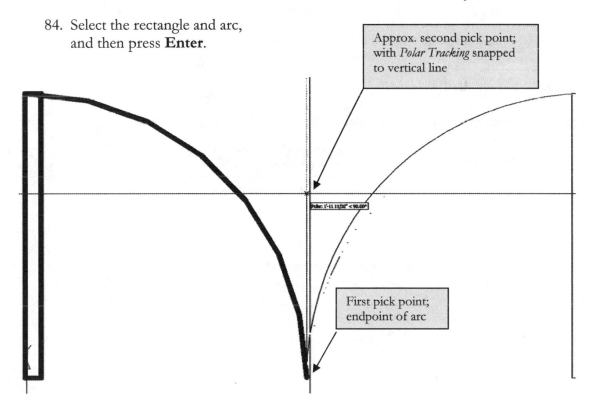

Approx. second pick point; with *Polar Tracking* snapped to vertical line

First pick point; endpoint of arc

Notice the current prompt:

> **FYI:** *Remember that Dynamic Input needs to be toggled on to see the on-screen prompts as shown above.*

85. Pick the two points described in the figure on the previous page.

Basically, you drew an imaginary line that is a plane about which to mirror the selected entities.

The figure below shows a few examples of different mirror lines and their results (each have the same first pick point). Notice the mirrored image is symmetrical about the mirror line.

Vertical
Mirror Line

Angled
Mirror Line

Horizontal
Mirror Line

FIGURE 3-2.10 Mirror command; door being mirrored, first point picked, in process of picking second point

Notice the *Command* prompt **Erase source objects? [Yes/No] <N>:**

And the on-screen prompt reads: Erase source objects?

You do not want the original door to be deleted here so…

86. Type **N** and press **Enter**.

> **TIP:** *Both the graphic and text prompt above indicate a default for the yes/no option; it is No. If the default is the setting you want, you can just press Enter instead of typing a Y or an N.*

87. **Save** your drawing.

filename: **Clg-Fan-1.dwg**

You will use the **Array** command while drawing this ceiling fan.

The **Array** command is used to copy entities in a rectangular pattern (e.g.,steel columns on a grid) or in a polar pattern (i.e., in a circular pattern).

You will use the polar array to rotate and copy the fan blade all in one step!

FIGURE 3-2.11
Dimensions for first part
of fan to be drawn

88. Start a new drawing and create the portion of drawing shown in Figure 3-2.11.*(The drawing origin should be the center of the circle.)*

89. Select **Array→ Polar Array** on the *Modify* panel on the *Home* tab.

You are now prompted to select the items to array. You will only select the fan blade, not the center circle. If you selected the center circle you would end up with several circles copied on top of it.

Next you will tell AutoCAD which entities you would like to array.

90. Select the entities that make up the fan blade.

91. Press **Enter** (to indicate you are done selecting).

> *TIP: You can also right-click rather than press Enter.*

Now you will specify the *center point* about which the fan blade will be rotated (which is the drawing origin and the center of the circle).

92. Using the *Center OSNAP*, **select** the center of the circle, and then **Enter**.

Notice the fan blade arrays around the center with a default of six items. All you have to do now is change the number of items to four (Figure 3-2.12).

93. On the *Ribbon*, for *Items* type **4**.

94. Press **Enter** to apply the change.

FIGURE 3-2.12 Arraying the fan blade.

95. To finish the Polar Array command, press **Enter** or select **eXit** on-screen.

96. **Save** your drawing.

In the next exercise you will see how AutoCAD can be used to parametrically adjust the number of fan blades!

filename: **Clg-Fan-2.dwg**

You could easily start this drawing from scratch, but instead you will learn how to edit an array. You will create a copy of the previous fan and edit it to have five fan blades.

97.   Open the **Clg-Fan-1.dwg** file.

98.   Select **Application Menu → Save-As**.

99.   Name the new file **Clg-Fan-2.dwg**.

100.   **Select** one of the ceiling fan blades.

You should now see the *Array* tab and a few grips appear as shown in Figure 3-2.13.

101.   Change the number of *Items* to **5**.

102.   Click the **Close Array** button on the *Ribbon*.

FIGURE 3-2.13 Modifying a polar array

The *Array* tab and the array grips should now be gone, and your fan should now have five blades!

103. **Save** your drawing.

filename: **HC-Symbol.dwg**

You may have some trouble drawing this symbol at this point. However, this will make you reflect on many of the commands you have covered thus far in this book (e.g.,Line, Rotate, Offset, Arc).

The distance between parallel lines should be 3½'. This is for the graphic, not the gridlines.

All other dimensions can be approximated so that your drawing looks as close to this one as possible.

You can draw the grid shown to help make your drawing more proportionally accurate. The lines are 1'-0" apart in each direction. When finished, erase the grid lines.

Exercise 3-3:
Using Layers

Using *Layers* in AutoCAD helps to separate different types of data. Mostly, you will use *Layers* to make things visible or invisible, and to control lineweights.

In a Floor Plan, for example, you will draw all the walls on one *Layer* and the doors on another *Layer*. You will also draw items such as windows, stairs, furniture, appliances, etc. each on its own *Layer*.

Many architectural firms have an Office Standard when it comes to *Layers*. This means that everyone in the firm uses the same *Layer* name (e.g., A-WALL) to draw walls on, for example. This helps make sharing drawings between projects more efficient; if you Copy/Paste from one drawing to another, and each project used a different *Layer* name for the walls, then you would have both *Layer* names in the drawing you pasted into (e.g., *A-Wall* and *AR-Wall*).

Example:
To see a quick example of how layers work you will open the *A1 First Floor Plan* drawing again and adjust some of the layer settings and then notice the effect those changes have on the drawing.

1. **Open** the *A1 First Floor Plan.dwg* located on the DVD (see page 1-17).

2. Switch to **Model Space** by clicking the *Model* tab at the bottom of the screen; see the image below.

3. Select the **Layer Properties** icon from the *Layers* panel on the *Home* tab.

You are now in the *Layer Properties Manager* where you can adjust the visibility and properties, such as lineweight, color and linetype, of the entities on a particular layer.

All drawings have a *Layer* named 0 (i.e., zero). You can add as many layers as you wish in a drawing file. Notice in **Figure 3-3.1** that the *current* drawing has several *Layers* (34 to be exact). Many of the layer *names* are descriptive enough for you to tell what information is drawn on each layer.

Clicking on a column heading will sort the list by that column. Right-click on the column heading and you can hide columns you never typically use (do not hide any columns at this time). Next you will *Freeze* (i.e., turn off the visibility of) three *Layers*.

FIGURE 3-3.1
Layer Properties Manager; three layers set to frozen (Step 4)

4.   In the column labeled "**Freeze**" click the *Sun* symbol (which will change the symbol to a B&W *Sun*) for the following *Layers(See Figure 3-3.1)*:

   o   A-Anno-Dims
   o   A-Area-Iden
   o   A-Door

   TIP: *The "Freeze" column may not display the full label; instead you will see a portion of the label (e.g. Fre…) as in the image above, which means the column is not wide enough to display the full label. You can, if you wish, stretch the column(s) wider with your mouse. You simply place the cursor between two labels and drag the mouse. This is helpful when the* Layer *names are long as well.*

5.   Click the "X" in the upper corner of the *Layer Properties Manager* to close the palette; there is no "OK" or "Apply" button as changes are made instantly.

Notice the changes to the *A1 First Floor Plan* drawing. Compare the "before" on the left to the "after" on the right in the image on the next page. The dimensions, doors and room names are no longer visible. However, it is important to realize that they still exist in the drawing file.

FIGURE 3-3.2
Sample drawing with layers frozen – original on left; notice doors, text and dimensions are hidden on the right

You should be able to see how this functionality is useful. If the electrical designer links the architectural designer's floor plan drawing into their drawing, they will want to turn off a few of the architectural *Layers* to "clean up" their drawing. For example, the electrical drawings might not need to see the dimensions, window tags and trees. When drawings are setup correctly, this task is easy!

Next you will change the color of a *Layer* to see the effect it has on the current drawing.

6. **Open** the **Layer Properties Manager** again.

7. Locate the *Layer* named **A-Wall**, and then in its *Color* column, **select the colors watch** listed for this *Layer* (which should be yellow).

You are now in the *Select Color* dialog box (Figure 3-3.3).

8. Select color **Blue** (color #5) shown selected in Figure 3-3.3.

9. Click **OK** to exit the *Color Selector* and then click **X** (in the upper left or upper right corner – shown in the upper left in the image below) to close the *Layer Properties Manager*.

FIGURE 3-3.3 Select Color dialog *(part of the Layer Properties Manager)*

Notice the walls are now blue.

10. **Close** the *Sample* drawing <u>without</u> saving any changes.

Now you will open a new drawing and walk through the basics steps of creating and using *Layers* in a drawing.

Creating Layers:

11. **Open** a new drawing and switch to *Model Space*.

    TIP: Remember to start with the correct template; Sheet Sets\Architectural Imperial.dwt.

12. **Open** the *Layer Properties Manager*.

    TIP: Notice some Layers already exist; they came from the template file you started with.

13. Click the **New** Layer icon.

A new row has been added to the list; by default you are immediately positioned to enter the *Layer* name.

14. Type the word **Circles** and then press **Enter**.

15. Repeat steps 13 and 14 to create the following layers:

    a. **Lines**

    b. **Rectangles**

    c. **Text**

FIGURE 3-3.4 Layer Properties Manager; with 4 new layers created

Next you will assign a new color to three of the new Layers.

16. Set the *Layer* colors as follows:

    a. **Circles**   Green *(color #3)*

    b. **Rectangles**   Red *(color #1)*

    c. **Text**   Cyan *(color #4)*

17. Click the **X** to close the *Layer Properties Manager*.

You now have four new *Layers*, each with a different color.

> *FYI: The Layer named Title Block is from your template file. Additional Layers can be added to template files to reduce new drawing setup steps.*

Drawing on Layers:

Now that you have *Layers* you will learn how to draw on different *Layers*. The easiest method is to set a *Layer* Current, and then all entities drawn after that will automatically be placed on that *Layer* (i.e., the current layer). Looking at Figure 3-3.4, notice in the upper left is the drawing's *Current Layer* (which is set to 0).

AutoCAD provides a few different ways to change the *Current Layer*. One is in *the Layer Properties Manager* (Figure 3-3.4). You simply click on the *layer name* you want to set to current and then click the **Current** icon (a green check mark). Another method is described next.

You can quickly set the *Current Layer* via the *Layers* panel (Figure 3-3.5); this is a dynamic toolbar. The toolbar will change its display per the following three scenarios:

- o No entities in the current drawing are selected (no grips visible).
  - ➢ The *Current Layer* is displayed.
- o One or more entities selected which are on the same *Layer*.
  - ➢ Displays which layer the selected entities are on.
- o A group of entities selected which are on two or more *Layers*.
  - ➢ Display is blank to indicate multiple layers.

FIGURE 3-3.5 Layers panel; Figure shows layer drop-down list in the dropped-down position

So, to change the *Current Layer*, you click the down arrow to the right of the display in the *Layers* panel (on the *Home* tab of the Ribbon) to view the drop-down list (which lists all the layers in the current drawing). Next, you click on the name of the layer you want to be current and that's it! *This only works if nothing is selected; otherwise you are changing which Layer the selected entities are on.*

Next you will change the *Current Layer* to *Rectangle* so when you draw rectangles they will automatically be drawn on the Rectangle layer.

18. Press the **Esc** key twice on the keyboard. This ensures that no entities are selected.

19. Click the **Down-Arrow** on the *Layers* panel (Figure 3-3.5).

20. Move the cursor over the *Layer* named *Rectangle* and click.

The *Rectangle* layer is now set current which means that anything drawn from now on (until the current layer is changed again) will be drawn on the *Rectangle* layer.

Be aware that the layer name in no way implies that only rectangles can be drawn on the *Rectangle* layer. That is the intention and the drafter's responsibility to make sure only rectangles go on the *Rectangle* layer. *Note that we could rename the* Circle *layer to* Ellipse *and it would have no effect on the circles previously drawn on that layer.*

21. **Draw a Rectangle** that is **28″** wide and **48″** tall (*with the lower left corner at the Origin*).

22. **Draw** two more rectangles per the dimensions provided in **Figure 3-3.6**. *(This can be accomplished using a combination of the following commands: Offset, Stretch and Move.)*

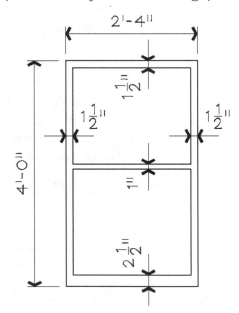

Next you will draw several lines, so you will need to change the *Current Layer*.

23. Making sure no entities are selected; use the *Layers* toolbar to make **Lines** the *Current Layer*.

24. Using the dimensions provided in **Figure 3-3.7**, draw the vertical lines shown. (*This can be achieved using either the Move or Offset commands.*)

You may have already figured out what you are drawing; it is a double-hung window in elevation view.

You have two more lines to draw.

25. **Draw** the two short horizontal lines shown in Figure 3-3.8. *(The lines are near each side towards the middle; compare with Figure 3-3.7.)*

FIGURE 3-3.7
More Rectangles drawn

FIGURE 3-3.8
Two short horizontal lines drawn
(cf. Figure 3-3.7)

26. Use the **Mtext** command to enter the text: "**Double-Hung Window**" directly below the window. Make the text 2¼″ high (Figure 3-3.9).

Oops:

If you were following the directions step by step, you missed a step. You forgot to change the *Current Layer* to *Text*.

You should notice one visual clue that the text is on the wrong layer; it's the same color as the lines previously drawn (*White*). If the text were on the correct layer it would be *Cyan* (the color you assigned to the text layer).

Next you will take a quick look at how to change which layer an entity is on without the need to erase and redraw.

Double-Hung
Window

Figure 3-3.9 Text added

Moving Entities from One Layer to Another:

Remember, when nothing is selected the *Layers* toolbar shows the *Current Layer* and when something is selected it shows which *Layer* the selected entity is on.

27. **Select the text**, make sure nothing else is selected (*press Esc key*) and click on the text. *(Notice the* Layers *panel is indicating that the text is on the* Lines *layer.)*

28. From the *drop-down* list, on the *Layers* panel, select **Text**.

Notice now, with the text still selected, the *Layers* panel indicates that the text is on the *Text* layer (Figure 3-3.10). The text should also now be the proper color: *Cyan*.

FIGURE 3-3.10 Text currently selected

29. Now press the **Esc** key to unselect the text.

Notice the *Layers* panel is now showing the *Current Layer* again. Try selecting and unselecting the various entities in your drawing to see the *Layers* panel change.

30. Make the *Circle* layer current and then draw a large circle around the window/text, similar to Figure 3-3.11.

Double-Hung
Window

FIGURE 3-3.11 Circle added

One More Look at Controlling Layer Visibility:

Before concluding this chapter you will take one more look at *Freezing* and *Thawing* layers, this time using your own drawing.

31. **Freeze** the *Lines* layer *(via the Layer Properties Manager)*.

Notice the lines all disappear from the screen.

32. **Thaw** the *Lines* layer.

33. **Freeze** the *Circle* layer.

You should have received a message stating that AutoCAD "cannot freeze the current layer" (Figure 3-3.12). To freeze the *Circle* layer you would have to set another layer as current first.

FIGURE 3-3.12 AutoCAD message

34. Set the *Rectangle* layer as *Current*.

35. Now *Freeze* the *Circle* layer.

Try a few more variations on the Freeze/Thaw scenarios before proceeding to the next step.

36. Make sure all *Layers* are turned **On** and **Thawed**.

37. **Print** the drawing showing all entities (including the circle).

38. **Save** the drawing as **Ex3-3 Layers.dwg**.

For extra practice on the basics, work on Chapter 12 on the DVD before moving on to Chapter 4!

What's the Difference between Freeze and Off?

On the surface there is no difference between Freeze and Off when it comes to controlling layer visibility. If you Freeze a layer, its contents are not displayed; the same is true when you turn a layer Off.

The difference has to do with display memory. When a layer is Frozen the information required to display it onscreen is not loaded into your graphics card's memory. On the other hand, when a layer is only turned Off, all the information required to display the entities on that layer is loaded into your graphics card's memory.

The Pro's and Con's:
The main benefit to turning a layer Off rather than Freezing it is:
> When you turn a layer back on, it will instantly display (without a regeneration).
> [*Negative:* slower panning and zooming on large / complex drawings]

The benefit to Freezing a layer rather than turning it Off:
> Faster Panning and Zooming without the extra baggage required in the graphics card
> [*Negative*: requires a time consuming Regen whenever a layer is Thawed]

Recommended use:
Freeze the following layers in your drawing if:
> The layer will typically "never" be on in the current drawing (e.g., doors and furniture in a reflected ceiling plan)

Turn a layer Off in your drawing if:
> The layer is generally always on but you want to make it invisible for a short period of time (e.g., hiding the *Text* and *Dimension* layers to print a "clean" floor plan).
>
> When using this method you can confidently select all the layers in the *Layer Properties Manager* and turn them all On without worrying about making a layer show up that shouldn't.

Self-Exam:

The following questions can be used as a way to check your knowledge of this lesson. The answers can be found at the bottom of this page.

1. There is no difference between *Freeze* and *Off*. (T/F)

2. A drawing's *Origin* is 0,0. (T/F)

3. Construction lines are useful drawing aids. (T/F)

4. Use the _____ command to create an oval shape.

5. When you want to make a previously drawn rectangle wider you would use

    the _____ command.

Review Questions:

The following questions may be assigned by your instructor as a way to assess your knowledge of this section. Your instructor has the answers to the review questions.

1. Use the *Offset* command to quickly create a parallel line(s). (T/F)

2. The *Explode* command will reduce a polyline (e.g., rectangle) to individual lines. (T/F)

3. With the *Stretch* command, lines completely within the *Crossing Window* are actually only moved, not stretched. (T/F)

4. You have to select entities and a center point when using *Polar Array*. (T/F)

5. Occasionally you need to draw an object and then move it into place to accurately locate it. (T/F)

6. Selecting this icon ( ) allows you to _____ two intersecting lines.

7. If an AutoCAD line looks like one line it should only be one line. (T/F)

8. Use the _____ command to create a reverse image.

9. You can use either _____ or _____ in the *Layer Properties Manager* to control the visibility of a layer.

10. When no entities are selected, the *Layers* toolbar displays the _____ layer.

Notes:

Lesson 4
Residential Project: FLOOR PLANS::

In this lesson you will jump right in and get started drawing your floor plans for the residential project. Throughout the lesson you will be introduced to a few new commands and you will study common methods used to draw floor plans.

Exercise 4-1:
Walls

Introduction:

Two lines, a certain distance apart, represent the walls in a floor plan. In AutoCAD these walls are drawn on a layer named *A-WALL*. The distance between the two lines is the same as the actual thickness of the wall (or very close to it); wall thicknesses are usually rounded off to the nearest ¼″.

The following is an overview of how walls are typically dimensioned in a floor plan. This information is intended to help you understand the dimensions you will see in the exercises, as well as prepare you for the point when you dimension your plans.

Stud walls (wood or metal) are typically dimensioned to the center of the walls. This is one of the reasons the walls do not need to be the exact thickness. Here are a few reasons why you should dimension to the center of the stud rather than to the face of the gypsum board:

o   The contractor is laying out the walls in a large "empty" area. The most useful dimension is to the center of the stud; that is where they will make a mark on the floor. If the dimension was to the face of the gypsum board, the contractor would have to stop and calculate the center of the stud, which is not always the center of the wall thickness (e.g., a stud wall with 1 layer of gypsum board on one side and 2 layers of gypsum board over resilient channels on the other side).

Dimension Example
– Two Stud Walls

o   The extra dimensions (text and arrows) indicating the thickness of the walls would take up an excessive amount of room on the floor plans; space that would be better used by notes.

Occasionally you should dimension to the face of a wall rather than the center. Here's one example:

o   When indicating design intent or building code requirements, you should reference the exact points/surfaces. For example, if you have uncommonly large trim around a door opening, you may want a dimension from the edge of the door to the face of the adjacent wall. Another example would be the width of a hallway; if you want a particular width you would dimension between the two faces of the wall and add the text "clear" below the dimension to make it known, without question, that the dimension is not to the center of the wall.

Dimensions for masonry and foundation walls:

o   Foundation and masonry walls are dimensioned to the nominal face and not the center. These types of walls are modular (e.g., 8″x8″x16″) so it is helpful, for both designer and builder, to have dimensions that relate to the masonry wall's "coursing" (which helps reduce waste).

Dimension Example –
Two masonry Walls

Dimensions from a stud wall to a masonry wall:

o   The rules above apply for each side of the dimension line. For example: a dimension for the exterior foundation wall to an interior stud wall would be from the exterior face of the foundation wall to the center of the stud on the stud wall.

Dimension Example
– Stud to masonry

Contos Residence

Image courtesy of Anderson Architects
Alan H. Anderson, Architect, Duluth, MN

Overview of the plans you will be drawing:

The following sketches will give you an idea of the floor plans you will draw in this lesson.

FIGURE 4-1.1 Sketch – First Floor Plan

FIGURE 4-1.2 Sketch – South Elevation

FIGURE 4-1.3 Sketch – Basement Floor Plan

FIGURE 4-1.4 Sketch – Second Floor Plan

Getting Started:

In this exercise you will draw just the walls for all three floor plans. Similar to the exercises in Lesson 3, you will draw each floor plan in a separate drawing.

Additionally, each drawing will have a common origin; this will make it easy to copy/paste and overlay the plans to make sure things lineup from floor to floor. You will use the upper left corner of the two-story portion of the residence as the origin.

Drawing walls involves extensive use of just a handful of commands, most of which you already know how to use. The most typical commands used in drawing walls are:

- Line
- Offset
- Stretch
- Trim
- Extend

The last two commands, Trim and Extend, have not been covered yet. You will study these commands in this exercise.

You will now start drawing the basement floor plan walls.

1. Start a new drawing named **Flr-B.dwg**.
   *Don't forget to use the correct template: App. Menu➔ **New** and then **SheetSets\Architectural Imperial.dwt**.*

2. Switch to *Model Space*.

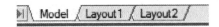

Setting the Drawing Limits

Next you will set the *Model Space* drawing limits. The drawing space does not actually have limits; this setting relates more to zooming and drawing regenerations.

3. Type **Limits** and then **Enter** *(make sure Dynamic Input is on; F12 toggles it on and off)*.

4. Type **-150'**, press the **Tab** key and then type **-130'**; **Enter**.

   a. Don't miss the minus sign in the two values above.

   b. FYI: If you are typing in the *Command Window* or *Dynamic Input* is off, you need to enter a comma in place of the tab.

5. Type **150'**, press the **Tab** key and then type **130'**;**Enter**.

6. Select **Zoom All** from the Zoom icon flyout *(Navigate 2D* panel, *View* tab)*. All

FYI: The Zoom All command will zoom to the drawing's extents or the drawing's Limits (whichever is greater). In this case, nothing has been drawn so you have no drawing extents; thus, the drawing limits are used. You are now viewing a drawing area 300´ wide and 260´ tall (based on the limits just set), with the drawing's origin (i.e., 0,0) centered in the view. This will allow you to start drawing the floor plan without having to stop and zoom (and regenerate the drawing). Try drawing a diagonal line like you did at the beginning of Lesson 2 and list the properties to verify this (see Page 2-4); be sure to erase the diagonal line before moving on.

7. Create the layer **A-WALL** (color: *White*; linetype: *Continuous*).

8. With *A-WALL* layer *Current*, draw the lines shown in **Figure 4-1.5** with either *ORTHO* or *Polar Tracking* turned on.

    *TIP: For drawing the first line, enter 0,0 for first point and then enter **24´** with Polar Tracking on and the cursor pointing down and snapped to the vertical.*

    a. Make sure *Dynamic Input* it toggled on (*Status Bar*).

    b. You do not need to draw the dimensions yet.

All the dimensions shown in the foundation perimeter drawing (Figure 4-1.5) relate to masonry coursing. See the *TIP* on the next page.

9. Use the **Measure \Distance** command (located on the *Utilities* panel under the *Home* tab) to double-check your dimensions before moving on. Now is the time to make corrections.

 Distance

FYI: Ortho is toggled on and off from the Status Bar, near Polar Tracking. When Ortho is toggled on you are only able to draw horizontal and vertical lines. Ortho needs to be turned off in order to draw angled lines. Polar Tracking gives you the "best of both worlds", i.e., angled lines and orthogonal lines. Sometimes Polar Tracking needs to be turned off when drawings angled lines which are really close to horizontal or vertical.

FIGURE 4-1.5 Foundation perimeter – Basement Floor Plan
The black dot represents the Origin (i.e., 0,0)

TIP: Concrete blocks come in various widths, and most are 16″ long and 8″ high. When drawing plans there is a simple rule to keep in mind to make sure you are designing walls to coursing. This applies to wall lengths and openings within CMU walls.

Dimension rules for CMU coursing in floor plans:

- *E′-0″ OR E′-8″*   *where e is any even number (e.g., 6′-0″ or 24′-8″)*

- *O′-4″*   *where o is any odd number (e.g., 5′-4″)*

The foundation walls consist of 8″ thick concrete blocks, so you will use the offset command to quickly create the interior side of the wall.

10. Use the **Offset** command to offset the lines previously drawn toward the center of the structure **8″** (Figure 4-1.6).

FIGURE 4-1.6 Preliminary Foundation perimeter - Basement Floor Plan

Notice in the figure above that the **Offset** command simply offsets a line of the same length as the original line. Thus, at outside corners the lines are too long and inside corners the lines are not long enough.

If you recall from the previous Lesson, the **Rectangle** command creates what is called a "closed polyline". If you had used the **Polyline** command to draw the perimeter the entire outline would have offset with perfect corners. You would then have to explode the polyline(s) in order to create the interior walls.

11. Use the **Fillet** command with the radius set to **0** (i.e., zero) to clean up all the corners. Do <u>not</u> Fillet the corner identified in Figure 4-1.7.

    *TIP: Use **Multiple**, a sub-command of Fillet, to perform several Fillets in a row.*

Do not Fillet this corner

FIGURE 4-1.7 Do not Fillet this corner
Basement Floor Plan

You should now have exterior walls with all but one "cleaned-up" corner.

Using the Extend Command:

You will use both Extend and Trim to complete the other major masonry wall in the basement. Both commands are located on the *Modify* panel under the *Home* tab (on the *Ribbon*); hover your cursor over the icon to view its tool-tip which displays the command name.

12. Select the **Extend** command (see the image to right).

You are now prompted to **Select boundary edges...**

The on-screen prompt reads:

This is what you want to extend to.

13. Pick the horizontal line identified in Figure 4-1.8.

14. Press **Enter** to tell AutoCAD you are done selecting.

a. Or, just right-click.

You are now prompted to **Select object to extend...**

The on-screen prompt reads:

15. Pick the short vertical line identified in Figure 4-1.8.

16. Press **Enter** to complete the line extension.

TIP: When you select tools from a fly-out icon, the selected tool rises to the top of the "stack". In the image above you see the default icon was Trim and once Extend is used it becomes the default (see image to the left). If the one you want is on top you simply click the icon rather than the down-arrow. Once AutoCAD is closed, the Ribbon reverts back to the defaults.

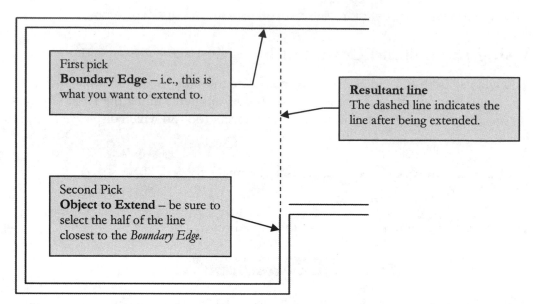

First pick
Boundary Edge – i.e., this is what you want to extend to.

Resultant line
The dashed line indicates the line after being extended.

Second Pick
Object to Extend – be sure to select the half of the line closest to the *Boundary Edge*.

FIGURE 4-1.8 Using the Extend command to extend a line

> *TIP: When selecting a line to extend, AutoCAD is aware of which side of the line's midpoint you select. This is because you can extend a line in both directions (assuming you selected lines to extend to <i.e., boundary edges> on each side). In the example above, you need to select the portion of the vertical line that is closest to the horizontal line.*

You will now draw the other line representing the 8″ concrete block wall between the basement and the unexcavated area below the garage. You have several ways in which you can draw this line. One is to Offset the line you just extended to the right 8″ and then Fillet the bottom corner. The following steps represent another option.

17. Draw a vertical **Line** from the *Endpoint* below to the *Perpendicular* point above (see Figure 4-1.9).

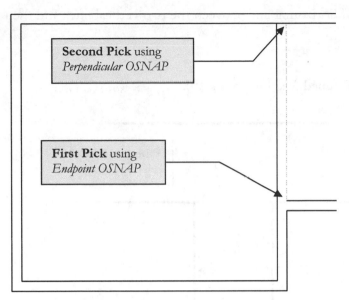

Second Pick using
Perpendicular OSNAP

First Pick using
Endpoint OSNAP

Figure 4-1.9 Drawing a line

Using the Trim Command:

Now you will use the Trim command to remove the portion of horizontal line between the two vertical lines you just created (at the top edge). In this example, the Trim command actually breaks one line into two lines. See Figure 4-1.10.

18. Select the **Trim** icon from the *Modify* panel.

You are prompted to: **Select cutting edges…**

The on-screen prompt reads: Select objects or <select all>:

These are the lines you want to trim to.

19. Select the two vertical lines you just drew.

20. Press **Enter** (or right-click) to tell AutoCAD you are finished selecting cutting edges.

You are now prompted to: **Select object to trim…**

The on-screen prompt reads: Select object to trim or shift-select to extend or

This is the portion of line you want to go away.

21. **Select** the portion of horizontal line between the two vertical lines and then press **Enter**.

The horizontal line is now trimmed (see Figure 4.1-10).

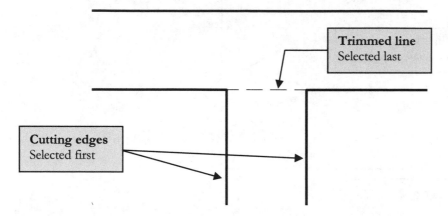

Trimmed line
Selected last

Cutting edges
Selected first

FIGURE 4-1.10 Trimming a line

Next you will complete the foundation wall at the south fireplace (towards the bottom).

22. Modify the drawing as shown in **Figure 4.1-11**.

   FYI: In the previous example of the Trim *command, if you had only selected one of the vertical lines, the entire portion of the horizontal line would be erased depending on which side of the vertical line you selected to trim.*

23. Modify drawing as shown in **Figure 4.1-12**.

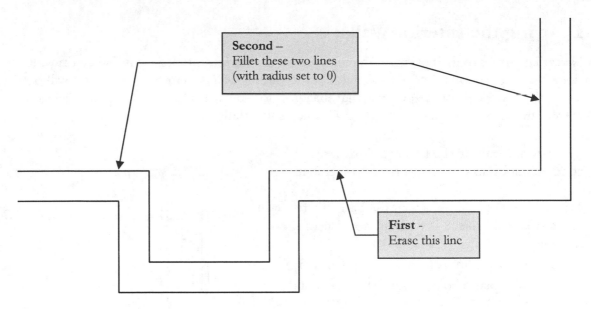

Second –
Fillet these two lines
(with radius set to 0)

First -
Erase this line

FIGURE 4-1.11 Creating and modifying walls

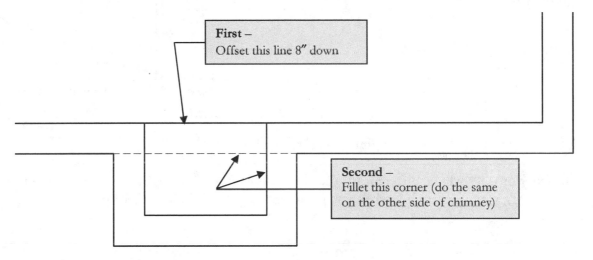

First –
Offset this line 8″ down

Second –
Fillet this corner (do the same
on the other side of chimney)

FIGURE 4-1.12 Creating and modifying walls

Drawing the Interior Walls:

Now that you have the perimeter drawn, you will draw a few interior walls. When drawing floor plans, it is good practice to sketch out the various wall systems you think you will be using; this will help you determine what thickness to draw the walls. Drawing the walls at the correct thickness helps later when you are fine-tuning things.

The exterior walls in the basement are simply 8″ concrete block so we did not need to sketch it.

Take a moment to think about the basic interior wall in a residential project. It typically consists of the following:

- o   2x4 wood studs (actual size is 1½″ x 3½″)
- o   ½″ gypsum board (⅝″is used for sound/fire control)

The wall system described above is sketched to the right (Figure 4-1.13).

FIGURE 4-1.13
Sketch – Plan view of interior wall system

All your interior walls should be drawn **4½″** for each floor.

The exterior walls will be different for the upper floors (the concrete block does not go up to the roof); you will sketch it when you get to drawing the main level floor plan.

You will now draw the interior walls to complete the walls for the basement floor plan.

24. Draw the interior walls shown in **Figure 4-1.14** using the **Line** command. Do not draw the dimensions at this time. Use the *Measure* tool to check for accuracy.

    FYI: *The dimensions shown are __not__ to the center here, for your convenience in drafting the walls.*

FIGURE 4-1.14 Interior walls to be drawn

Notice (in Figure 4-1.14) where one wall system meets another, the lines are not trimmed. This helps to delineate the extents of each wall. You would, however, trim the lines between two stud walls of varying thickness.

For now you are done with the basement floor plan. You have drawn several 8″ CMU (i.e., Concrete Masonry Units, or Concrete Blocks) and a handful of interior stud partitions (i.e., walls). After saving this drawing you will move on to the main level plan.

25. **Save** your **Flr-B** drawing file.

Drawing the Main Level Floor Plan:

Before starting the main level floor plan you will sketch the exterior wall system (see Figure 4-1.15). Notice the siding is out past the face of the concrete block foundation wall. Even though the outside face of the exterior wall is technically not aligned with the outside face of the foundation wall below, you will ignore the thickness of the siding in plan view. This allows you to draw the outside of the exterior walls in the same position as the outside face of the foundation wall below. This makes it easier to draft and for the contractor to read the dimensions on the blue prints. All the contractor needs to know is the face of the exterior sheathing is flush with the face of the foundation wall below.

SIDING
AIR BARRIER
1/2" OSB SHEATHING
2x6 STUDS at 16" O.C.
FULL-FIT BATT INSULATION
VAPOR BARRIER
1/2" GYPSUM BOARD

This wall system will be studied more closely later in the book. However, a brief explanation will be provided. This is a fairly standard wall design. The ½″ OSB (oriented strand board) extends all the way down to the top of the foundation wall. Again, as previously mentioned, notice how the exterior face of the sheathing aligns with the exterior face of the foundation wall. Often, rigid insulation is placed on the exterior side of the foundation wall to conserve heat and protect the waterproofing.

FIGURE 4-1.15 Sketch – Exterior wall in section view

26. Start a new drawing named **Flr-1.dwg**, set the drawing **Limits** as previously instructed (see page 4-5; i.e., template plus limits), and then **Zoom All**.

27. Using the **6½″** exterior wall dimension shown in Figure 4-1.15, draw all the walls shown in Figure 4-1.16.

   *NOTE: The garage is only one story in height, so the walls do not need to be constructed with 2x6's; **draw the exterior garage walls at 4½″ thick**. The interior garage wall will still be a 2x6 wall to maintain a higher R-value incase the garage door is accidentally left open in the middle of winter!*

28. Be sure the *Origin* is in the same relative position as the basement floor plan. If it is not, use the *Move* command to move the entire first floor plan into its correct position.

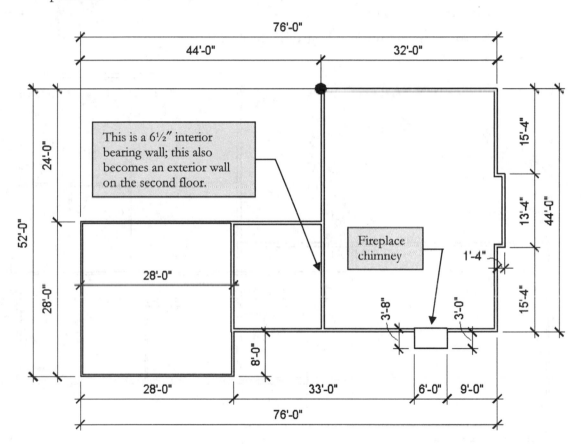

FIGURE 4-1.16 Exterior walls – First floor plan; the black dot represents the Origin

Notice, with the exception of a few added dimensions, all the dimensions given in Figure 4-1.16 are the same as those given for the basement floor plan. (See Figure 4-1.5.)

Now you will draw the interior walls.

29. Draw the interior walls shown in **Figure 4-1.17**, keeping the following in mind:

   a. Remember to use the **4½″** dimension from Figure 4-1.13.

   b. Again, the dimensions shown are to the face of the walls.

   c. Trim all intersections except at the southern fireplace.

   d. The two major horizontal interior walls are to align with the inside face of the exterior wall as shown.

   e. North is straight up as indicated by the north arrow.

Figure 4-1.17 Interior walls – First floor plan

FYI: Unless there are unusual circumstances, north is always UP on architectural plan drawings (i.e., floor plans, site plans, etc.).

Notice the dimensions within the rectangles above; they relate to wall dimensions from the basement floor plan (Figure 4-1.14). Each is related to a stairway that, of course, passes between floors so the walls, by necessity, need to align from floor to floor. (Notice the dimension changes for the stair near the garage as the exterior basement wall is thicker than the first floor exterior wall.)

Drawing the Second Level Floor Plan:

Here you will use the same wall thicknesses previously identified.

       Exterior Walls: 6½″
       Interior Walls: 4½″

30. Start a new drawing named **Flr-2.dwg**, set the drawing **Limits** as previously instructed (page 4-5), and then **Zoom All**.

31. Using the same relative **Origin**, draw the second floor exterior walls shown in **Figure 4-1.18**.

    FYI: The fireplace chimney is smaller at this level than below; the smaller size is centered on the larger size below. You will see this better when you draw the elevations.

FIGURE 4-1.18 Exterior walls – Second floor plan; the black dot represents the Origin

Again, you should notice several of the dimensions in Figure 4-1.18 match dimensions shown on the two lower floor plans; this floor is considerably smaller than the other floors.

32. Draw the interior walls shown in **Figure 4-1.19**.

FIGURE 4-1.19 Interior walls – Second floor plan

33. **Save** your floor plan drawings.

This concludes the exercise on drawing walls for your floor plans. You should now have a good working knowledge of *Offset*, *Trim*, and *Extend*, as well as using the *Distance* command to verify your drawings.

In the next exercise you will use *Offset*, *Extend* and *Trim* to locate and create door openings in the walls. Additionally, you will learn how to insert pre-drawn symbols (called blocks) into your drawing. In this case you will insert the door symbols previously drawn in Lesson 3.

Exercise 4-2:
Doors

Now that you have drawn the walls, you will add the doors. This involves locating where the door opening will be in the wall and then trimming the wall lines to create the opening. Finally, you insert a door symbol that indicates which side the hinges are on and the direction the door opens.

New doors are typically shown open 90 degrees in floor plans, which helps to avoid conflicts such as the door hitting an adjacent base cabinet. Additionally, to make it clear graphically, existing doors are shown open only 45 degrees.

Door symbol Example – New Door drawn with 90 degree swing

Door symbol Example – Existing Door shown with 45 degree swing

One of the most powerful features of any CAD program is its ability to reuse previously drawn content. With AutoCAD you can insert entire drawing files as symbols into your drawing. Most of the individual drawings you drew in Lesson 3 will be inserted as symbols (AutoCAD calls them blocks), into the three floor plans.

For those new to drafting, you may find this comparison between CAD and hand-drafting interesting. When hand-drafting, one uses a straightedge or a plastic template that has doors and other often used symbols to trace.

Hand Drafting Template – Plastic template with holes representing common residential shapes (at ¼″ – 1′-0″)
Image used by permission, Timely Templates www.timelytemplates.com

Doors in stud walls are dimensioned to the center of the door opening. On the other hand, and similar to dimensioning masonry walls, doors in masonry walls are dimensioned to the face (see example below).

Door Dimension Example – Dimension to the center of the door opening

Door Dimension Example – Dimension the opening size and location

Placing a door usually involves the following commands: Offset, Extend, Trim, and Insert.

Getting Started:

First you will locate all the openings in the plans. This includes trimming the wall lines.

1. Open your **Flr-1.dwg** drawing file.

2. **Zoom** into the area shown in **Figure 4-2.1**.

FIGURE 4-2.1 Zoom into area shown

3. **Offset** the vertical line **2′-6″** to the West (to the left) as shown in **Figure 4-2.2**.

Offset vertical line
2′-6″ to the West

FIGURE 4-2.2 Offset vertical line 2′-6″

4. **Extend** the new line South, to the outside face of the exterior wall (Figure 4-2.3).

FIGURE 4-2.3 Extend new line south

5. Now **Trim** the line so its length equals the depth of the wall (Figure 4-2.4).

FIGURE 4-2.4 Trim the new vertical line

Next you will *Offset* the new line; the offset distance will be the width of the door.

If your line is located in the center of the door opening, you would offset it each direction with the offset distance being half the width of the door opening. Then you would delete the center line.

6. **Offset** the line **3'-0″** to the west (Figure 4-2.5).

New line offset 3'-0″ to locate door jambs

FIGURE 4-2.5 Offset to define the door opening

Finally, you will use *Trim* to remove the wall lines within the door opening.

7. **Trim** the wall lines within the door opening (Figure 4-2.6).

    TIP: Select both vertical lines as the Cutting Edge and then pick the portion of the line you want to remove (the portion between the two vertical lines in this example).

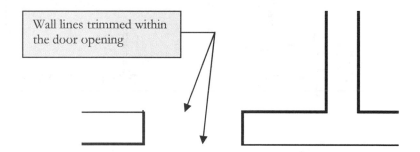

Wall lines trimmed within the door opening

FIGURE 4-2.6 Trim the wall lines within the door opening

That completes the steps necessary to accurately locate a door opening in a wall. Next you will create the rest of the openings for both the first and second floors (the basement has no doors).

> ## What layer do the new jamb lines go on?
>
> The two vertical lines (jamb lines) just drawn go on the same layer as the wall.

Locate and Size the Remaining Openings:

8. Using the following four drawings (Figures 4-2.7, .8, .9, .10), create the door openings for the first and second floors.

9. Be sure to **Save** often to avoid losing work in the event you have a power outage or the AutoCAD program crashes.

FIGURE 4-2.7 Door opening; First floor LOCATIONS

FIGURE 4-2.8 Door/opening sizes; First floor SIZES

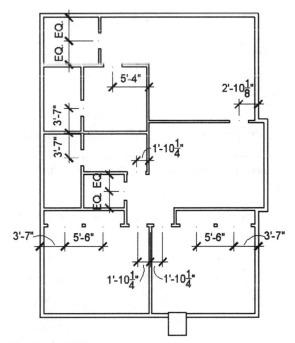

Figure 4-2.9 Door locations; Second floor

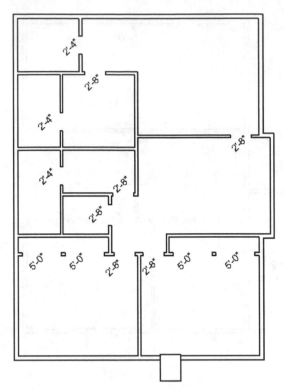

Figure 4-2.10 Door/opening sizes; Second floor
- *angled number represents size of opening*

Inserting the Door Symbols (a.k.a., Blocks):

Now that you have created all the door openings you will insert the door symbols. AutoCAD refers to these symbols as *Blocks*.

Blocks have several advantages compared to simply drawing individual lines for everything.

o   A Block contains a group of entities so you can easily move it without having to meticulously select each entity that makes up the symbol.

o   Blocks can also be redefined, meaning that you can add or remove the amount of detail in a block. When it's redefined, all the instances of that block in the current drawing are automatically updated.

o   Blocks can consist of an entire drawing located on your hard drive. Thus, they can be used in multiple drawings as needed.

o   Blocks help reduce the drawing file size.

You will insert the door *Blocks* you created in the previous lesson. You may occasionally need to Rotate and Mirror the *Block* once it is inserted. Additionally, you will need to create additional *Blocks* as needed throughout this book.

Door *Blocks* go on their own *Layer*, called *A-DOOR*. Next you will set this up.

10. In the first floor plan, create a *Layer* named **A-DOOR** and set its color to ***Yellow*** (Color #2).

11. Set the **A-DOOR** layer to be the *Current Layer*.

12. Select **Insert** in the *Block* panel under the *Insert* tab.

Insert

You are now in the *Insert* dialog (Figure 4-2.11), which allows you to insert *Blocks* that already exist in the current drawing and other drawings located on your hard drive.

13. Click the **Browse...** button *(you will pick a DWG file)*.

14. Browse to the location where you saved the **Door-36** drawing created in Lesson 3.

15. Click **Open**.

FIGURE 4-2.11 Insert dialog; allows you to insert *Blocks* into the current drawing

16. **Insert** the **Door-36** drawing using *OSNAPs* to accurately position the door *Block* within the opening. Insert the doors as shown in Figure 4-2.12.

> ***TIP #1:*** *Use Rotate and Mirror (previously covered) as required to indicate the required swing.*

> ***TIP #2:*** *Doors should be yellow if the layer was setup correctly and was current when the door block was inserted.*

Notice the block insertion point?

Notice that the hinge side of the door *Block* is attached to the center of the cross-hairs. This relates to the drawing *Origin* (0,0) of the Door-36 drawing file.

If the drawing *Origin* had been located on the latch side of the door in drawing Door-36, the latch side of the door would have been attached to the cross-hairs during insert.

You may have noticed that you have not created a 2'-8" wide door yet. Simply follow the steps outlined in Lesson 3, creating the door symbol in a separate drawing file.

17. Create the 32" wide door drawing; name the file **Door-32**.

18. Insert the 2'-8" wide doors using the **Door-32** file.

FIGURE 4-2.12 Door-36 and Door-32 blocks inserted; First floor

19. Insert the **Door2-36** drawing file as a *Block* at the main entry as shown in **Figure 4-2.13**.

FIGURE 4-2.13 Door2-36 added

Next you will insert the doors on the second floor.

20. **Save Flr-1.dwg** and **Open** the second floor drawing file **Flr-2.dwg**.

21. Insert the doors for the second floor as shown in **Figure 4-2.14**.

NOTE: On the second floor all swing doors are 32" wide doors.

FIGURE 4-2.14 Door-32 blocks inserted; Second floor

Sliding Pocket Doors:

Sliding pocket doors are doors that slide into the wall rather than swinging open into a room. This type of door is convenient when the door will be open most of the time and you do not want, or have room for, an open door. On the other hand, if the door will be used often, like the door from the hallway into the bath room, you should use a swinging door for ease of use and long-term durability.

One important thing to keep in mind when designing a room with a sliding door: the entire width of the door is in the wall when the door is fully open. That means you need space in the wall next to the door that equals the width of the door plus a few inches depending on the manufacturer (this includes plumbing and electrical that might be in the wall).

Next you will create the 2'-4" and 4'-0" wide Sliding Pocket Doors.

22. **Open** a new drawing file and name it **Pocket-28.dwg**.

23. **Create** the 2'-4" wide pocket door (show the door 2" thick) shown in **Figure 4-2.15**. This is basically two rectangles.

> *TIP: Do not draw the dimensions or the black dot. Also, the dashed lines in the figure below represent a wall (not to be drawn). Finally, make sure everything is on Layer 0 (i.e., zero).*

FIGURE 4-2.15 Pocket-28; First and Second floor

This *Block* (Pocket-28) will show the door in the fully closed position; you can adjust this to be partially open if you prefer.

24. **Insert** the 2'-4" wide pocket door in the three locations shown in Figure 4-2.16 (make sure the current layer is set to *A-DOOR* before inserting the blocks; also, you may need to stretch the opening location a little so the pocket door fits in the wall).

25. Do a **Save-As** to save the Pocket-28 to a file named **Pocket-48**.

26. Use the **Stretch** command to create the 48" pocket door.

27. Insert the 48" wide pocket door in two locations, as shown in Figure 4-2.17, on the first floor.

FIGURE 4-2.16 Pocket-28; three locations; Second floor

FIGURE 4-2.17 Pocket-48; two locations; First floor

ROUGH OPENING IN WIDTH IS 2 TIMES THE DOOR SIZE PLUS 2" (50.8mm). R.O. IN HEIGHT IS 4" (101.6 mm) MORE THAN DOOR HEIGHT.

ROUGH OPENING

FRAME INSTALLED IN ROUGH OPENING.

FRAME AND DOOR INSTALLED. READY FOR DRYWALL.

POCKET DOOR EXAMPLES – Double door and Single door photos (top); Installation illustration (bottom); *Images used by permission, KrisTrack www.kristrack.com*

Drawing Closet Doors:

These doors will be drawn right in the Flr-1 and Flr-2 drawings (on layer *A-DOOR*); not everything needs to be a *Block*.

28. **Draw** two rectangles, each 1½″ thick, per Figure 4-2.18.

29. Do the same on the second floor (4 closet openings total).

FIGURE 4-2.18 Closet door added; First floor

Garage Doors:

Now you will add the garage door. The exterior face of the door aligns with the interior face of the wall; see garage door jamb detail at right.

30. Similar to the closet doors, you will simply draw a rectangle (place on layer *A-DOOR*); see Figure 4-2.19.

31. **Save** your drawings.

FIGURE 4-2.19 Garage door added; 2″ thick door shown

Exercise 4-3:
Windows

In this exercise you will add exterior windows to your plans. This is similar to placing doors, discussed in the previous exercise.

One difference between drawing doors and windows is that windows are drawn on two separate layers:

A-GLAZ	The window frame and glass (a.k.a., glazing) are drawn on this layer.
A-GLAZ-SILL	The sill lines are drawn on this layer. (This represents the portion of wall that continues below the window.)

Lineweights:

The primary reason that two *Layers* are used is to control lineweights. The thickness of a line (i.e., lineweight) is commonly controlled by which *Layer* it is on. One benefit to this is that you can adjust the lineweight setting in one location and all the lines on that *Layer* are updated. You will more about setting lineweights later in this book; for now, do not make any changes related to lineweights unless specifically instructed to do so.

When thinking about how lineweights relate to a window in plan, you need to consider whether the line is in section or not.

The diagrams below show the different components that make up a window in plan view.

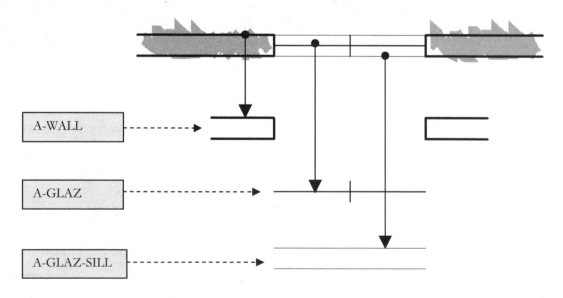

Window Opening Example   Components / Layers for a window

You can think of floor plans as cutaways of the 3D building. The cutting plane is usually about 4′- 5′ above the floor level. Notice in the following illustration that the wall is in section but the window sill is not. The sill is technically in elevation (i.e., plan view) while looking down.

Wall lines; the lines are in section, so they will be heavier lines

Window sill lines; the lines are in elevation, not section, so they will be a lighter line

FIGURE 4-3.1 Window Isometric; floor plan cutting plane

Drawing the Windows:

The windows could be *Blocks*, similar to the doors, but you will simply draw lines to create the windows in this exercise. Again, the advantages of *Blocks* are that you can pick any part of a *Block* and the entire thing will highlight; you can also redefine a *Block* and all occurrences of it in the current drawing will automatically be updated.

1. Create the openings in your exterior walls the same way you created the door openings on page 4-20 (Figures 4-3.3, 4-3.4, and 4-3.5):
    a. The [wider] double windows are **6′-8″**.
    b. The single windows are **3′-2″**.
    c. The basement windows are as dimensioned in plan.
    d. See the *extra credit* option towards the end of this exercise (page 4-41).

2. Create the following *Layers*:
   A-GLAZ (color *Yellow*); **A-GLAZ-SILL** (color *Red*)

3. Draw the "window lines" per the example shown in Figure 4-3.2; draw a line in the center of the window for the double wide windows. *(This indicates two window frames mulled together.)*

Add center line at double wide windows (layer *A-GLAS*)

FIGURE 4-3.2 Window Lines; note that EQ. is an abbreviation of 'Equal'

4. **Save** your drawings.

FIGURE 4-3.3 Window Locations; Basement floor

Window Dimensions in Masonry Walls?

Dimensioning windows in masonry openings is similar to dimensioning doors (discussed in the previous exercise).

The mason laying the block typically has nothing to do with the windows; they just want to know how big to make the opening and how far it is from the previous opening.

On the other hand, the carpenter typically builds the walls and installs the windows. Additionally, dimensioning windows to the center is beneficial because the window manufacturer used to draw the details may not be the one used in the project. Window sizes can vary from manufacturer to manufacturer.

FIGURE 4-3.4 Window Locations; First floor

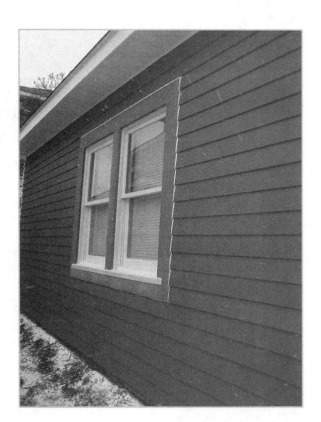

Double Window Example
Two Double-Hung windows

FIGURE 4-3.5 Window Locations; Second floor

Software Offered by Window Manufacturers?

Some window manufacturers offer software to insert their windows into your AutoCAD floor plans. One such manufacturer's program, offered free via the internet, is Marvin Windows and Doors.

The program is called **Marvin Design System** (MDS) and can be downloaded via the following URL: **http://pros.marvin.com/resources/marvin-design-system/**

If you are taking this course for credit, your instructor may offer extra credit if you use this program to insert your windows into the floor plans.

NOTE: In a classroom lab setting you need to make sure you have permission to install software!

Exercise 4-4:
Annotation and Dimensions

As previously mentioned in Lesson 2, annotations (text; notes) and dimensions allow the designer/drafter to accurately describe the drawing.

To complete this lesson you will add room names and dimensions to your floor plans.

Room Names:

Now you will add the room names to the floor plans.

1.   **Open** your basement floor plan drawing (Flr-B.dwg).

2.   Create the layer **A-ANNO-TEXT** (color 4) and set it *Current*.

3.   Using the **Multiline Text** command, create **9″ Arial** type text in the center of the floor plan that reads: "UNFINISHED BASEMENT". See Figures 4-4.1 and 4-4.2.

A

Text

   TIP: Refer back to Exercise 2-4 for more on MText.

Figure 4-4.1 Mtext command; 9″ high Arial text

4.   Looking at **Figures 4-4.3** and **4-4.4**, add the room names to the first and second floors; remember to create the appropriate text layer.

> **REMINDER:**
> *Double click on **MText** to edit it in **Text Editor** mode.*

UNFINISHED BASEMENT

FIGURE 4-4.2 Text added; Basement floor plan

Residential project created in *Residential Design Using Autodesk Revit 2014*.

FIGURE 4-4.3
Text added; First floor plan

UPPERCASE vs. Lowercase text:

Text, on architectural drawings, is typically all uppercase. The lowercase letters can be hard to read, especially when they overlap lines or the printer made the strokes of the letters too thick.

One exception might be a large body of general notes that are off to the side of the plans.

FIGURE 4-4.4 Text added; Second floor plan

Dimensions:

A floor plan has all the major elements dimensioned on them. It is not desirable to leave the location of these major components to be scaled off the blue prints; in fact, for many larger residential projects and most commercial projects, the contract prohibits the contractor from scaling the drawings; they are instructed to request the information from the Architect or Designer.

Next you will dimension all the Walls, Doors and Windows on the exterior walls.

5. Type **Units**, and set the *Length Precision* to **0'-0 1/32"**.

   FYI: You need to do this so you can set the text height to 3/32" in a later step.

6. Create the layer ***A-ANNO-DIMS*** (color 30) and set it *Current*.

7. On the *Annotate* tab, click the **Dimension Style** link (small arrow in lower right).

FIGURE 4-4.5 Dimension Style Manager; Standard style selected

8. Click the style **Standard** (on left), and then click **Modify...**

You are now in the dialog box that allows you to control how the dimensions look when you draw them. You will adjust a few of these settings (Figure 4-4.6a).

9. Make the changes identified with a star (★) in Figures 4-4.6A, 4-4.6B, 4-4.7, 4-4.8, and 4-4.9.

FIGURE 4-4.6A
Modify Dimension Style;
Lines tab

FIGURE 4-4.6B
Modify Dimension Style;
Symbols and Arrows tab

FIGURE 4-4.7
Modify Dimension Style;
Text tab

FIGURE 4-4.8
Modify Dimension Style;
Fit tab

FIGURE 4-4.9
Modify Dimension Style;
Primary Units tab

10. Click the **OK** button.

11. Click **Close** to exit the *Dimension Style Manager.*

Many of the changes you just made are self-explanatory by the description and the preview images which change as you adjust the settings.

12. At the bottom of the screen, on the *Application Status Bar* menu, right-click on the **Automatically Add Scales…** icon and select the **Automatically Add Scale to Annotative Objects** option.

13. Just to the left of the previous item, click the *Annotation Scale* listed (should be 1:1) and select **¼"=1'-0"** from list (see image below).

14. From the *Annotate* tab select **Linear** (on the *Ribbon*).

   TIP: *The top Dimension button starts the Linear tool – just click it.*

Now when you add dimensions to this drawing, the height will automatically be set based on the scale selected at the bottom of the screen; this scale can be changed on-the-fly, instantly updating the height of all text in the drawing. You will try this next.

15. Draw the dimension shown in **Figure 4-4.10**.

FIGURE 4-4.10 Dimension Added; Basement floor plan

Try setting the *Annotation Scale* to ½″ = 1′-0″ and notice the text and arrows on the dimensions change size. Set the scale back to **¼″ = 1′-0″** before moving on.

16. Complete the dimensioning of the exterior (for each floor plan) per the following figures (Figures 4-4.11, 4-4.12, and 4-4.13).

   TIP #1: *Make sure you draw on the correct layer.*

   TIP #2: *Use OSNAP to accurately pick points to dimension to.*

   TIP #3: *When creating a string of dimensions, use OSNAP for the third pick to make sure the dimensions line up perfectly.*

FIGURE 4-4.11 Dimensions added; Basement floor plan

TIP: If you right-click on the grip of a selected dimension, you have the option of entering "Continue" mode. This mode allows you to point points on your drawing and AutoCAD will align the dimension with the previous one.

Figure 4-4.12 Dimensions added; First floor plan

TIP: **Dimensioning Shortcut**

AutoCAD has a command that allows you to quickly draw a **continuous** string of dimensions. First you add one dimension using the Linear command. Then, from the *Dimensions* panel you select the **Continue** icon. Finally, you start picking points along the wall and AutoCAD automatically places the dimension and aligns it with the first one you added! This feature can save a lot of time. Also, the drawings look better when a continuous string of dimensions aligns perfectly.

GOOD
EXAMPLE

BAD
EXAMPLE

Figure 4-4.13 Dimensions added; Second floor plan

17. **Save** your drawings.

18. **Print** each floor plan "**scaled to fit**" on **8½ x 11** paper; refer back to Exercise 2-5 for an overview on printing.

> *TIP: If you use the Print Display option, per Exercise 2-5, you will need to position the floor plan as large as possible on in the Drawing window. You may want to try using the Plot Window option at this point, so you can tell AutoCAD exactly what you want to print.*

This concludes the "Floor Plans" exercise. Next you will develop the exterior elevations while taking a look at additional AutoCAD features like *Bhatch* (which fills an area with a pattern) and *Grip Editing* (which allows you to manipulate lines without using AutoCAD commands).

It is highly recommended that you complete the Additional Tasks at the end of this chapter.

Self-Exam:
The following questions can be used as a way to check your knowledge of this lesson. The answers can be found at the bottom of this page.

1. *Offset* is very useful for drawing floor plans. (T/F)

2. You dimension to the center of masonry walls. (T/F)

3. It does not matter which half of the line you pick when using *Extend*. (T/F)

4. Use the _____ command to remove a portion of a line between two crossing lines.

5. All walls go on the _____ layer.

Review Questions:
The following questions may be assigned by your instructor as a way to assess your knowledge of this section. Your instructor has the answers to the review questions.

1. Text on architectural drawings is typically uppercase. (T/F)

2. The *A-GLAZ-SILL* layer is meant to be a lighter line. (T/F)

3. It does not matter which *Layer* dimensions are drawn on. (T/F)

4. Use _____ _____ to control dimension text size.

5. You cannot mirror a *Block*; such as your door blocks. (T/F)

6. These icons() allow you to _____ and to _____ respectively.

7. For masonry coursing, what are the two options; 6'- ____" and 6'- ____".

8. In plan view, a door open 90 degrees is a _____ door; and a door open 45 degrees is a _____ door.

9. What *Layer* do jamb lines go on? _____.

10. When inserting a drawing as a *Block*, the insertion point for the block is the same as the drawing origin (i.e., 0,0) it was created with. (T/F)

Additional Tasks:

Task 4-1: Fireplace – North

Draw all the lines shown on Layer *A-WALL*. Copy/Paste this line work from the basement floor plan to the first floor plan.

Commands used: Offset, Trim, Extend, Fillet, Layer Manager, Circle

TASK 4-1 (1) Fireplace (north); Basement floor plan view (First floor is similar).

TASK 4-1 (2) Fireplace (north); Second floor plan view.

Drawing Multileaders

A *Multileader* is a line with an arrow on one end and text on the other end. Multileaders are very customizable and can have various symbols on the "arrow" end and a *Block* (e.g., a circle with a number in it) or nothing at all. You will need to use this feature in the next exercise (adding notes and pointing to various parts of the drawing) so you will take a moment to learn about it now.

A *Multileader* system is similar to the dimensioning system in that you first setup the style (of which you can have several, if needed) and then draw the leader and enter the text. If the style is modified, all instances of *Multileaders* that were created using that style will be modified.

First you will setup the style; these steps could be done in a template file so you would not have to repeat them each time you created a new drawing.

1. Start a new drawing (SheetSets\Architectural Imperial).

2. On the *Annotate* tab, in the *Leaders* panel, click the **Multileader Style Manager** link (Figure Task 4-1 (3)).

TASK 4-1 (3) Found on the *Annotate* panel

3. In the *Multileader Style Manager*, with **Standard** style selected, click the **Modify...** button (Figure Task 4-1 (4)).

   FYI: Notice how this looks just like the style manager for dimensions.

TASK 4-1 (4) Multileader Style Manager dialog

4. Make the changes shown in the following three images (Figures Task 4-1 (5)A thru Task 4-1 (5)C).

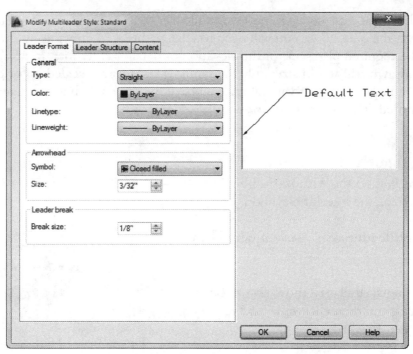

TASK 4-1 (5)A: Leader Format tab: Modify Multileader Style dialog

TASK 4-1 (5)B: Leader Structure tab   **TASK 4-1 (5)C:** Content tab

5.   When finished, click **OK** and then **Close** to exit these two dialog boxes.

You are almost ready to use your newly modified multileader style, but first you need to set the *Annotation Scale* via the *Status Bar*. You will need to change this on a drawing-by-drawing basis according to the required plot scale of the elevation or detail. Remember, in *Model Space* everything is always drawn real-world size; only the symbols and text are scaled up or down so that a sheet with multiple details of varying scale all have the same relative text height when the sheet is printed. This is where *Annotation Scale* comes in handy!

6. On the *Status Bar*, set the **Annotation Scale** to ¼″ = 1′-0″. This is the scale of the next exercise (i.e., the interior elevations).

7. Click the **Multileader** icon, *Annotate* tab (Figure Task 4-1 (6)).

Figure Task 4-1 (6):
Multileader tool

8. Click three points, similar to those shown below, type some text, and then click *Exit Text Editor* on the *Ribbon* when finished.

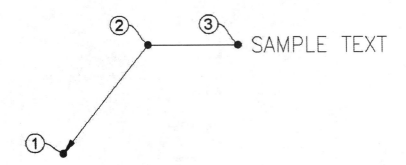

Try changing the *Annotative Scale* and notice the text and arrow size changes automatically. You can now apply this technique throughout the remaining lessons of this textbook.

Task 4-2: Main Stairway

Draw all the lines shown on Layer *A-FLOR-VERT* (color *Yellow*). Copy/ Paste this line work from the basement floor plan to the first floor plan and then modify for that condition. Handrail lines are 1½″ apart. You can use the Array (Polar) to create the angled lines (or Rotate –90 degrees divided by 3). Actually drawing the line with the arrow (i.e., Multileader) has not been covered yet but is very simple. Select the **Multileader** icon from the *Annotate* tab and pick points on the screen.

Draw the text on layer *A-ANNO-TEXT* (color 4).

The angled line that trims off part of the stair indicates where the stairs pass through the imaginary cutting plane for the floor plan; draw these lines on the *A-FLOR-VERT* layer (color 2).

Approximate the line work not dimensioned; *TYP.* Means typical (i.e., they are all the same dimension).

Commands used: Line, Offset, Trim, Extend, Fillet, Layer Manager, Array, Leader, Mtext

> *TIP:* The 'Maximum Leader Points' within the MultiLeader properties needs to be increased to 4 to create this three legged leader.

TASK 4-2 (1) Main Stair; Basement floor plan view.

> *NOTE:* You can add the leaders with no text (just press Enter when prompted to type text) and then add regular Mtext to position where you want it as shown in this task. When you type the text (i.e., Up or Down) as part of the MultiLeader you are limited in where you can place the text relative to the leader.

TASK 4-2 (2) Main Stair; First floor plan view.

TASK 4-2 (3) Main Stair; Second floor plan view.

Task 4-3: Secondary Stairway

Similar to the previous Task; draw this stairway.

FYI: *You will learn later, when you develop the stair section, that this stair is not in the correct location.*

TASK 4-3 (1) Secondary Stair; Basement floor plan view.

TASK 4-3 (2) Secondary Stair; First floor plan view.

Task 4-4: Porch

Draw the porch per the dimensions shown.

Draw the large columns (12"x12") and outside lines on layer *A-WALL* and the railings and steps on layer *A-FLOR-VERT*.

You do not need to draw the dimensions (unless instructed otherwise).

TASK 4-4 Porch; First floor plan

Task 4-5: Garage Steps

Draw the steps from the garage into the house per the dimensions shown.

NOTE: It is common to have the garage slab lower than the house floor to prevent any spills or snow melt from entering the house. Draw the lines on layer A-FLOOR-VERT.

TASK 4-5 Garage Steps; First floor plan

Task 4-6: South Fireplace

Add the following detail to the south fireplace (similar to Task 4-1).

TASK 4-6 Fireplace (south); First floor plan

Lesson 5
Residential Project: EXTERIOR ELEVATIONS::

In this lesson you will draw the exterior elevations based on the floor plans previously drawn. You will also take a look at a few new commands and tools like *GRIP* editing.

Exercise 5-1:
Elevation Outlines

Introduction:

When designing a residence, one needs to be sensitive to the massing and proportions of each elevation and the various elements within. The exterior elevations are the drawings used to develop the outward aesthetic of the structure. Too often this is not given enough thought and time, thus resulting in harsh, unappealing homes with vast amounts of siding and awkwardly sized and positioned windows.

In this section you will look at blocking out the exterior elevations based on information previously drawn in the floor plans. The vertical dimensions will be given to you (which will also be used to draw your sections).

You will start a new drawing to draw all four elevations in. Each elevation will align horizontally, which aids in aligning windows, doors, roof edges, etc.

South Elevation (Figure 5-1.1):

1. Create a new drawing named **Exterior Elevations.dwg**.

2. Create *Layer* **G-Detl-Medm** (color *Green*), and set it *Current*.

First you will draw the outline for the garage.

3. Looking at your printed out and dimensioned floor plans (on page 4-6), notice that the garage is 28'-0" wide.

4. Draw a horizontal line **28'-0"** long.

5. Draw a vertical line **9′-6½″** tall at each end of the horizontal line previously drawn (Figure 5-1.3).

FIGURE 5-1.1 Completed South Elevation to be drawn in this lesson

FIGURE 5-1.2 Outline of South Elevation to be drawn in this exercise

FIGURE 5-1.3 Garage elevation; first three lines

Next you will draw the angled line representing the sloped roof edge. This roof has an 8/12 pitch. That means that for every 12″ horizontally, the roof drops (or rises) 8″.

The easiest way to draw this line is to draw temporary lines per the description above and then draw an angled line that connects the dots; you will do this in the following steps:

6. At the top of the vertical line on the left, draw a horizontal line 12″ long towards the right (Figure 5-1.4).

7. Now draw a vertical line 8″ long (Figure 5-1.4).

8. Draw the angled line using the endpoints of the temporary lines as snap points (Figure 5-1.5).

9. **Erase** the temporary lines (Figure 5-1.6).

10. **Mirror** the angled line, using the Midpoint of the 28′-0″ horizontal line (Figure 5-1.7).

FIGURE 5-1.4
Temporary lines used to create roof edge (left side)

FIGURE 5-1.5
Angled line drawn using OSNAPs

FIGURE 5-1.6
Temporary lines erased

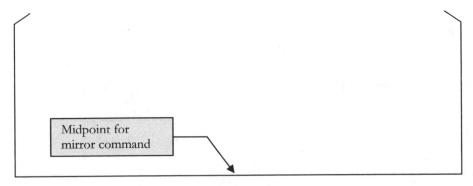

Midpoint for mirror command

FIGURE 5-1.7 Garage elevation; angled line mirrored

You will now use the *Fillet* command to extend the two angled lines up to the peak.

11. Select the **Fillet** command. Make sure the Radius is set to **0″**, and then select the two angled lines (Figure 5-1.8).

FIGURE 5-1.8 Garage elevation; roof line completed

Next you will *Offset* your two vertical lines inward. These lines will represent the vertical trim boards that the siding ties into.

12. **Offset** the two vertical lines **5½″** inward (Figure 5-1.9).

13. Use the **Extend** command to extend the trim lines up to the angled lines.

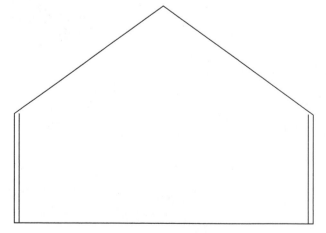

FIGURE 5-1.9 Garage elevation; corner trim

14. **Offset** the two roof lines outward **10½″** (Figure 5-1.10).

FIGURE 5-1.10 Garage elevation; fascia lines

15. **Fillet** the two new lines to form the ridge at the top.

Next you will develop the overhang. It is sometimes helpful to sketch the roof edge detail (you will draft it later in this book) so you can draw it correctly and not have to go back and tweak the elevations later. Figure 5-1.11 is our sketch, showing a total of 10½″ for the fascia and a 1′-0″ overhang.

Then you will draw the roof edge in your elevation.

FIGURE 5-1.11 Typical Roof edge; similar condition at garage

16. Draw the roof edge profile as shown in **Figure 5-1.12**.

   a. Draw the temporary line (shown dashed in Figure 5-1.12) and *Offset* it down **5⅞″**, and then delete the temporary line.

   b. Make sure you use *ORTHO* or *Polar Tracking* to assure horizontal and vertical lines.

FIGURE 5-1.12 Typical Roof edge profile

17. Use the **Mirror** command to mirror the roof edge to the other side of the garage.

This completes the outline of the garage. Next you will work on the house.

Referring to your dimensioned plans (or page 4-7), notice the overall dimension is 76'-0" and the garage takes up 28'-0" of that dimension. So the remaining portion to be drawn is 48'-0".

18. Draw a line **48'-0"** to the right (Figure 5-1.13).

The first floor of the house is higher than the garage floor (to keep the snowmelt from getting into the house for us northerners!), so you need to move this line up; recall the steps drawn in Task 4-5(page 4-62).

19. **Move** the 48'-0" line up **1'-4"** (Figure 5-1.14).

FIGURE 5-1.13 48'-0" line drawn to the right

FIGURE 5-1.14 48'-0" line moved up 1'-4"

20. Draw two vertical lines **19'-1⅝"** long and **32'-0"** apart; note the two story portion of the building is 32'-0" wide on your dimensioned plans.

FIGURE 5-1.15 Vertical lines 32'-0" apart; 19'-1⅝" long lines

21. The vertical trim, roof edge and pitch are the same as the garage, so follow the same steps to complete the roof as shown in **Figure 5-1.16**.

FIGURE 5-1.16 Roof outline added to two story portion of house

22. **Offset** the first floor line **12'-5 9/16"** up to establish the ridge line; extend and trim as required (Figure 5-1.17).

> **TIP:** *Knowing the building is 20'-0" wide below the portion of roof in question, you could draw a section through this area to calculate the height of the ridge line (this roof and the porch only have a 4/12 pitch).*

FIGURE 5-1.17 South Elevation; added roof ridge line

Taking a look back at Figure 5-1.2 you will notice that the fascia of the porch roof aligns with the garage roof. Therefore you can draw horizontal lines extending from the endpoints of the garage roof edge.

23. Draw two horizontal lines as shown in **Figure 5-1.18**; the length does not matter at this time.

FIGURE 5-1.18 South Elevation

24. Draw an **8′-6″** line as shown in Figure 5-1.19.

FIGURE 5-1.19 South Elevation

25. At the edge of the 8′-6″ line just drawn, you will draw one of the porch columns per the dimensions shown in Figure 5-1.20.

FIGURE 5-1.20 South Elevation; porch column

26. Using the same roof edge profile, draw the porch roof with a **4/12** pitch as shown in **Figure 5-1.21**. Extend the sloped roof line up to the face of the building as shown.

27. Draw the horizontal line where the porch roof meets the wall, and then trim the vertical lines to the new horizontal line as shown in **Figure 5-1.22**.

28. Draw the rest of the columns; locate them using the floor plan dimension previously provided (or use Xref, described next).

FIGURE 5-1.21 South Elevation; porch roof

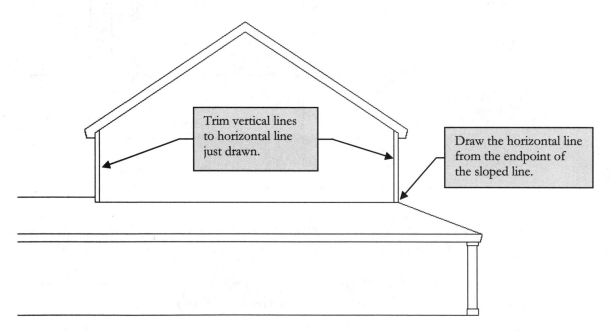

Trim vertical lines to horizontal line just drawn.

Draw the horizontal line from the endpoint of the sloped line.

FIGURE 5-1.22 South Elevation; porch roof

External References:

We will digress for a moment and take a look at *External References*. Basically, this is a way to bring another drawing into the current drawing. AutoCAD remembers where the file is located on the computer's hard drive and reloads it every time the drawing is opened. This saves disk space and assures the referenced drawing stays current.

You will use *DWG Reference* (Xref) to bring in a floor plan so you can project lines off of it, which can speed the elevation process. When you are done you will use the *External References* palette to detach the drawing.

29. In the **exterior elevations.dwg** file select the **Attach** icon from the *Insert* tab (*Reference* panel).

Attach

30. Browse to the location of your **flr1.dwg** file and then select **Open** (Figure 5-1.23).

   a. Make sure *Files of Type* is set to **All files (*.*)** or **Drawing (*.dwg)**.

FIGURE 5-1.23 Insert External Reference (browse)

31. Next, check **Specify On-screen** under *Insertion Point* (if not already checked) and then click **OK** (Figure 5-1.24).

32. Pick a point to the upper left of your elevation for an insertion point.

33. **Rotate**, and **Move** if needed, the floor per **Figure 5-1.25**.

34. You can now use the floor plan and elevation to project temporary lines to quickly block out the new elevation (West).

FIGURE 5-1.24 Insert External Reference dialog

Temporary Xref used to project lines which aid in the creation of the exterior elevations

Temporary lines to help create exterior elevations.

FIGURE 5-1.25 Inserted External Reference; rotated flr1 drawing

When you are finished using the *External Reference* (Xref) you can easily detach it from your drawing.

35. Select **External Reference** link from the *Insert* tab – the arrow to the right of the *Reference* panel title.

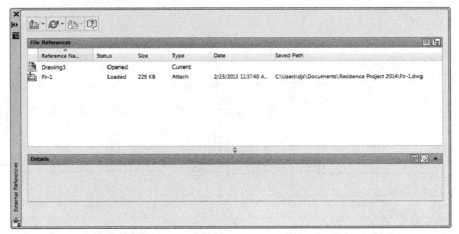

FIGURE 5-1.26A External Reference Palette

36. Right-click on **Flr1** under *Reference Name* and then click **Detach** from the context menu (Figures 5-1.26A and B).

It is also possible to select *Unload* (Figure 5-1.26B) rather than *Detach*. This gives you the ability to *Reload* the Xref whenever you want without having to pick the insertion point again. This keeps the Xref in the same location making alignment automatic.

FIGURE 5-1.26B
External Reference Palette; right-click

Finishing the Exterior Elevation Outlines:

You should now have enough information to complete the outlines of the remaining exterior elevations.

37. Using the dimensions from the floor plans and the portion of elevation previously drawn, complete the outline of the four elevations per Figures 5-1.27, 5-1.28, 5-1.29 and 5-1.30.

38. **Save** your drawing.

   TIP: You can find more information on how to draw the dormer-type roof, shown with dashed lines, by looking at Figure 5-1.29. **Do NOT draw the lines dashed.**

FIGURE 5-1.27 South elevation

FIGURE 5-1.28 West elevation

FIGURE 5-1.29 East elevation

FIND THE MISSING ELEMENT!

Comparing this elevation with the floor plan and other elevations, find the portion of elevation that is missing from Figure 5-1.30; add it to your elevation to correct the problem.

When drawing elevations, you need to thoroughly scan the plans and elevations to make sure you get everything. See Figure 5-2.7c for an image with missing elements.

FIGURE 5-1.30 North elevation

Image courtesy of Anderson Architects
Alan H. Anderson, Architect, Duluth, MN
Interior Design, Steven W. Sanborn, A.I.A., Santa Rosa, CA

Exercise 5-2:
Windows

In this section you will add the windows to the exterior elevations. You will also study the *Block* feature a little more.

Drawings the Windows:

First, you will draw each window type in a separate drawing, similar to the drawing completed in Exercise 3-3.

1. Start a **new** drawing.

2. On *Layer 0* (zero), draw the window shown in **Figure 5-2.1**. Set the bottom middle as the *Origin* (i.e., 0,0).

Carter Residence   *Image courtesy of LHB*
                          www.LHBcorp.com

FIGURE 5-2.1 Window-1 drawing

3. Save the window drawing as **Window-1.dwg**.

4. **Save-As** to a drawing named **Window-2.dwg**.

5. Create the window shown in **Figure 5-2.2**.

> ***NOTE:*** *It is the same size as the window previously drawn so you can copy it over to create the second window.*

FIGURE 5-2.2 Window-2 drawing

6. **Save** your drawing (as Window-2.dwg).

The third window type is similar to Window-2 except taller. The next steps will have you save a copy and stretch the window to the correct size.

7. **Save-As** to a drawing named **Window-3.dwg**.

8. Use the **Stretch** command to quickly create the window shown in **Figure 5-2.3**.

FIGURE 5-2.3 Window-3 drawing

9. **Save** your drawing.

10. **Save-As** to a drawing named **Window-4.dwg**.

11. **Erase** one of the windows and use **Fillet** to create the window shown in **Figure 5-2.4**.

You may recall from Exercise 3-3 that the vertical lines in the upper sash were more detailed in that you drew two lines, whereas, here you only drew one.

Detail such as this is either added or removed depending on what scale the drawing will be printed at. Lower detail, like the window to the right, is more appropriate for smaller scale prints, such as ⅛″ = 1′-0″ or ¼″ = 1′-0″. Higher detail would be better on larger scale details, like ½″ = 1′-0″ or ¾″ = 1′-0″.

Too much detail on a smaller scale print usually produces a drawing where the lines run together, creating what looks like one really heavy line.

Now that you have created the various window types, you will insert them into the exterior elevations the same way you inserted the door symbols into the floor plans.

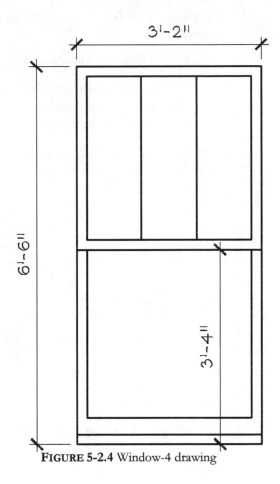

FIGURE 5-2.4 Window-4 drawing

12. **Open** the **Exterior Elevations** drawing.

13. Create a new *Layer* named ***Windows*** and set it to color *Yellow*; you will place the window *Blocks* on this *Layer*.

14. Select **Insert** in the *Block* panel via the *Insert* tab.

15. *Browse* to the location where you saved the **Window-1** drawing.

16. **Insert** the **Window-1** *Block* into the location shown in Figure 5-2.5, noting the following:

    a. The dimension shown is from the garage floor to the window sill.

    b. The horizontal dimension is to be derived from the plans; make sure you use the center of the window as a snap point if you are using an Xref'ed floor plan to locate the windows.

FIGURE 5-2.5 Window-1 block inserted - North elevation (garage area)

Once a *Block* (an external drawing in this case) has been inserted into your drawing, you can copy it around to additional locations; you do not have to use the Insert command every time.

17. **Insert** instances of **Window-1, Window-2, Window-3** and **Window-4** as *Blocks* per **Figure 5-2.6**.

    a. Do not worry about the windows overlapping the porch roof and columns right now; you will adjust this later.

    b. Make sure you insert the window *Blocks* on the *Layer* named ***Windows***.

FIGURE 5-2.6 Window blocks inserted - South elevation

18. Using the sill-height dimensions and procedures previously described, insert the remaining windows based on the window locations shown in the plan (Figures 5-2.7A, B *and* C).

Align top of window-1 with top of window-3 here; window-1 is over the cabinets in the kitchen area.

FIGURE 5-2.7A Window blocks inserted – West elevation

FIGURE 5-2.7B Window blocks inserted - East elevation

FIGURE 5-2.7C Window blocks inserted - North elevation

Advantages of using Blocks:

In addition to the window being one object when it is a *Block*, which is easy to pick and move around, you can also make changes which instantly apply to all instances of the block in a particular drawing.

Next you will modify the *Block* by adding trim, which is part of the siding. You will do this before adjusting the windows that are behind the porch roof and columns.

WHEN SHOULD I USE A *BLOCK*?

Anytime something is repetitive and exactly the same (or with few variations like your windows in elevation), you should use a block. This makes the drawing size smaller and any changes much quicker.

---

19. **Open** each of the four window type drawings and add a **5″ wide trim board** to three sides and extend the sill lines as shown in **Figure 5-2.8**.

FIGURE 5-2.8 Revised windows (siding trim added)

20. **Save** each of the four window type drawings (Window-1.dwg, Window-2.dwg, Window-3.dwg, and Window-4.dwg).

21. In the *Exterior Elevations* drawing, **Zoom In** on the south elevation.

Notice the window elevations are as they were when you originally inserted them. After the next step they will all automatically update.

22. Per steps previously outlined (starting with step 14), insert the four window types again; note the following:

    a. When you are prompted to redefine the *Block*, click **Redefine Block** (Figure 5-2.9).

    b. When you are at the final stage, where you are prompted to pick a point on the screen to insert the *Block*, you can press the **Esc** key; this cancels the insert, but not before updating the block definition in the current drawing.

    c. Or, you can insert the window *Blocks* off to one side and delete them.

FIGURE 5-2.9 Re-define block prompt

You should review the south elevation again; notice the windows have been all updated automatically (Figure 5-2.10)! The other three elevations are updated also. This feature can save a lot of time.

FIGURE 5-2.10 Re-defined blocks in South elevation

Exploding Blocks:

The Explode command allows you to reduce a *Block* to its basic components (i.e., lines, arcs, text, etc.). Only the *Blocks* selected are exploded. And, even if you Explode all the instances of a particular *Block* in a drawing, the definition of the *Block* will still exist in the drawing; this allows you to insert the *Block* without having to browse to the original drawing on your hard drive (i.e., C: drive).

Next you will Explode the *Blocks* at the porch and trim the portion of window covered by the porch roof and columns.

23. Select the **Explode** icon from the *Modify* panel.

24. Select the two windows on the south elevation and the two windows on the east elevation that are covered by the porch roof.

The four windows are now exploded to their original lines. Next you will trim the windows so you only see the lines that are not obstructed from sight by another building element.

25. **Trim** and **Erase** the window lines as shown in **Figures 5-2.11** and **5-2.12**.

FIGURE 5-2.11 Exploded windows (original lines trimmed and erased); East elevation

FIGURE 5-2.12 Exploded windows (original lines trimmed and erased); South elevation

After exploding the *Blocks* you should have noticed that the lines changed color (from *Yellow* to *White*). If you recall, you created the window on *Layer 0* in the original drawings and placed the window *Blocks* on the *Windows* layer in the 'Exterior Elevations' drawing. When a *Block* is exploded, you get the original line-work on the original *Layers*.

So, to clean house, you need to move the exploded window lines to the *Windows* layer.

26. Revise the drawing so the exploded windows are on the **Windows** layer.

Exercise 5-3:
Doors

In this exercise you will add exterior doors to your plans. In the process you will take a quick look at using a feature called "Grip Edit".

1.   **Open** the exterior elevations.dwg drawing file.

2.   Create a new *Layer* named **Doors**; set the color to *Green*.

The elevations, as a whole, do not have more than two instances of any door; plus two of the doors need to be trimmed because they are behind other architectural elements.

Thus it is not beneficial, in this case, to create blocks of each door. So you will draw each door type in-place and then copy the entities to the second location (if applicable).

3.   On the *Doors* layer, draw the door shown in **Figure 5-3.1** on the east elevation.

The door/frame elevation shown in Figure 5-3.1 represents two doors that are mostly glass and a glass transom above the doors that aligns with the tall windows on either side (not shown in Figure 5-3.1).

FIGURE 5-3.1 Door elevation; East elevation

Notice that the double doors you just drew correspond to the double doors you drew in the first floor plan.

4.   Draw the portion of door shown in **Figure 5-3.2** on the west elevation (door into garage); you will draw more of the door in subsequent steps.

FIGURE 5-3.2 Partial door elevation; West elevation

RESIDENTIAL DOOR SIZES

Doors come in many shapes and sizes.

THICKNESS: 1⅜″, 1¾″ and 2¼″
The 1⅜″ door is most often used in residential construction and the 2¼″ door is typically only used on exterior doors for high-end projects, i.e., big budget.

SIZE: ranges from 1'-0″ x 6'-8″ to 4'-0″ x ′0″
The height of a residential door is usually 6′-8″. This writer recently worked on a project where 7′-0″ high doors were specified. The contractor was so used to the standard 6′-8″ dimension; he framed all the exterior openings at 6′-8″. To top it off, the exterior walls where concrete (ICF system), so the openings could not be modified. Thus, 6′-8″ doors were used.

You can find more information on the internet; two examples are
algomahardwoods.com   and   madawaska-doors.com
(wood veneer door mfr.)   *(custom solid wood door mfr.)*

NOTE: Do not jump ahead here; follow the next few steps closely!

5. Using the **Offset** command, offset the previously drawn lines inward, as shown in Figure 5-3.3.

FIGURE 5-3.3 Door elevation with lines offset; West elevation

Using the Grip Edit Feature:

Next you will use the **Grip Edit** feature to modify the lines to represent the window in the door panel.

Grip Edit allows you to modify lines without having to activate a command first. Basically you select a line, then select one or more of the visible *Grips* and then reposition the *Grips* by selecting another point.

6. Without any commands active, select the horizontal line shown in **Figure 5-3.4**.

FIGURE 5-3.4 Line selected for editing; West elevation

7. Select the *Grip* on the right; simply click the mouse button with the cursor over the *Grip*; do <u>not</u> drag the mouse button (Figure 5-3.4).

8. Move the mouse to the left. Using **OSNAPs**, select either *Perpendicular* or *Intersection* of the vertical line shown in **Figures 5-3.5a** and **5-3.5b**.

FIGURE 5-3.5A Perpendicular snap   **FIGURE 5-3.5B** Relocated snap

9. Finally, press the **Esc** (i.e., Escape) key, on the keyboard, to clear the *Grips* (and unselect the horizontal line).

Essentially, you just trimmed a line without using the *Trim* command.

10. Using the same technique just described, modify the lines using *Grips* to look like **Figure 5-3.6.**

AutoCAD also allows you to select more than one *Grip* at a time. You will try this next to adjust the bottom of the (4) vertical lines.

11. Select the (4) vertical lines; you can click each line individually or use a *Crossing Window (by clicking right to left)*.

12. Holding the **Shift** key, **click** each of the lower *Grips* on the (4) vertical lines; the selected *Grips* will turn red.

13. Releasing the **Shift** key, click the lower right *Grip*.

    REMEMBER: *Do not drag the mouse; i.e., do not hold the mouse button down continuously (Figure 5-3.7).*

14. Moving the mouse straight up, use the *Endpoint OSNAP* to accurately select the lower horizontal line.

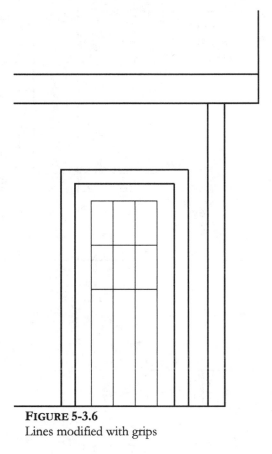

FIGURE 5-3.6
Lines modified with grips

Your door is now complete and should look like **Figure 5-3.8.**

FIGURE 5-3.7 Modifying multiple grips at once

FIGURE 5-3.8 Completed door elevation

Before moving on, here are a few additional comments on the Grip Edit command that you may want to investigate further on your own.

o You select the middle *Grip* to move the entity.

o If you select a *Grip* and then right-click, you get additional modification options. (Figure 5-3.9)

o The *Grip* that is selected is, by default, the base point for the *Mirror* command.

15. **Copy** the door just created to the other two locations (per the floor plans); also make sure the doors are placed in the correct floor elevation. (See **Figures 5-3.10** and **5-3.11**.)

FIGURE 5-3.9
Right-click with grip selected

FIGURE 5-3.10 Door added and trimmed – South elevation

You will proceed with the idea that the owner will build steps from this door down to grade.

FIGURE 5-3.11 Door added - North elevation

Garage Doors:

16. Draw the **garage door** shown in **Figure 5-3.12**.

   a. All panels are to be equally spaced.

   b. **Copy** or **Mirror** the door to the other location.

   c. **Save** your drawing!

NOTE: *This is all the information you need to draw the garage door; it requires you to do a little math.*

FIGURE 5-3.12 Garage Door

Exercise 5-4:
Chimney, Railing and Siding

In this exercise you will draw the chimneys, the railing at the porch and the siding and brick patterns.

Chimney:

1. Open your **Exterior Elevations** drawing.

2. Draw two vertical lines at the first floor that represent the width of the fireplace; refer to the first floor plan for location and width. (Place on *Layer* G-Detl-Hevy, color White.)

3. Draw the upper portion of the chimney as shown in Figure 5-4.1 (with the 2'-8" portion centered on the first floor lines):

    a. Trim the fascia as shown.

    b. You will finish the bottom/porch roof intersection next.

FIGURE 5-4.1 Chimney – South elevation

Next you will draw the side view of the chimney. Once you are done with this view you will be able to complete the front view.

4.   On the East elevation, draw the chimney as shown in Figure 5-4.2.

Added chimney lines

FIGURE 5-4.2 Chimney – East elevation

Now you can project a line from this elevation over to the South elevation to determine where the chimney intersects the porch roof.

5.   Draw a line from where the upper chimney intersects the porch roof, over to the South elevation (Figure 5-4.3).

Notice how the side view of the chimney helps determine where the chimney intersects the porch roof in the front view of the chimney.

FIGURE 5-4.3 Chimney – South elevation
FYI: *This technique is called Orthographic Projection.*

6.   Complete the chimney as shown in Figure 5-4.4.

FIGURE 5-4.4 Chimney – South elevation

7.   Zoom into the top of the chimney and draw a concrete chimney cap shown in Figure 5-4.5.

FIGURE 5-4.5 Chimney Cap

8.   Copy the chimney cap to the other elevation.

9.   Draw the chimney in the other two elevations (Figures 5-4.6 and 5-4.7).

FIGURE 5-4.6 Chimney – West elevation

FIGURE 5-4.7 Chimney – North elevation

You will draw the other chimney later.

CHIMNEY CAPS!

You can buy prefabricated chimney caps in all shapes and sizes. Here are a couple of websites that sell/make them:

http://www.ejmcopper.com/chimneycaps/
http://classiccopper.com/store
http://chimneycapdesign.com/

Porch Railing:

10. Create a *Layer* named ***Railing*** (color *Red*).

11. **Zoom In** to the porch on North elevation.

12. Draw the railing shown in Figure 5-4.8. Do not add the shading.

FIGURE 5-4.8 Railing – North elevation; shading added for clarity

13. Draw the rest of the railings on the other elevations (Figures 5-4.9 and 5-4.10).

FIGURE 5-4.9 Railing – East elevation

FIGURE 5-4.10 Railing – South elevation

14. **Trim** any lines that extend behind the 3½″ boards or the 1½″ top and bottom rails (Figures 5-4.9 and 5-4.10).

Using the Hatch Command:

The tool used in AutoCAD to draw patterns, such as bricks, siding and shingles, is called **Hatch**. This tool allows you to quickly fill an enclosed area with one of many predefined patterns. You will use this feature to add the shingles, siding and bricks to your elevations.

First you will draw the roof shingles.

15. **Zoom In** to the East elevation.

16. Create a *Layer* called **Shingles**; color *Blue*.

17. You can start the **Hatch** command in one of the following ways:

   a. Click the **Hatch** icon on the *Draw* panel.

   b. Type **hatch** at the *Command prompt* or *On-Screen*.

You should now see the *Hatch Creation* tab on the *Ribbon* (Figure 5-4.11).

FIGURE 5-4.11 Hatch and Gradient dialog box

This is called a contextual tab. It only appears while the *Hatch* command is active or when a hatch element is selected in the drawing. This tab gives you access to all the settings related to hatch patterns, scale, transparency, etc. With the *Hatch* command active, you set things the way you want them on the *Ribbon* and then move your cursor into the *Drawing Window*. When your cursor moves within an enclosed area, that area will automatically get a temporary hatch pattern so you can see the final result before actually clicking to create the hatch. When your cursor moves out of the enclosed area the temporary hatch goes away. If you want to create the hatch you simply click the left mouse button within the enclosed area. Once you are done creating hatch patterns you click *Close Hatch Creation* on the *Ribbon*. The contextual tab goes away and the hatch command is no longer active.

18. Click the down-arrow in the *Pattern* panel and select **AR-RSHKE** (Figure 5-4.12).

FIGURE 5-4.12 Hatch Creation tab – pattern selected

Next you will pick a point in the drawing that is completely enclosed.

19. Click the Add: **Pick Points** button (this should be the default already).

20. Click anywhere in the roof; see **Figure 5-4.13**.

21. After picking an area, **right-click** and then click **Enter** from the pop-up menu. Finally, select **OK** to close the *Hatch* dialog.

Click anywhere in the enclosed area when using **Pick Points**

FIGURE 5-4.13 Boundary Hatch; one enclosed section hatched

22. Click the **Close Hatch Creation** button to finish the hatch creation process.

23. Use the **Hatch** tool to draw the rest of the roof shingles.

Close
Hatch Creation

> **TIP:** *Only Hatch one area at a time; it is easier later when you have to re-hatch an area due to a change (Figures 5-4.17 – 19.).*

Next you will draw the brick at the chimney.

24. Use the **Hatch** tool to draw the brick at the chimney:

    a. Do not draw the brick pattern behind the railing; this would create too much clutter.

    b. Use the pattern named: **AR-BRSTD**.

    c. See fully hatched **Figures 5-4.17 – 19**.

    d. Create on *Layer* named ***Brick***.

Finally you will draw the siding; this will be a little different.

25. Create a *Layer* named **Siding**, color *Blue*.

26. Initiate the **Hatch** command.

27. Select **User Defined** next to *Type*.

28. For *Spacing* enter **4** (this means the lines will be 4″ apart). (Figure 5-4.14)

FIGURE 5-4.14 Boundary Hatch; User Defined pattern

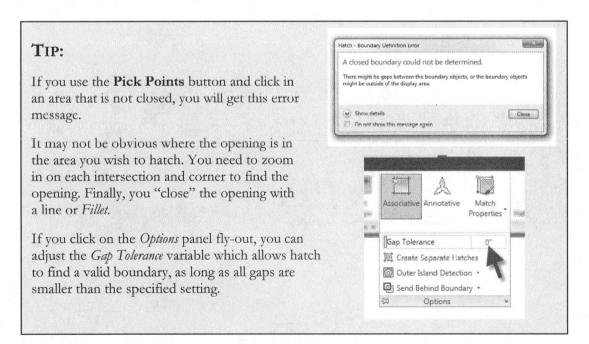

TIP:

If you use the **Pick Points** button and click in an area that is not closed, you will get this error message.

It may not be obvious where the opening is in the area you wish to hatch. You need to zoom in on each intersection and corner to find the opening. Finally, you "close" the opening with a line or *Fillet*.

If you click on the *Options* panel fly-out, you can adjust the *Gap Tolerance* variable which allows hatch to find a valid boundary, as long as all gaps are smaller than the specified setting.

29. Zoom into the West elevation and use the **Pick Points** button to select one area at a time to hatch with the siding pattern (Figure 5-4.15).

FIGURE 5-4.15 Boundary Hatch; User Defined pattern used to draw 4″ siding

30. Use this technique to draw the rest of the siding, hatching one area at a time (see Figures 5-4.16 to 5-4.19).

TIP: You can select several areas at one time and check the "Create separate hatches" option in the Options panel fly-out dialog box (see image to the right).

TIP:
You can select a hatch pattern to display the Hatch Editor tab on the Ribbon. This tab is basically the same as the one used in creating the hatch pattern. Here you can change the pattern or adjust the scale and/or spacing.

FIGURE 5-4.16 Hatching complete – East elevation

FIGURE 5-4.17 Hatching complete – North elevation

FIGURE 5-4.18 Hatching complete – South elevation

FIGURE 5-4.19 Hatching complete – West elevation

This concludes Exercise 5-4; don't forget the *Additional Tasks* at the end of this chapter. It is strongly recommended that you complete them before moving on as they contain many new concepts not yet covered.

Self-Exam:

The following questions can be used as a way to check your knowledge of this lesson. The answers can be found at the bottom of this page.

1. You do not need to create a *Block* if the item to be drawn only exists once in the drawing. (T/F)

2. You can use Grip Edit to adjust the length of a line. (T/F)

3. Use the Hatch command to draw the brick pattern in elevation. (T/F)

4. When drawing the exterior elevations, the horizontal location for the windows and doors comes from the_____ drawings.

5. All doors go on the _____ layer.

Review Questions:

The following questions may be assigned by your instructor as a way to assess your knowledge of this section. Your instructor has the answers to the review questions.

1. The Hatch command does not have very many patterns to select from. (T/F)

2. Redefining a *Block* causes all instances to automatically update. (T/F)

3. You can project lines from another elevation and from the plans to locate where the chimney intersects the sloping roof below it, also referred to as orthographic projection. (T/F)

4. Name the command that links a drawing to the current drawing:

    _____

5. You can select on a hatched area to edit its properties. (T/F)

6. This icon (   ) allows you to _____ a *Block*.

7. A 6/12 pitch means; for every 12"_____ the roof rises 6"_____

8. Name the Hatch pattern used to draw the brick _____

9. What is the most often used door thickness? _____.

10. You should use a *Block* when something in the drawing is repetitive and exactly the same. (T/F)

Additional Tasks:

Task 5-1: Grade Line

Draw the grade lines shown in the images below.

Create a *Layer* named **Grade** and set its color to *Magenta*.

Use the **Polyline** command via this icon on the *Draw* panel.

Polyline

After picking your first point, type **W** for width; enter **4″** (for both the starting width and end width). Alternatively, you can draw the polyline and then adjust the width afterwards using the **Pedit** command (or with the Polyline selected, by adjusting the *Global Width* option in *Properties*).

Draw the grade as close as possible to that shown below. Extend the lines at the corners of the building down to the grade line.

All grade lines should be at the same vertical location for common corners on each of the two elevations showing that corner.

Commands used: Polyline, Pedit, Layer Manager

Task 5-1 (1) North elevation with grade line added; grade line is approx. 2′-2″ below porch floor

Task 5-1 (2) East elevation with grade line added; grade line is approx. 2′-2″ below porch floor

Task 5-1 (3) South elevation with grade line added; grade line is approx. 2′-2″ below porch floor

Task 5-1 (4) West elevation with grade line added

Task 5-2: Draw the Other Chimney

Draw the other chimney based on reference lines from the floor plan and other elevations. Draw as much as you can in each elevation and then use orthographic projection to complete the task.

Draw the same chimney cap and use the same hatch pattern used to draw the first chimney. Do this for all four elevations.

Commands used: Line, Trim, Extend, Hatch

Task 5-2 (1) South elevation with other chimney added

Task 5-2 (2) West elevation with other chimney added

Task 5-3: Print Content from a Website

Using your Internet web browser, print one page of information from one of the websites mentioned in Lesson 5. HAND IN ONLY ONE PAGE.

Task 5-4: Adding Foundation Lines

First you will draw the lines and then adjust the lines so they look dashed.

> *FYI: Dashed lines typically represent lines that are hidden from view but are still helpful to show. The foundation walls and footings are below the ground - so the ground is hiding them. However they need to be seen on the drawings.*

1. Create a *Layer* named **Foundation**; set its color to *Red*.

2. Draw the lines as shown below (4 images), and then proceed to Step 3 for instruction on making the lines dashed.

Task 5-4 (1) West elevation with foundation lines added

Task 5-4 (2) South Elevation with foundation lines added

Task 5-4 (3) East elevation with foundation lines added

Task 5-4 (4) North elevation with foundation lines added

Creating dashed lines:

3. Open the **Layer Properties Manager**.

4. In the *Foundation* (layer name) row, click the linetype name (which should be <u>Continuous</u> at the moment).

You are now in the Select Linetype dialog.

You will notice that the current drawing only has one linetype loaded. Next you will load another linetype into the current drawing.

5. Click the **Load...** button.

You are now in the Load or Reload Linetypes dialog.

6. Scroll down to the **HIDDEN2** linetype; select it and click **OK**.

Now, back in the *Select Linetypes* dialog box...

7. Select **HIDDEN2** and click **OK**.

8. Click **OK** to close the *Layer Properties Manager*.

The next three system variable adjustments will make the hidden lines correct in both *Model* and *Paper Space*.

9. Type **LTSCALE** and **Enter**; then type **1** and then **Enter**.

10. Type **PSLTSCALE** and **Enter**; then type **1** and then **Enter**.

11. Type **MSLTSCALE** and **Enter**; then type **1** and then **Enter**.

Next you will set the *Annotation Scale* which controls the spacing of the lines, as well as the size of text and dimensions when set to Annotative.

12. Set the **Annotation Scale** to **1/4″ = 1′-0″**.

13. Type **REGEN** and then **Enter**.

14. **Save** your drawing.

Lesson 6
Residential Project: SECTIONS::

In this lesson you will create simple building and wall sections. A section helps the builder understand how the structure is to be constructed; it also shows the vertical relationships, such as floor and ceiling locations.

Exercise 6-1:
Building Sections

Introduction:

Building sections show an overall section through the structure.

The building sections are typically the same scale as the exterior elevations.

Because the building section generally has the same outline as one of the exterior elevations, you can copy the elevation and use it as a starting point for your building section.

You will do this next.

Building Section Outline:

1. **Open** your drawing named **Exterior Elevations.dwg**.

2. **Save-As** to a drawing file named **Building Section.dwg**.

3. **Zoom In** on the South elevation (Figure 6-1.1).

4. **Erase** and **Trim** all inner lines to create an outline of the building as shown in **Figure 6-1.2**.

   TIP: The information on the next page starts to get things set up for applying line-weights, but does not actually fully implement it. This is covered in more detail later in the book. Please do not worry about adjusting the lineweights column in the Layers Properties Manager.

FIGURE 6-1.1 South elevation drawn in previous lesson

Typical Non-Plan Layers:

Non-plandrawings typically have a handful of *Layers* whose names represent the thickness of the lines drawn on that *Layer*. These drawings do not need the same level of control as floor plans so the layering system is simplified (e.g., you would never need to *Freeze* a layer that contained the steel beams).

The general concept with lineweights is this:

Things in section	Lines should be heavy
Things in elevation	Lines should be a middle-of-the-road (medium) lineweight
Hatch patterns	These are the lightest lines

5. Create the following *Layers*:
   a. **G-Detl-Hevy**   White   Heavy lines
   b. **G-Detl-Medm**   Green   Medium lines
   c. **G-Detl-Lite**   Red   Light lines

6. Modify the remaining lines (in Figure 6-1.2) to the *Layers* just created (i.e.,change the outline to *G-Detl-Hevy*, the shingle hatch to *G-Detl-Lite*, etc.).

FIGURE 6-1.2 Modified South elevation; outline to start building section

FIGURE 6-1.3 Building Section – see page 5-6 for enlarged rawing

TIP: Once the sections are developed you can go back and update the dashed footing and foundations line in your exterior elevations (if needed). Those lines are often approximated when first drawing the elevations and then refined as the sections are developed and other conditions arise.

7. Begin generating the building section based on the information provided in Figure 6-1.3 and the following guidelines; See Fig. 6-1.5 for enlarged drawing:

   a. The wall thicknesses and locations are to be derived from the Xref'ed floor plans. (See Figure 6-1.4.)

      NOTE: The heavy dashed line below represents the section location.

   b. Make the footings (below the foundation walls) 1'-8" wide.

   c. The first and second floor thickness is 1-4¾"; the top of the concrete block foundation wall starts 1½" below the floor thickness (to accommodate a 2x wood nailer; see Figure 6-2.3).

   d. The two trusses (shown in elevation) have equally spaced vertical members with the diagonals drawn last (all 2x4 framing – i.e., 3½" with 2x6 top cord).

   e. Trusses shown over Mud Room: 2x4's (i.e., 1½") at 2'-0"o.c.

   f. The horizontal lines in the foundation wall are 8" apart; which represents the individual concrete masonry units (CMU).

   g. Draw the dimensions shown.

   h. Dimensions at ceiling are to the bottom of the truss; draw a ½" thick gypsum board ceiling below the trusses.

   i. The garage/basement slabs are 5" thick.

   j. Add the room labels. *TIP: Copy them from the floor plans.*

   k. Extend the truss lines into the overhang/fascia area (simple).

FIGURE 6-1.4 Building Section; with Xref'ed plan and temp. reference lines

FIGURE 6-1.5 Building Section enlarged

Exercise 6-2:
Typical Wall Section

Introduction:

Wall sections are similar to building sections in that they show how a building is constructed and the vertical relationships (e.g., floor-to-floor heights). The difference between a wall section and a building section is implied by their names; a wall section is just one wall in section; a building section is a section through the entire building. Wall sections are also drawn at a larger scale than building sections.

On smaller projects, where the building section can be drawn larger, you may not need a wall section because everything can be clearly drawn and noted on the building sections.

The wall sections are typically as large as possible, so that it will still fit on the sheet. Occasionally a large repetitious area will be removed with break lines to allow the section to be larger (see Figure 6-2.1).

Wall sections are usually started after the building sections have been substantially developed. You can use the linework from the building section to start your wall section.

You will do this next.

FIGURE 6-2.1 Wall section with break lines and section without. Note that section with break lines is larger.

Wall Section Linework:

1. **Open** your drawing named **Building Section.dwg**.

2. **Save-As** to a drawing file named **Wall Section.dwg**.

3. Erase and Trim portions of the building section so it looks similar to the ½″ = 1′-0″ wall section shown in Figure 6-2.1.

   TIP: Draw a temporary vertical line to trim to.

4. Use the same *Layers* as Exercise 6-1.

You are now ready to begin developing the wall section. Your section will look similar to Figure 6-2.2. You will use the information in the enlarged details, Figures 6-2.3 and 6-2.4, to draw the wall section.

5. Draw the wall section shown in **Figure 6-2.2** per the following information:

   a. Use the information in the roof edge detail (**Figure 6-2.4**) to draw items, such as the roof sheathing and gypsum board, the correct size.

   b. Use the information in the rim joist detail (**Figure 6-2.3**) to draw the joist, siding, floor sheathing and sill plate.

   c. Draw the second floor rim joist condition based on the information provided in the similar condition identified in item "b" above (Figure 6-2.4).

   d. Do not add any notes or dimensions at this time.

6. **Save** your drawing.

FIGURE 6-2.2
Wall section to be drawn in this exercise.

SIDING (6"x 1/2")
AIR BARRIER
1/2" OSB SHEATHING
2x6 STUDS at 16" O.C.
FULL-FIT BATT INSULATION
VAPOR BARRIER
1/2" GYPSUM BOARD

3/4" PLYWOOD FLOOR
SHEATHING GLUED AND
NAILED TO JOISTS

16" WOOD FLOOR
TUSSES @ 16" O/C

INSULATED RIM JOIST

2X8 TREATED SILL
PLATE SET ON SILL
SEALER

1/2"X10" ANCHOR BOLTS @ 32" O/C

FIGURE 6-2.3 Rim joist detail

NOTES ON THE RIM JOIST DETAIL

The 2x8 sill plate creates a flat surface for the joists to sit on and be nailed to. The sill plate is set on a foam sill sealer that fills the voids between the irregular concrete block and the smooth wood; which helps to decrease air infiltration. The L-shaped anchor bolts are set in grout and help hold the sill plate down (with a nut and washer on top).

The first siding board rests on a "starter strip" which places the board at the correct angle (which matches the other boards above).

The air barrier goes on just before the siding; it helps to reduce air infiltration into the building. Air barriers allow moisture to pass through; this is not a vapor barrier.

The vapor barrier goes just behind the finish (on the warm side of the wall). This prevents moisture from condensing within the wall. Avoid double vapor barriers as the moisture cannot escape and creates mold. This is why air barriers are not vapor barriers.

ASPHALT SHINGLES

WATERPROOF SHINGLE UNDERLAYMENT

1/2" PLYWOOD ROOF SHEATHING

INSULATION BAFFLES

2X12 SUB-FASCIA

METAL EDGE TRIM

1x4 FASCIA BOARD

1x8 FASCIA BOARD

1x12 FASCIA BOARD

3" CONTINUOUS SOFFIT VENT

7/16" SOFFIT PANEL

BLOWN FIBERGLASS INSULATION TO ACHIEVE R80 INSULATION VALUE

2x4 FASCIA FRAMING @ 24" O.C.

6$\frac{1}{2}$"

1/2" GYPSUM BOARD OVER VAPOR BARRIER

SIDING (6"x 1/2")
AIR BARRIER
1/2" OSB SHEATHING
2x6 STUDS at 16" O.C.
FULL-FIT BATT INSULATION
VAPOR BARRIER
1/2" GYPSUM BOARD

NOTE: *See page 5-6 for soffit and fascia dimensions. This standard detail has a different pitch so the soffit blocking will look a little different in your drawing.*

FIGURE 6-2.4 Roof edge detail

NOTES ON THE ROOF EDGE DETAIL

The "waterproof shingle underlayment" (i.e., Ice and Water Shield) is required on overhangs and valleys in colder climates. This helps prevent melted snow, which freezes at overhangs and then backs up under the shingles, from leaking though the roof sheathing. This product is occasionally applied over the entire roof in place of felt to create a second layer of waterproofing on the roof.

The insulation baffles are thin panels attached between the trusses. The baffles maintain an air space between the roof sheathing and the blown-in attic insulation. The air space helps keep the underside of the roof sheathing at the same temperature as the top side, which helps prevent ice-damming.

The soffit vent allows outside air into the attic space. This helps the attic space to maintain the same temperature as the outside air, which reduces the possibility of condensation at the shingles/sheathing plane; this helps to prevent mold.

Similar to the wall condition, the vapor barriers go just behind the finish (on the warm side of the ceiling), between the truss and the gypsum board in this case.

Exercise 6-3:
Adding Annotation to Wall Section

In this exercise you will add notes and dimensions to your wall section.

1. **Openwall section.dwg** drawing file.

2. Create a new *Layer* named **G-Anno-Text**, set the color to *Cyan*.

3. Setting up a drawing for text.

   o The ideal way to work with text in AutoCAD requires a few settings be adjusted first. This will have to be done in each new drawing, but could be setup in an office template file in the workplace.

   o Once things are set up properly, any text added will automatically be the correct height based on the intended plot scale. If the plot scale (i.e., annotation scale) is changed, all the text in the drawing will be updated to the correct height.

   o Specific steps to perform:
      - On the *Application Menu* → *Drawing Utilities*, select the **Units** tool from the fly-out list (see image to right).
      - Set the precision to **0'-0 1/32"**.
      - Click **OK** to save the change.

   0.0 **Units**
   Controls coordinate and angle display formats and precision

Additional steps to perform:

4. On the *Annotate* tab, in the *Text* panel, click the **Text Style** link (small arrow in the lower right corner). You are now in the dialog box shown on the next page.

   o In the *Text Style* dialog, select **Roman** under *Styles* (it should already be selected)

   o In the *Size* area, check **Annotative** and set the *Paper text height* to **3/32"**. (This is the size the text will be on paper regardless of the drawing scale.)

   o Click **Set Current**, and then click **Yes** if prompted to save changes.
   FYI: This will make it the default text style.

   o Click **Apply** and then **Close**.
   FYI: The Cancel *button becomes the* Close *button when something changes in the dialog.*

5. At the bottom of the screen, on the *Application Status Bar*, right-click on the **Automatically Add Scales…** icon and select the **Automatically Add Scale to Annotative Objects** option. (You only need to click this if the icon is gray, i.e., not active.)

6. Just to the left of the previous item, click the *Annotation Scale* listed (should be 1:1) and select **½"=1'-0"** from the list (see image on next page).

Now when you add text to this drawing the height will automatically be set based on the scale selected at the bottom of the screen; this scale can be changed on-the-fly, instantly updating the height of all text in the drawing. You will try this next.

The previous steps allow you to add text to your wall section at the proper scale. This is meant for any *Multiline Text* (without leaders). For notes that point to something, you will use a *Multileader* which allows you to add the arrows, lines and text all as one object. You can also use the *Multileader* align tool (see icon to the right) to make sure the notes line up.

7. Add the notes for the wall construction shown in **Figure 6-3.1**:

   a. Use the **Multileader** command (Annotate tab).

   b. Place all text on *Layer **G-Anno-Text***.

   Multileader

   c. All text to be aligned as shown.

   d. Adjust the *Multileader Style* settings; refer back topage 4-55 if needed for more information.

8. Add the four dimensions shown in Figure 6-3.1; draw them on *Layer **G-Anno-Dims*** (color 30). Be sure to setup the *Dimension Style*; see page 4-45 if needed.

9. **Save** your drawing.

Try changing the *Annotation Scale* (see image above) to see the notes and dimensions automatically update; make sure to **Undo** these changes before moving on (i.e., *Annotation Scale* should be set to ½″ = 1′-0″).

ASPHALT

½"OSB ROOF SHEATHING

BLOWN FIBERGLASS
INSULATION TO ACHIEVE
R80 INSULATION VALUE

ENGINEERED WOOD TRUSS

½" GYPSUM BOARD
OVER VAPOR BARRIER

¾" PLYWOOD FLOOR
SHEATHING GLUED AND NAILED
TO JOISTS

16" FLOOR TRUSSES @ 16" O/C

½" GYPSUM BOARD

INSUL RIM JOIST, TYPICAL

SIDING, AIR BARRIER, ½" OSB
SHEATHING, 2X6 STUDS @ 16'
O/C, FULL-FIT BAT INSULATION,
VAPOR BARRIER ½" GYPSUM
BOARD

INSUL RIM JOIST, TYPICAL

¾" PLYWOOD FLOOR
SHEATHING GLUED AND
NAILED TO JOISTS

16" FLOOR TRUSSES @ 16" O/C

2X8 TREATED SILL
PLATE SET ON SILL
SEALER

½" X 10" ANCHOR BOLTS @ 32" O/C

8" CONCRETE BLOCK
FOUNDATION WALL

5" CONCRETE SLAB

CONCRETE FOOTING

FIGURE 6-3.1 Wall Section

Exercise 6-4:
Stair Section

In this exercise you will draw and dimension a simple stair section.

1. **Open** the **building section.dwg** drawing file.

You will draw a simple profile of a stair in this exercise. Unless the stair is very complex or unique in some way, you do not need to draw a large scale section because contractors build stairs regularly and lumber yards sell standard treads and risers that simplify the construction process.

First you will use an Xref'ed first floor plan to locate the first riser.

2. Align the first floor plan with your building section and extend a line from the top riser (in plan) to the building section (Figure 6-4.1).

FIGURE 6-4.1 Building section with line extended from plan to locate top riser

3. Erase the portion of floor and wall shown dashed in Figure 6-4.1.

    FYI: Looking back at the basement floor plans, you will notice there is no wall where you are deleting the basement wall; the floor and wall above will be supported by a steel beam due to the heavy load.

4. Modify the remaining linework to look like Figure 6-4.2; draw the steel beam per the following information:

    a. Add the steel beam on *Layer G-Detl-Hevy*.

    b. Use the enlarged beam drawing for dimensional information only; do not draw the larger beam.

    c. Center the beam on the wall above.

    d. The top of the beam should be directly under the floor sheathing, i.e., ¾″ below the first floor line.

FIGURE 6-4.2 Building section with line extended from plan to locate top riser

Sizing the beam and floor trusses is beyond the scope of this tutorial. The same is true for the vertical position of the beam; but note the following points. The beam is either below the floor truss (or joist) so the floor truss can bear on it similar to the way it bears on a wall, or the beam is "upset" within the floor truss system as in our example above. An "upset" beam creates a special bearing condition for the floor truss. The floor truss needs to be top cord bearing or steel brackets can be hung off the steel beam that supports the bottom edge of the floor truss. This condition allows for more headroom.

Calculate Tread/Riser Size:

The *riser* is typically calculated to be as large as building codes will allow. Occasionally a grand stair will have a smaller riser to create a more elegant stair.

Similarly, the *tread* is usually designed to be as small as allowable by building codes.

The largest riser and shortest tread creates the steepest stair allowed. This takes up less floor space (see **Figure 6-4.3**). A stairway that is too steep is uncomfortable and unsafe.

Building codes vary by location; for this exercise you will use 7″ (max.) for the risers and 9″ (min.) for the treads.

Codes usually require that each tread be the same size, likewise with risers.

Calculate the number and size of the risers:

    Given:
        Risers: **7″** max.
        Floor to floor height: **9′-0″** (from Exercise 6-1)

    Calculate the number of risers:
        9′-0″ divided by 7″ (or 109″divided by 7″) = 15.429

Seeing as each riser has to be the same size, we will have to round off to a whole number. You cannot round down because that will make the riser larger than the allowed maximum (9′-0″ / 15 = 7.2″). Therefore you have to round up to 16. Thus: 9′-0″ divided by 16 = 6.75

So you need **16** risers that are **6¾″** each.

FIGURE 6-4.3 Stair rise / run comparison

Drawing the Tread/Riser Profile:

Next you will use the Array command to create several lines appropriately spaced.

5. Use the **Array** command to "copy" the top concrete slab line up to create the tread lines:
   a. Select the **Rectangular Array** icon.
   b. **Select** the top line of the concrete basement floor slab.
   c. **Right-click** (to indicate you are done selecting items to array).
   d. On the *Array Creation* contextual tab:
      i. Type **16** for number of *Rows*.
      ii. Type **6.75** for the <u>row</u> *Spacing*.
      iii. Type **1** for number of *Columns*.
      iv. Click **Close Array**.

FIGURE 6-4.4 Array options on the Ribbon

You should now have horizontal lines as shown in Figure 6-4.5.

FIGURE 6-4.5 Horizontal lines arrayed to aid in creating stair profile

Here is an example of another use for the *Array* tool: Notice that if you set the *Row Offset* to 8″ in the Array command, you could have drawn the concrete block in elevation (on the foundation wall beyond).

Next you will array the vertical line to create the stair riser lines.

6. Array a vertical line to the right (you will need to draw one):
   a. Columns: **16**
   b. Column offset: **9″**
   c. See Figure 6-4.6

Your drawing should now have the lines necessary to create the stair profile (see Figure 6-4.6).

MUD ROOM

FAMILY DINING

UNFIN

FIGURE 6-4.6 Vertical lines arrayed to aid in creating stair profile

Before you can modify the lines produced by the *Array* you need to explode it. Currently selecting any line will bring the *Array* tab back on the *Ribbon*. Once exploded, you will just have lines and not an *Array*.

7. Select **Home → Modify → Explode**, and then select one of the lines in the array.

Finally, you need to modify the linework so it looks like a stair. The following image has the stair profile superimposed over the temporary reference lines to help you understand the task at hand (Figure 6-4.7).

8. Use the **Trim** or **Fillet** command to create the stair profile shown in **Figure 6-4.7**.

FYI: The original grid has been left as a background underlay (in Figure 6-4.7) so you can see the start point (i.e., the grid), and the end point (i.e., the stair profile). When you are done using the Trim command, only the stair profile will remain.

FIGURE 6-4.7 Vertical and Horizontal lines with desired stair profile superimposed

If you want to show more detail in the stair section, you can do so by using the following information as a guide (also see theAdditional Tasks for even more detailed information):

- **Tread** thickness: 1⅛″ (offset the profile line downward)

- **Riser** thickness: ¾″ (offset the profile line, horizontally, in the up-run direction)

- Show a **stringer** line below the stair profile (usually cut from a 2x12 (**FYI:** *Actual size of a 2x12 is 1½″ x 11¼″)* so draw a Line from the top nosing to the bottom nosing, Offset it downward 11¼″ and then Erase the first line. (See Additional Task 6-4 for more information).

- Before erasing the line mentioned in the previous item, you can also Copy (not Offset) that line vertically, and upward, 6′-8″ to make sure you have plenty of **headroom** (code minimums vary on this).

- A 1½″ **handrail** can be shown 30″–34″ above the treads (check local code; many also require that the handrail ends return to the wall).

Stair Annotation and Dimensions:

To complete this exercise you will create a note and two dimensions.

9.   Add the **Multileader** shown in Figure 6-4.8:

   a.   Set the **Annotation Scale** to¼″ = 1′-0″

   b.   You can modify the *Multileader Style* if you would like to use curved leader lines as shown.

   c.   Text should read: **WOOD STAIR WITH THREE 2x12 STINGERS AND A WALL MOUNTED HANDRAIL**.

FIGURE 6-4.8 Annotation added to section

Next you will add dimensions to your stair and learn how to add additional text to the dimension line.

10.   Add a horizontal and vertical dimension (linear), as shown in Figure 6-4.9.

Next you will modify the dimension line text.

E | MUD ROOM | FAMIL

WOOD STAIR WITH THREE
2x12 STRINGERS AND A WALL
MOUNTED HANDRAIL

11'-3"

9'-0"

FIGURE 6-4.9 Two dimensions added to section

11. Select the horizontal dimension line.

12. Right-click and select **Properties**.

13. Locate the *Text Override* field and enter the following (Figure 6-4.10):
    15T. @ 9″ = <>

    NOTE: The line just typed means the stair has 15 treads that are 9″; all added together you get 11'-3″. The <> symbol tells AutoCAD to insert the current dimension (try stretching the dimension to see the number change).

14. Similarly, modify the vertical dimension to read (Figure 6-4.11):
    16R. @ 6¾″= <>

    TIP: If you double-click on the dimension text you can edit it there as well (see image below).

15T. @ 9″= 11'-3"

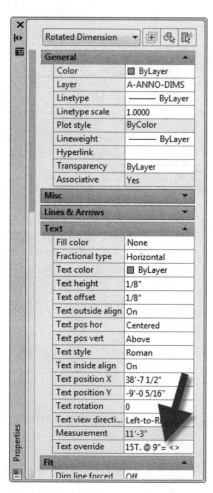

Rotated Dimension		
General		
Color	ByLayer	
Layer	A-ANNO-DIMS	
Linetype	—— ByLayer	
Linetype scale	1.0000	
Plot style	ByColor	
Lineweight	—— ByLayer	
Hyperlink		
Transparency	ByLayer	
Associative	Yes	
Misc		
Lines & Arrows		
Text		
Fill color	None	
Fractional type	Horizontal	
Text color	ByLayer	
Text height	1/8"	
Text offset	1/8"	
Text outside align	On	
Text pos hor	Centered	
Text pos vert	Above	
Text style	Roman	
Text inside align	On	
Text position X	38'-7 1/2"	
Text position Y	-9'-0 5/16"	
Text rotation	0	
Text view directi...	Left-to-R	
Measurement	11'-3"	
Text override	15T. @ 9"= <>	
Fit		
Dim line forced	Off	

FIGURE 6-4.10 Properties; horizontal dimension selected

FIGURE 6-4.11 Stair with modified dimensions

15. **Save** your building section drawing.

16. Now go back and update your basement floor plan so the first riser coincides with the stair section just developed. This is not unusual, as you may not know the floor to floor height when you start designing the floor plan. A corrected version of the plan is shown below (Figure 6-4.12). Note the wall has not been modified, which is fine as sometimes having the last few steps open helps with moving furniture.

FIGURE 6-4.12 Basement floor plan updated to match stair section

Self-Exam:

The following questions can be used as a way to check your knowledge of this lesson. The answers can be found at the bottom of this page.

1. The *Layer* name in non-plan drawings relates to the thickness of lines on that *Layer*. (T/F)

2. You can Xref the plans to locate interior walls in your building sections. (T/F)

3. You should know what scale a wall section will be printed at before adding text and dimensions so its size is correct. (T/F)

4. What is the feature that controls the size of dimensions?_____.

5. The Leader command can also add text.(T/F)

Review Questions:

The following questions may be assigned by your instructor as a way to assess your knowledge of this section. Your instructor has the answers to the review questions.

1. A vapor barrier is installed on the cold side of a wall. (T/F)

2. A wall section is typically as large as possible and still fit on the sheet. (T/F)

3. Lineweights help drawings to be more readable. (T/F)

4. Name the three non-plan *Layers* created in this Lesson:

   _____   _____   _____.

5. A *Sill Sealer* helps to reduce air infiltration into a building. (T/F)

6. What command was used to locate the stair treads quickly?_____.

7. What command creates an arrow with a line behind it? _____.

8. What command allows you to set the drawing precision? _____.

9. What *Layer* should text go on in section drawings? _____.

10. Things in section are the lightest lines in a drawing. (T/F)

Additional Tasks:

Task 6-1: Additional Building Sections

Draw additional building sections, using the exterior elevations as a starting point (similar to exercise (Task 6-1). This section is through the front entry. The image below shows a double-stud super-insulated exterior wall system. (You can use the typical exterior wall in your building section.)

Task 6-1 Building Section (section centered on front door / dormer)

Task 6-2: Wall Section at Garage

Draw a wall section at the garage (similar to exercise 6-2).

> *TIP: Remember the exterior garage walls only have 2x4 walls.*

Task 6-3: Hatch Wall Sections

Per your instructor's direction, add hatching to your section (e.g., concrete block, concrete footing and batt insulation).

Task 6-4: Stair Detail

In a new drawing file, draw the stair detail shown below; add the notes and dimensions shown. For the purpose of determining the text height and *Dimscale* setting, the drawing will be printed at 1½″ = 1′-0″.

The dashed line and 11¼″ dimension are provided for your information only and do not need to be drawn.

This is how you draw the stringer: Draw the dashed Line (it is a temporary line), Offset it 11¼″ (this is the size of the 2x12), and Erase the temporary line.

COMMENTS: *The treads and risers may have different finishes depending on where the stair is in the house. The basement stair may be plain/painted wood or carpeted. The upstairs may be a high-end stained wood (maybe with a carpet runner) or simply all carpet. The basement stair may have no finish on the bottom (like the detail below), whereas the upper stairs would likely have gypsum board attached to the bottom of the stringers and joists to create the finished ceiling for that area (additional wood blocking should also be called out in the notes).*

Task 6-4 Stair detail; to be printed at 1½″ = 1′-0″ scale

Lesson 7
Residential Project: PLAN LAYOUT & ELEVATIONS::

In this lesson you will further develop the floor plans and create interior elevations. You will add plumbing fixtures to the bathrooms and add furniture to the plans.

Exercise 7-1:
Bathroom Layout

Introduction:

In this exercise you will layout the bathroom fixtures. This typically involves thinking about where the plumbing is coming from and how it will get to each fixture without conflicting or compromising the design; also, things like circulation and door swings should be considered.

Like your floor plan, all fixtures are drawn (or inserted) into *Model Space* at full scale.

1. **Open** your second floor plan drawing **Flr-2.dwg**.

2. **Zoom In** to the bathroom area shown in **Figure 7-1.1**.

FIGURE 7-1.1 Second floor plan; zoomed into bathroom area

The first plumbing fixture you will insert is the tub, but first you will double-check your wall locations to make sure it will fit. If you refer back to the tub you drew in Lesson 3 (page 3-18), you will notice the tub is 5'-0" long. This is a standard size for a tub.

3. Use the **Distance** command (or draw a dimension and then erase it) to verify you have exactly **5'-0"** between the exterior wall and the interior wall as show in Figure 7-1.2. If you do not have exactly 5'-0", use the *Stretch* command to adjust the interior wall location.

FIGURE 7-1.2 Second floor bathroom; verify wall locations

As you have already seen, when you insert an external drawing file, like you are about to do with the *Tub* drawing, it comes in as a *Block* (i.e., a named group of entities). The *Block* will be inserted on the current *Layer*.

You can easily change the *Layer* by selecting the *Block* and then picking the desired *Layer* from the *Layer Control* drop-down list on the *Ribbon*.

However, in anticipation of the fact that you will be inserting several plumbing fixtures, you will create a *Layer* and set it to current before inserting the *Blocks*.

4.   Create a *Layer* named **A-Flor-Pfix**, set its color to **Green**.

5.   Set the *A-Flor-Pfix* layer to be the **Current Layer**.

6.   Use the **Insert** command to insert the **Tub.dwg** file you previously created (Figure 7-1.3).

    a.   Make sure you use *OSNAPs* to accurately pick the corner of the wall.

    b.   The more rounded side of the *Tub* is the back; the other side is where the faucet/piping is; make sure the faucet is on the interior wall as shown in Figure 7-1.3.

FIGURE 7-1.3 Second floor bathroom; tub block added

FIXTURE LOCATIONS IN COLD CLIMATE REGIONS

As you know, whether you live in a cold climate or not, water expands when it freezes. When this happens in a pipe, the pipe bursts under the extreme pressure exerted by the expanding water/ice. The problem is further compounded by the fact that the pipe is usually buried in the wall behind cement board and ceramic tile.

Therefore, whenever possible, you should avoid placing plumbing fixtures on an exterior wall in cold climates (at least the faucet/piping side in the case of a tub).

The problem usually only occurs when the heating system fails and the residents don't notice the problem right away, are on vacation, or the property is vacant. However, the problem can still occur during extreme weather condition (e.g., minus 40 to minus 60 degrees F).

If you must place the fixtures on an exterior wall you should build a second wall in front of the insulated exterior wall and provide grilles at the top and bottom of the wall to allow the warm room air to enter the wall cavity.

7. Use the **Insert** command to insert the **Water-Closet.dwg** file you previously created (Figure 7-1.5).

   a. Insert a *Toilet* (aka, water closet) at a corner of the room (see Figure 7-1.4); this puts the fixture in a known location, which then can be moved.

   b. Locate the fixture 18″ away from the side wall; also, move the toilet so there is 1″ between the fixture and the backwall. (Figure 7-1.5)

FIGURE 7-1.4 Second floor bathroom; *Toilet Block* inserted with *OSNAP*

FIGURE 7-1.5 Second floor bathroom; *Toilet Block* moved into place

Next, you will add two sinks to the plans. The sinks are in base cabinets, so you will **draw the lines** that represent the cabinets first.

Also, remember that in floor plans you should separate each building element onto **different** *Layers*; this helps to have better control over visibility and lineweights of those elements. So, you will create a *Layer* to draw the base cabinets on as follows:

Name	**Color**	**Linetype**	**Descriptions**
A-Flor-Case-L	Yellow	Continuous	Base cabinets
A-Flor-Case-U Red	Hidden2	Wall cabinets	

8. Create the two *Layers* described above.

Now you will draw the countertop/vanity. The top is typically 21″ deep.

9. Draw the base cabinets, on *Layer **A-Flor-Case-L**,* as shown in **Figure 7-1.6**.

> ***TIP:*** *Offset the wall lines to create the countertop in plan and then use Trim to clean up the lines; finally, change the lines to the correct layer.*

FIGURE 7-1.6 Second floor bathroom; offset wall lines to create vanity/countertop

10. **Offset** the wall line as shown in Figure 7-1.7; these lines will be erased after the sinks have been inserted.

FIGURE 7-1.7 Second floor bathroom; offset wall lines to help locate sinks

11. **Insert** the **Lav-2** drawing file, previously created, using the Insert command (on the Block panel of the *Insert* tab, via the Ribbon); then move the sink down **1″** with *ORTHO* turned on. (See Figures 7-1.8 and 7-1.9.)

FIGURE 7-1.8 Second floor bathroom; *Sink* inserted at intersection of temp. line and wall

FIGURE 7-1.9 Second floor bathroom; *Sink* moved 1″ out from wall

12. Repeat these steps to insert the other sink (Figure 7-1.10).

13. **Erase** the temporary lines (Figure 7-1.10).

FIGURE 7-1.10 Second floor bathroom; with tub, toilet and sinks added

This completes the bathroom layout.

In the next exercise you will draw the interior elevation of the cabinets.

> *FYI:* *You will see why the sinks are spaced the way they are.*

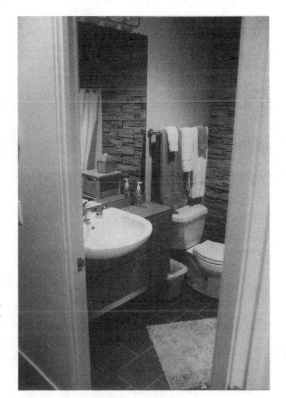

Image courtesy of Anderson Architects
Alan H. Anderson, Architect, Duluth, MN
Interior Design, Steven W. Sanborn, A.I.A.,
Santa Rosa, CA

Exercise 7-2:
Bathroom Elevation

Introduction:

The purpose of interior elevations is to show information that is not easily described on a floor plan. For example, you can show how high a countertop is, how tall a door is or the layout of wall and base cabinets.

Floor plans typically have horizontal dimensions and interior elevations typically have all the vertical dimensions. However, interior elevations are usually drawn larger than the floor plan (¼″ = 1′-0″ floor plans and ½″ = 1′-0″ interior elevation); so you may have additional horizontal dimensions that would be hard to read on a smaller plan.

In this exercise you will draw the interior elevation for the bathroom. You will use an *Xref* of the floor plan to get started and learn how to use a feature called *DesignCenter* to insert blocks contained in other drawings.

1. **Open** AutoCAD.

2. Start a new drawing named **Bathroom Elevation**.

3. **Xref** your second floor plan (**Flr-2**) into the drawing.

Next you will use a feature called **Clip,** which allows you to crop an Xref (i.e., external reference drawing). This will allow you to position the bathroom area close to your interior elevation drawing.

4. **Zoom Extents** so you can see the entire drawing.

5. Zoom **In** to the bathroom area (Figure 7-2.1).

6. Select **Clip** from *Reference* panel, which is on the *Insert* tab.

Clip

7. **Select** the Xref'ed floor plan and then press **Enter** two times, *or*

    a. If you have *Dynamic Input* on, select the following on-screen prompts:
        *   New Boundary
        *   Rectangular

8. Click twice to select a window as shown in **Figure 7-2.1**.

    TIP: You should turn OSNAP off so it does not interfere with your picks.

FIGURE 7-2.1 Second floor plan; bathroom area to select for Clip

MORE ABOUT CLIP

This section is meant to give you a little more information about the **Clip** command. You can also Clip Blocks and Images (i.e., photos).

Removing a Clip from an Xref
Click **Clip**, select the Xref, and then type **D** (for the **Delete** sub-command); then press **Enter**. You will now see the entire Xref again.

Irregular shaped clips
You can either create the outline before using the **Clip** command or after.

> If you create it before, you need to create a *Polyline*; you can even use **Pedit** to smooth (spline) the outline. Once the *Polyline* is created you enter the **Clip** command, select the Xref, and then press **Enter** twice.

> Now enter **S** for the **Select Polyline** sub-command. Finally, select your *Polyline* and you are done.

> Or, you can also follow the prompts and create the outline within the Clip command. However, you cannot get a smooth outline like you can with the method previously described.

You can experiment with the other sub-command features by looking at the prompts while the Clip command is active.

Now that the Xref is in place you can use it to quickly locate several lines in your elevation; you will do this next.

9. Arbitrarily draw a horizontal line and then draw the 8 vertical lines (snapping to the *Xref* for position), as shown in Figure 7-2.2.

Looking back at the *Wall Section* from Exercise 6-3 you can see the 8'-1⅛" dimension represents the floor to truss bearing height. If you subtract ½" for the ceiling gypsum board, you have the ceiling height for your elevation: 8'-0⅝".

10. **Offset** the horizontal line **8'-0⅝"** upward (Figure 7-2.3).

    TIP: Type 8'0-5/8 at the Command prompt.

11. **Trim/Extend** the wall lines to the horizontal floor and ceiling lines (Figure 7-2.3).

FIGURE 7-2.2 Interior Elevation: lines extended from Xref

FIGURE 7-2.3 Interior elevation: lines trimmed and extended

Using AutoCAD DesignCenter:

AutoCAD **DesignCenter (DC)** allows you to quickly access drawings (whether currently open or not), and drag items such as *Blocks*, *Linetypes*, *Layer* definitions, etc. into the current drawing. You will use the DC to insert a toilet in elevation from a preinstalled sample drawing (a file that comes with the AutoCAD software).

12. From the *Insert* tab select the **DesignCenter** icon (shown to the left) on the *Content* panel.

  TIP: You can also press Ctrl + 2.

You should now see the dialog box shown in **Figure 7-2.4**. This is the default view. Notice the full path listed at the bottom of the image; use the folder tree structure to browse to this same location if not already there (see step 13).

If you only see the vertical title bar shown to the left of Figure 7-2.4, then it is set to **Auto-Hide**. Simply hover your cursor over the title bar and the full image will show. This feature is meant to save space on your screen (i.e., larger drawing window).

To disable the Auto-Hide feature:
Right-click on the title bar and uncheck the **Auto-Hide** option (see right-click menu to the right).

Similar to the *Properties* palette, the *DC* dialog is modeless. That means it can be open while you are drawing (whereas the *Hatch* dialog box must be closed before you can continue drawing).

> ***TIP:*** *If you are running a dual screen system, you can drag both the Properties dialog and the DC dialog over to the second screen so you have the convenience of having them open without sacrificing valuable drawing area.*

Also, on the title bar right-click options is the ability to **Allow Docking**. If this is checked, the dialog will snap to the side of the AutoCAD window. Some people prefer this option so it does not cover the drawing window in an awkward fashion.

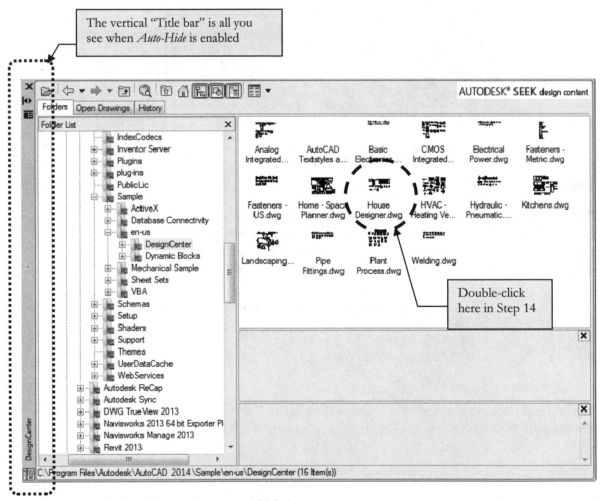

FIGURE 7-2.4 AutoCAD DesignCenter; initial view

13. First, verify you are in the correct area in *DesignCenter* (DC):

    a. Click on the **Folders** tab.

    b. In the *Folder List* pane, browse to the following folder:
C:\Program Files\Autodesk\AutoCAD 2014 - English\Sample\en-us\DesignCenter.

TIP: You may have to scroll horizontally and vertically to see everything, or stretch the Folder List pane wider.

    c. Your DC should look like Figure 7-2.4.

14. In the right pane, double-click **House Designer.DWG**.

You can now see the various categories of information you have access to (see Figure 7-2.5). Notice that the selected drawing file is highlighted on the left, in the *Folder List* pane.

FIGURE 7-2.5 AutoCAD DesignCenter; *House Designer* sample file selected

15. Double-click on the **Blocks** icon in the right pane.

You can now see a thumbnail image of all the *Blocks* within the *House Designer* sample drawing file.

> *TIP: If you do not see thumbnail images, click the __View__ icon and select __Large icons__.*

FIGURE 7-2.6 AutoCAD DesignCenter; blocks within the *house designer* sample file

Take a minute to notice the *Blocks* available for insertion into your drawing. You will only be inserting two of these *Blocks* for this drawing: the elevation of the *Toilet* and the elevation of the *Faucet*.

16. Double-click on the ***Toilet - front*** block.

You are now in the standard *Insert Block* dialog box with the *Toilet - front* block selected.

FIGURE 7-2.7 Insert dialog; initiated from DC

17. Click **OK**.

18. Using *OSNAPs*, select the *Intersection* of the floor line and the temporary vertical line projected from the toilet in the Xref'ed floor plan (Figure 7-2.8).

Insertion Point
(use *Intersection OSNAP*)

FIGURE 7-2.8 Bathroom elevation; toilet block inserted

Now you will draw the cabinets.

19. Draw the countertop and cabinets shown in Figure 7-2.9:

    a. You do not have to draw the dimensions.

    b. Notice that the two vertical lines from the sink are centered on their respective cabinets.

    c. Notice the other two vertical lines will locate the tall cabinets for you.

    d. The extra space on the right will be a filler panel; this allows for some flexibility when building the walls; the filler panel can also be ascribed to an irregular shaped wall.

    e. The two horizontal lines, 1½" apart, represent the countertop; the line 3" above that represents the backsplash.

FIGURE 7-2.9 Bathroom Elevation; countertop and cabinet outlines

Next you will add more detail to the cabinets and draw the remaining elements required for this exercise.

20. Draw the remaining elements shown in Figure 7-2.10.

    a. The mirrors are 2'-0" wide and 2'-6" tall, centered on the sink below.

    b. The vanity lights above the mirror are the same width as the mirror and 6" tall; draw the rest to look like the drawing.

    c. Use *DesignCenter* to *Insert* the **Faucet – Bathroom front** *Block* from the *Home Designer* drawing.

    d. Use the dimensions in the drawing below (you do not have to draw the dimensions at this time).

FIGURE 7-2.10 Bathroom Elevation; remaining elements to be drawn

Depending on the project you could add much more detail to the elevation.

For example, you could add:

- o electrical outlets and switches to make sure they end up where you want them;
- o the ceramic tile pattern and indicate the accent tile pattern as well (using hatch patterns);
- o the location of the pulls on the cabinets;
- o towel bars that might be in this particular elevation;
- o the toilet paper holder, especially if it is recessed in a tiled wall.

NOTES ON CABINET SIZES AND DESIGN

Bathroom and kitchen cabinets come in several standard sizes. They usually start at 12″ wide and increase in size by 3″ increments.

In kitchens,

- ♦ Wall cabinets are typically 12″ deep
- ♦ Wall cabinet heights: 18″, 24″, 30″, 36″, 42″
- ♦ Base cabinets are 24″ deep with a 25″ deep countertop
- ♦ Base cabinets are 36″ high (to the top of the countertop)
- ♦ Cabinets up to 24″ wide have one door; 27″- 48″ wide have two doors

In bathrooms,

- ♦ Vanity cabinets are typically 21″ deep
- ♦ Vanity cabinets are 33″ (or 36″) high (to top of countertop).

The Internet is loaded with information on designing kitchens. A few examples to get you started are:

www.kohler.com Major plumbing fixture manufacturer; web site is packed with kitchen and bath design information.

www.merillat.com *National Cabinet Manufacturer*; full line of cabinets including details and specifications.

www.kraftmaid.com Cabinet manufacturer with *Design tools*

www.doityourself.com/scat/designingkitchens

You will now complete the elevation by adding notes and dimensions.

21. **Erase** the temporary vertical guidelines.

22. Select **External References** link (***REMINDER:*** *small arrow in the lower right*) from the *Insert* tab (to enter the *External References* palette) and **Detach** the *Flr-2* Xref from the *Bathroom Elevation* drawing (right-click on the Xref name and select Detach from the pop-up menu).

23. Using ***MultiLeader***, and *Annotation Scaling*, add the notes shown in **Figure 7-2.11**.

    TIP: *Make sure they go on Layer A-ANNO-TEXT.*

24. Using the **Linear** *Dimension* tool, add the dimensions shown in Figure 7-2.11.

    TIP: *Make sure the dimensions go on Layer A-ANNO-DIMS.*

25. **Save** your **Bathroom Elevation** drawing.

FIGURE 7-2.11 Bathroom Elevation; notes and dimensions added

Don't Forget about LineWeights:

Don't forget to draw your lines on the different non-plan *Layers* (previously discussed on page 6-2) based on how heavy the linework should be. For interior elevations:

- ♦ **Heaviest Lines**:   The outline of the room should be the heaviest line.
- ♦ **Medium Lines**:   Objects out from the wall, like cabinets, should be the next heaviest.
- ♦ **Lightest Lines**:   Any lines on the wall (e.g., the mirror) should be the lightest lines
- ♦ **Light Gray Lines**:   Hatch patterns for ceramic tile or brick joints should be a light and gray line so it is not too intense. (This has not been covered yet.)

The actual implementation of lineweights will be covered in Lesson 10.

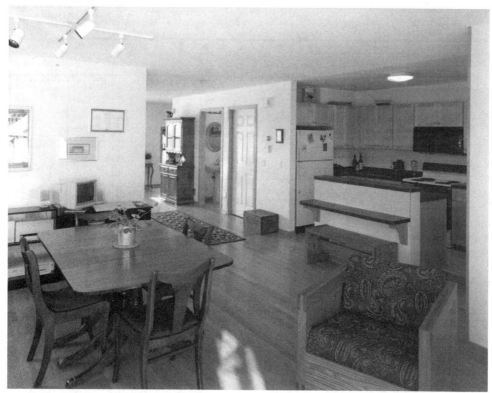

Carter Residence

Image courtesy of LHB
www.LHBcorp.com

Exercise 7-3:
Adding Furnishings to Your Floor Plans

In this exercise you will add *Blocks* that represent various furnishings. Laying out furniture helps both you and the client to verify that your floor plan design is functional. You will see that *Blocks* are available from several sources; this is in addition to the ones you drew at the beginning of this book.

First you will start with the *Master Bedroom*.

1. **Open** the "Flr-2" drawing file.

2. Create a *Layer* named **A-FURN**; set color to **Red**.

3. Set the **A-FURN** layer *Current*.

4. Zoom **In** to the *Master Bedroom* area.

Next, you will insert a few of the symbols you created in Lesson 3.

5. **Insert** the following *Blocks*, created in Lesson 3 (Figure 7-3.1):
   a. **Bed-king**   c. **Dresser-1**
   b. **Night-stand**   d. **Chair-2**

FIGURE 7-3.1 Master Bedroom; *Blocks* inserted

Now you will use *DesignCenter* to insert a *Block* located in a sample drawing file that was installed with AutoCAD.

6. Similar to Exercise 7-2, use *DesignCenter* to browse to the sample drawing file named **Home - Space Planner.dwg** (Figure 7-3.2).

7. Insert **Plant - Rubber or Philodendron** from the *Blocks* category (Figure 7-3.3).

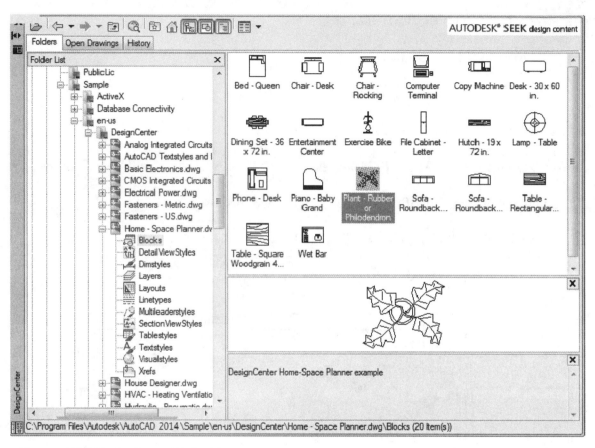

FIGURE 7-3.2 DesignCenter; *Blocks* to insert

FIGURE 7-3.3 Master Bedroom; *Plant* block inserted between chairs

ADDITIONAL CONTENT RESOURCES

In addition to the design content you have drawn and have found in *DesignCenter*, you can acquire additional content from other sources. Below are a few examples:

DesignCenter	click the **SEEK** link (Figure 7-3.4)
Sweets Online:	www.sweets.com
CAD Block Exchange Network	www.cben.net
AutoCAD Block Library	www.cadmonkey.com/blocks.htm
Wood Panel Systems	www.newenglandclassic.com
Fireplaces	www.firespaces.com

Many manufacturers have CAD blocks on their websites for download or will mail you a CD if you ask them.

WARNING!
Keep in mind that some of the symbols available on the Internet, or elsewhere, may not be accurate for a number of possible reasons. You should verify the size and accuracy of important symbols!

Notice the *SEEK* button in the upper right, gives you access to a significant amount of online content for use in your drawings! You must be connected to the internet for this link to work.

FIGURE 7-3.4 Website interface for Autodesk Seek

Notice you can also search for online content within the *Content* pane on the *Insert* tab (see image to the right). Give it a try… type: TOILET.

One last comment about SEEK; you may upload drawings (e.g., blocks) from the *Application Menu* → *Publish* fly-out. User based content needs to be checked for accuracy before using.

Share with Autodesk Seek
Share product related design files with the design community through Autodesk Seek

Walk-In Closet:

It is helpful to draw as much information as possible to better understand the complete design concept and make sure everything is coordinated. Drawing the clothes racks, for example, will show which walls are open and would be more accessible for an electric outlet. You will do this simple task next.

8. **ZoomIn**to the *Walk-In Closet*.

9. **Offset** both the south and west wall lines into the room **12″** (Figure 7-3.5).

10. **Trim** the two new lines and change them to *Layer* **A-FURN** (Figure 7-3.5).

Next you will draw lines to represent hanging cloths.

11. Draw a line **18″** long (on *Layer A-FURN*) and randomly copy and rotate it as shown in Figure 7-3.6.

FIGURE 7-3.5 Master Bedroom Walk-in Closet; lines offset for hanging rod

FIGURE 7-3.6 Master Bedroom Walk-in Closet; lines (i.e., hangers) added

That completes the *Master Bedroom* layout.

12. **Save** your drawing.

Image courtesy of Anderson Architects
Alan H. Anderson, Architect, Duluth, MN
Interior Design, Steven W. Sanborn, A.I.A., Santa Rosa, CA

Exercise 7-4:
Using Tool Palettes

Tool Palettes are a feature, introduced in AutoCAD 2004, which helps to organize content (*Blocks*) and frequently used hatch patterns. First you will explore the standard, out-of-the-box, *Tool Palettes*. After looking at the *Tools* provided, you will learn how to customize the *Tool Palettes*.

Overview of the "Out-of-the-Box" Tool Palettes:

First you will open one of your floor plans, so you can test the *Tool Palettes*.

1. **Open** the "Flr-1" drawing file.

2. Click *View* → *Palettes* → **Tool Palette** icon if the *palette* is not currently displayed; the *Tool Palette* icon toggles the visibility on and off.

The initial view of the *Tool Palettes* should look like **Figure 7-4.1**. Notice, down one side, are *Tabs*, similar to file folder tabs, which allow you to organize different groups of hatches, content and commands. The current *Tab* should be the one labeled "**Architectural**"; click this *Tab* if not current.

TIP: *If you only see the Title Bar show up when toggling the Tool Palettes icon, simply hover your cursor over the Title Bar and the palettes will display. This is caused by a feature called Auto-Hide (see page 7-12).*

The next page consists of definitions...

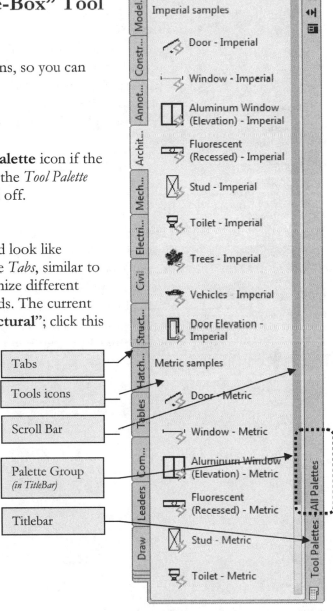

FIGURE 7-4.1 Tool Palettes; Architectural tab

Move Up
Move Down
View Options...
Paste
New Palette
Delete Palette
Rename Palette

Right-click menu

Tabs:

Used to organize *Blocks*, *Hatch Patterns* and *Commands* that are used regularly. You can add new *Tabs* as well as rename and reposition existing *Tabs*. When you right-click on a *Tab* you see the menu to the left.

Redefine
Block Editor
Cut
Copy
Delete
Rename
Update tool image
Specify image...
Properties...

Right-click menu

Tools icons:

You can store *Blocks*, *Hatch Patterns* and *Commands* on *palettes*. Each *Icon* has various settings to control, such as the scale and layer *Blocks* are inserted. Similarly, you can control properties like *Hatch Pattern* Scale and Color. These predefined properties will be covered next. When you right-click on a tool you see the menu to the left.

Move
Size
Close
✓ Allow Docking
Anchor Left <
Anchor Right >
Auto-hide
Transparency...
New Palette
Rename
Customize Palettes...
Customize Commands...
Annotation and Design
Parametric Design
Architectural
Civil
Structural
Manufacturing
Electrical Engineering
3D Make
Tables
Leaders
Materials
Generic Lights
Photometric Lights
Cameras
Visual Styles
✓ All Palettes

Right-click menu

Title Bar:

This is the area you select when you want to move the *Tool Palettes* window on the screen (click and drag). When *Auto-Hide* is turned on, the *Title Bar* is all you see when the *Tool Palette* is open. *Auto-Hide* and other options are set via the right-click menu shown to the left. When you have *Palette Groups* (which are several *Palette Tabs*), you can toggle between them via the list of *Groups* that would be displayed at the bottom of the right-click menu.

Inserting a Dynamic Block from a Tool Palette:

Now you will insert a *Dynamic Block* from the *Tool Palette*; you will insert a car in the garage. *Dynamic Blocks* were introduced in AutoCAD 2006. You will learn how to insert one and edit it with the special controls that are visible when the *Dynamic Block* is selected. Creating and editing *Dynamic Blocks* is beyond the scope of this tutorial.

3. **Zoom** into the *Garage* area (Figure 7-4.2).

4. From the *Architectural* tab on the *Tool Palettes*, click (not drag) on the **Vehicles – Imperial** icon.

5. Click near the center of the garage, centered on the left overhead door (i.e., garage door). See Figure 7-4.2A.

Oddly, your drawing should look like Figure 7-4.2A. One of the interesting things about *Dynamic Blocks* is that they can store multiple representations of the same or similar objects.

When you select the inserted *Dynamic Block*, a special symbol is displayed near the block. Clicking the symbol displays a list of display representations you can toggle between for the particular insertion. (This will not change any other insertions for that same block.)

Default view for the *Vehicle – Imperial* block inserted in the *Garage* from the *Tool Palettes*

FIGURE 7-4.2A
First Floor Plan; (default view) Vehicle – Imperial block inserted in Garage

Next you will change the *Dynamic Block* to display a top view of the vehicle block.

6. Click the car symbol just inserted; notice the symbol that is now visible (Figure 7-4.2B).

7. Click on the triangle-shaped *Grip* to see a list of display options.

8. Select **Sports Car (Top)** from the pop-up menu displayed (Figure 7-4.2C).

FIGURE 7-4.2B
Dynamic Block selected; notice special *Grip*

You will notice from the pop-up menu that the *Vehicle – Imperial* block has 12 different display options associated with it. The image below is the same drawing file with the same block (*Vehicle – Imperial*) inserted 12 times, and each insertion is set to display a different representation (Figure 7-4.2D).

9. Rotate the car *Block* negative 90 degrees so the front of the car points into the garage (Figure 7-4E).

FIGURE 7-4.2C
Dynamic Block display options listed

FIGURE 7-4.2D Dynamic Block display options

FIGURE 7-4.2E Dynamic Block rotated into place

Dynamic Blocks have many other capabilities such as stretching a table and having additional chairs added as the table is stretched. Additional control *Grips* can be added to quickly Mirror and Rotate the selected symbol. To create and edit *Dynamic Blocks*, you use the *Block Editor* which has a *Tool Palette* loaded with tools to create complex symbols.

Another *Dynamic Block*, listed in the *Tool Palettes*, is the **Door – Imperial** block. This is a very useful *Block*. You can adjust its size between several standard door widths; you can flip, change the open angle and rotate the symbol via the special control *Grips* (Figure 7-4.2F) to adjust the door swing. The built-in jamb lines would need to be edited in your project as they are not adjustable to the exactwidth of your walls.

FIGURE 7-4.2F Dynamic Block:
Door - Imperial

Notice when you clicked the *Tool Palettes* icon, you did not see the standard *Insert* dialog (Figure 7-2.7). This is because all the settings you are normally prompted for from the *Insert* dialog have been pre-assigned to each *Block* stored in a *Palette*. You will explore these settings next.

10. Right-click on the **Vehicles – Imperial** icon (Figure 7-4.1).

11. Select **Properties...** from the pop-up menu.

Take a minute to observe some of the settings available for the selected tool (*Vehicle – Imperial*). The main settings are:

Source file: AutoCAD imports the *Block* from an external drawing file, so the file must always exist in the location specified.

Scale: This is set to *1* for "real-world" items like furniture and fixtures; they are drawn actual size and don't need to be scaled. However, annotation symbols (e.g.,the detail bubble) need to be scaled relative to intended plot scale.

Color: This should almost always be set to *ByLayer*, which means the *Layer* the block is inserted on controls the color of the *Block* (assuming the lines in the *Block* were drawn on *Layer0* <zero>).

Layer: When set to *use current*, the *Block* is inserted on the current *Layer*, just like the standard Insert Block command. However, unlike the standard Insert Block command, you can pre-specify a *Layer* for the *Block* to be inserted on. So in the example below, you know the *Block* should always be inserted on the *A-SITE-CARS* layer. Simply setting the *Layer* property to *A-SITE-CARS* assures you that it will always be inserted on the correct *Layer*, regardless of the *Current Layer* setting; the Layer will even be created if it does not exist in the current drawing!

FIGURE 7-4.3
Tool Properties; Vehicle - Imperial tool

Using a Hatch Tool on the Tool Palettes:

Next you will use one of the standard *Solid Hatch* patterns predefined on the *Hatches* tab.

You will be using the Solid Hatch tool to fill in the walls, which will make them stand out more when printed.

The first thing you will do is create a separate *Layer* for the wall fill pattern to go on; this will allow you to *Freeze* it when you do not want it to show.

12. Open the second floor plan, **Flr-2.dwg** and create a *Layer* named *A-Wall-Patt*; leave the color set to *7* (*White*).

    *NOTE: Do **NOT** set this Layer to be Current!*

To show how you can predefine the *Layer*, you will adjust the *Layer* setting for one of the Hatch tools before filling the walls.

13. Right-click on the third icon located on the **Hatches** tab on the *Tool Palettes* darker blue swatch).
    - If you do not see the *Hatches* tab, right-click on the icon at the bottom of the title bar and select "All Palettes".

14. Select **Properties**.

15. Click on the word **"use current"** next to the *Layer Property* (this will cause a down-arrow to show up on the right).

16. Click the down-arrow to display the list of *Layers* in your drawing.

17. Select **A-Wall-Patt** and then select **OK** (Figure 7-4.4).

    TIP: The layer will not show up in the list if it has not been previously created.

Now you are ready to fill a section of wall with the Hatch tool.

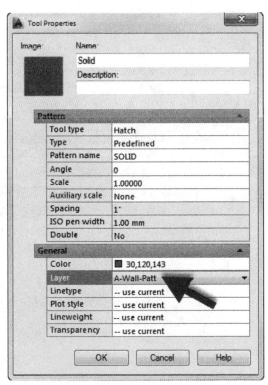

FIGURE 7-4.4 Tool Properties; Solid tool

18. Click the **Hatch** icon you just modified.

19. Click within the wall area in the upper-right corner of the *Master Bedroom* (Figure 7-4.5).

> *TIP:* *If you get the error "Valid hatch boundary not found", you should zoom in on all corner- and end-points to verify they are truly connected; AutoCAD needs to find a "perfectly" closed area in order to draw a hatch pattern.*

Click here (i.e., with-in wall) for Step 19

FIGURE 7-4.5
Second Floor Plan; area to click to specify area to be hatched

20. **Zoom Extents** to see the entire plan.

The selected portion of wall is now *Hatched* (Figure 7-4.6). It is good practice to only Hatch one or two closed areas at a time. If you were to Hatch all the walls for the entire floor at one time, you would have to do it all over again to accommodate one change. Whereas, you would only need to redo the fill pattern directly adjacent to the change.

21. Repeat steps 18-19 to Hatch the rest of the walls **on each floor**.

FIGURE 7-4.6
Portion of wall hatched

TIP: *You only need to adjust the Tool Palette settings once, not for each drawing (i.e., you don't need to change the Hatch tool Layer setting for the first floor; it will even create the Layer for you).*

All your walls should now be hatched (Figure 7-4.7).

FIGURE 7-4.7
Flr-2 walls hatched

Notice how the floor plan reads more clearly with the walls hatched; there is no question where a wall starts and ends.

FYI: *Extra furniture and toilet room layout is based on the "additional task" section.*

Next you verify the Solid Hatch was drawn on the correct *Layer* (even though that *Layer* was not set *Current* when drawing the Hatch).

22. In the *Layer Manager*, **Freeze** layer ***A-Wall-Patt***.

All the wall hatching should no longer be visible.

23. **Thaw** layer ***A-Wall-Patt***.

You should also notice that the color for the *Solid Hatch* has been set *ByEntity* rather than *ByLayer*. So, even though the *A-Wall-Patt* layer has its color set to 7, the *Solid Hatch* is set to <u>True Color 30,120,143</u> per the color property in the *Tool Properties (see Figure 7-4.4)*.

Adding Custom Content to a Tool Palette:

Now you will create a custom *tab* and add some of the *Blocks* you have previously created.

Content is added to the *Tool Palettes* by "dragging and dropping" *Blocks* from the *DesignCenter*, *Drawing Window* or *Windows Explorer*. So, similar to inserting *Blocks* from the *DesignCenter*, you browse to a drawing (open or closed) and open its *Blocks* category. Then you drag the desired *Block* to the *Tool Palette*. Finally you can specify the scale, *Layer*, etc. if desired.

First you will create a custom *Tool Palette* tab; this creates a storage area for your frequently used symbols (i.e., *Blocks*).

24. Right-click on one of the existing tabs and select **New Palette** from the pop-up menu (see page 7-28).

25. Enter the tab name: ***My Symbols*** in the area provided and then press **Enter**.

You now have a custom *tab* ready to hold your *Blocks* or hatch patterns. (See Figure 7-4.8.)

Make sure your Flr-2 drawing is open before proceeding.

26. Open the *DesignCenter* palette.

27. Click on the *Open Drawings* tab (near the top).

28. Expand the **Flr-2** drawing to view its categories (i.e., click the plus symbol) *if necessary*.

29. Select the **Blocks** category (Figure 7-4.9).

FIGURE 7-4.9
DesignCenter; *Open Drawings* tab - Flr-2\Blocks selected

FIGURE 7-4.10
Custom content added
to Tool Palette

30. Drag your *Blocks* (the ones you created) from *DesignCenter* to the "My Symbols" *Tool Palette*. (Figure 7-4.10)

31. Set the *Layer* to *A-Furn* (cf. 7-4.4) for each furniture symbol and A-Flor-Pfix for each plumbing fixture.

32. Save your **Flr-1** and **Flr-2** drawings.

Keep in mind that the Flr-2 drawing file cannot be moved or renamed as the *Tool Palette* will extract the symbols out of this file every time the symbol is needed (in other drawings).

Self-Exam:

The following questions can be used as a way to check your knowledge of this lesson. The answers can be found at the bottom of this page.

1. Base cabinets should be placed on the *Layer A-Flor-Case-L.* (T/F)

2. Interior elevations are typically drawn at ½″ = 1′-0″. (T/F)

3. You can use an irregular shaped polyline to *Clip* an external reference. (T/F)

4. What type of *Block* can have multiple graphics?_____.

5. *DesignCenter's SEEK* link only has a handful of *Blocks* available.(T/F)

Review Questions:

The following questions may be assigned by your instructor as a way to assess your knowledge of this section. Your instructor has the answers to the review questions.

1. *Clip* permanently deletes all of the clipped lines. (T/F)

2. In this lesson you used *DesignCenter* to insert *Blocks* contained within other drawing files. (T/F)

3. You can *Offset* wall lines to quickly create a temporary reference line. (T/F)

4. In *DesignCenter*, to access drawings on your hard drive, you must have the

   _____tab selected (one of the three tabs near the top of *DC*).

5. You can draw lines from your *Clipped* floor plan to position walls and fixtures in your interior elevation. (T/F)

6. Typing *Clip* does what?_____.

7. This icon ( ) allows you to open _____.

8. All furniture should be drawn on *Layer*_____.

9. All *Blocks* (symbols) downloaded off the Internet are 100% accurate. (T/F)

10. You cannot create your own *tabs* in the *Tool Palette*. (T/F)

Additional Tasks:

Task 7-1: Toilet Room Plan Layouts
Using the techniques learned in this lesson, add the plumbing fixtures to the two remaining toilet rooms. Refer back to Figures 4-1.1 and 4-1.4 for the fixture locations.

Task 7-2: Toilet Room Elevations
Using the techniques learned in this lesson, draw the interior elevations for the wall with the toilet and sink for the plans drawn in the previous task (Task 7-1).

Task 7-3: Furniture Layout
Using the techniques learned in this lesson, place furniture symbols throughout the house. Use your own ideas for this task. Imagine it is your house and decide where you would put the couch, the chair, the television, etc. Create new blocks for any symbols you may need but cannot find.

Notes:

Lesson 8
Residential Project: SITE PLAN::

This lesson will introduce you to the basic site plan drafting concepts. First you will draw the existing site conditions from a survey. Secondly, you will draw the building footprint, driveway and walks on the site. Finally, you will draw new contours indicating finished grade and drainage for the site.

Exercise 8-1:
Draw Existing Survey

Introduction:

The first thing you typically do when preparing a site plan is draw the existing site conditions. A survey crew will gather the site data and then draw a site plan indicating the location of any buildings, trees, and paved surfaces, as well as contours describing the shape of the land.

Ideally, you would get an AutoCAD file from the surveyor which would allow you to pretty much start drawing the new conditions. One thing to understand, in this case, is that you will usually have to adjust the scale (i.e., size) of the drawing. The reason is that surveyors use one AutoCAD unit as a foot whereas architects use one AutoCAD unit as an inch. Therefore, if you were to list the distance of a line (from a survey drawing) that is 48' in a drawing (with its units set to architectural), you will get 4'-0" (see the following chart):

Drawing	Line	Units	Length	Adjustment
Survey	48 Acad units	Decimal	48'	n/a
Site Plan	48 Acad units	Architectural	48"=4'	48x12=576"=48'

Thus, you scale the survey drawing up 12 times to make it the correct scale in your site plan file (or any file that has the units set to architectural). AutoCAD will do this automatically in most cases, but this is good for you to know when things don't work correctly.

If you do not get an AutoCAD file of the survey, you will have to draw it from the blueprint provided. This can be more challenging than reproducing an existing floor plan drawing because of the curved lines; curved lines are more difficult to create. In this lesson you will draw a site survey from a "hardcopy only" drawing.

Create Layers:

The first thing you will do is create the required *Layers*.

1. In a new drawing file, set the *Limits* to **280′ x 160′**, and then **Zoom All**.

2. Create the following *Layers*:

Layer Name	Color	Linetype
a. C-ANNO-TEXT	YELLOW	CONTINUOUS
b. C-PROP	MAGENTA	PHANTOM2
c. C-TOPO	YELLOW	HIDDEN2
d. C-TREE	CYAN	CONTINUOUS
e. C-WATR	CYAN	CONTINUOUS

Draw the Property Lines:

Now you will draw the property line. This will involve entering decimal feet for lengths and degrees-minutes-seconds for angles.

3. On the correct *Layer*, draw the property line shown in Figure 8-1.1. Note the following:

   a. Entering the length 134.6254′
   You can directly enter the decimal foot property line lengths listed. Consider a similar example: when drawing a line you can enter 1′6″ or you can enter 1.5′; in either case AutoCAD will draw the line the same length.

   b. Entering the angle 101°56′
   Entering angles by inputting Degrees-Minutes-Seconds requires a particular format: 101d56′ (for this example). If you are in the Line command, you can enter the following to draw the line the correct length/angle: @122.653456′<78d4′. If you need to dimension angles using this format, you would change the *Units* (from *Application Menu* → *Drawing Utilities*) to Deg/Min/Sec.

4. Set the variables related to the linetype scale:
   a. **LTSCALE= 1**
   b. **PSLTSCALE = 1**
   c. **MSLTSCALE = 1**
   d. *Annotation Scale:* this will be set in a later step

   FYI: Just type 'LTSCALE' and press enter to set the system variable to 1.

FIGURE 8-1.1
Site Survey; current/existing conditions

Drawing the Contours:

You have a few options for getting the contours into your cad file. One is to scan the drawing and place it in AutoCAD at the correct scale; then you can draw/trace over the image. The second involves using a grid to approximately transfer the curved contour lines from the "hard copy" to the drawing file; you will try this next.

Normally you would hand draw a 10'-0" x 10'-0" grid on a blueprint of the survey using an engineer's scale and a parallel bar or drafting board. However, this step will not be necessary for this tutorial; the grid is already added in Figure 8-1.3.

    5.   Using the **Pline** command (i.e., Polyline), draw the contours on the correct *Layer* per the comments below:

          a.   Use the site plan with the 10'-0" x 10'-0" grid overlay in Figure 8-1.3.

    b. Draw a 10'-0" x 10'-0" grid overlay on your site plan; aligned with orthographic property lines as shown in Figure 8-1.3.

    c. Draw each contour using the various locations the contour crosses the 10' x 10' grid as a reference (Figure 8-1.2). For example:

        i. Draw one contour at a time, following and noting where the line intersects the grid.

        ii. You only need to pick points where the contour line intersects a grid line; you will smooth out the line in a later step.

        iii. Notice that the contours cross exactly at some of the grid intersections; these are the easiest points to locate.

        iv. All other intersections can be approximated to be ¼, ½ or ¾ distance between two grid lines.

    d. You want to be as accurate as possible, but it is not necessary to be as accurate as you need to be when drawing the floor plans.

6. Select all the contours then, from the *Properties* palette, set the *Linetype Generation* to **Enabled**.

    FYI: *This setting makes the dashes consistent in your dashed lines. When this feature is disabled, dashes are calculated for each line segment in the polyline, many of which may not be large enough to show a dash at all; making portions of the line look continuous.*

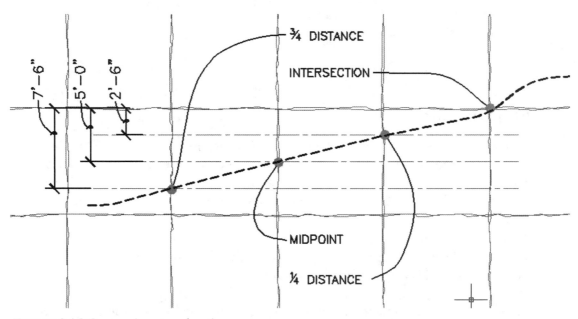

FIGURE 8-1.2 Contour layout explanation:
The image above shows the four primary points where the counter line crosses the vertical grid lines; the same process is used on horizontal grid lines.

FIGURE 8-1.3
Site Survey; with 10'-0" square grid overlay

Smoothing the Segmented Contours:

Now you will use the **Pedit** (aka, Polyline-Edit) command to smooth out the segmented contour lines. If you recall, you used the Pedit command to adjust the width of the grade line (which was a polyline) on your exterior elevations. Another sub-feature of the Pedit command is to smooth out a segmented Pline. The Pedit command has two methods available for smoothing a line: *Spline* (aka, Spline Fit) and *Fit* (aka, Curve Fit).

You can see the effect each option has on a polyline in Figure 8-1.4. The top figure indicates the original "segmented" polyline where the dots represent the points you picked while drawing the Pline. The second (or middle) image shows what happens when you use the *Spline* option of Pedit. Finally the bottom image shows how the *Fit* option modifies a Pline.

Seeing as the points you pick to create the polyline (i.e., contour) are defining the path, you will want to use the *Fit* option on your contours.

ORIGINAL SEGMENTED PLOYLNE

PEDIT --> SPLINE

PEDIT --> FIT

FIGURE 8-1.4
PEDIT Options; compare results of Pedit:Spline and Pedit:Fit

7. Type **Pedit**, press **Enter**, and then select one of the contour lines.

You now see the following in the *Command Window*: **Enter an option [Close/Join/Width/Edit vertex/Fit/Spline/Decurve/Ltype gen/Undo]:**

8. Type **F** (for Fit) and then press **Enter**.

The line is now smoothed and you get the same prompt as before, which would allow you to further modify the polyline if necessary.

9. Press **Enter** to complete the *Pedit* command.

You can also select the *Pline* and right-click to access the options just covered (see image to the right).

10. Repeat the previous three steps to smooth out each contour line.

11. Using the information just covered, draw the creek:

    a. Draw the lines on *Layer* **C-WATR**.

    b. Smooth the lines using Pedit.

Adding the Trees and North Arrow:

Once again, thanks to one of AutoCAD's sample drawings you have access to the pre-drawn trees and a north arrow shown in Figure 8-1.1. You will place these items next.

12. Using **DesignCenter** (and steps previously covered in this book), browse to the folder shown in Figure 8-1.5.

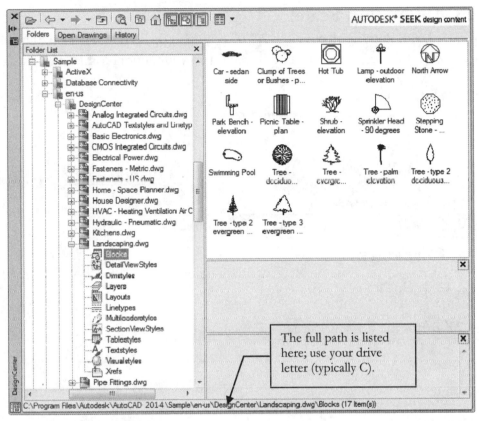

FIGURE 8-1.5
DesignCenter: landscape blocks available via the sample files

13. Drag and drop "**Clump of Trees or Bushes – plan**" and "**Tree – deciduous plan**" into your site plan; the trees should automatically be placed on the correct *Layer*: *C-Tree*.

14. Copy the *Blocks* around the drawing using Figure 8-1.3 as a reference for quantity and location.

> *FYI: You are drawing existing conditions, not designing a new site, therefore you should not deviate from the prescribed drawing at this time.*

> *TIP: You can (and should) Scale and Rotate the tree blocks so they don't all look the same and thus will better account for current conditions.*

Insert the **North Arrow** drawing from the *DesignCenter*.

15. Draw all the text shown in Figure 8-1.1, including the contour elevation labels, property line lengths and the creek label (all of which should be on the *C-ANNO-TEXT* layer).

    a. Rotate the text to align with the contours and property lines.

Adding a New Annotation Scale:

The template you started with does not have a 1″=20′-0″ option in the list of scales (1:20 is not the same; it is 1″=20″). You will learn to add it to the list so your annotation is correct.

16. From the scale list, select **Custom** (Figure 8-1.6).

FIGURE 8-1.6 Annotation scale

17. Click **Add**.

18. Enter **1″ = 20′-0″** for the name (Figure 8-1.7).

19. Set the following:

    a. Paper unites: **1**

    b. Drawing units: **20′**

FIGURE 8-1.7 Custom scale

20. Click **OK** to close the open dialog boxes.

21. Set the annotation scale to **1″=20′-0″**.

FIGURE 8-1.8 New annotation scale

In addition to the items just drawn, you might expect to find the following items on a survey/site plan:

- **Utilities**– water, gas, storm, sewer, cable, etc.

- **Land Features**– exposed ledge, rock, ponds, etc.

- **Easements/Covenants**– areas you cannot build on so access to utilities can be maintained.

- **Setbacks**– how close a building can be to the front, back and side property lines based on local zoning codes.

- **Soil Boring Locations**– where soil tests have been done to determine the footing size and depth.

The items listed above are added by the survey based on what has been contracted for when the survey was ordered. If you (or the client) only paid for property line locations, that is all you get! Typically, the client directly pays the surveyor to lessen the Architect/Designer's liability related to the survey's accuracy and potential of unknown conditions (e.g., buried foundation wall).

You now have the existing site plan drawn and ready for you to place the new elements such as the building, walks, driveway, etc.

> **TIP:** *It is good practice to save an unmodified copy of any original drawing. This helps if you decide to start over and have made several changes to the drawing. It also helps to quickly go back and verify existing conditions; maybe you accidentally erased a tree and did not realize it until later. You could open the archived existing drawing and copy/paste the missing tree into your new drawing. In your new drawing, once all the existing conditions have been drawn, it is a good idea to Lock the "existing" Layers to keep from accidentally changing existing linework. You should never erase anything existing; rather, place it on a demolition Layer (whose linetype is dashed).*

Exercise 8-2:
Add House, Driveway and Walks

Introduction:

This exercise locates the outline of the building on the site as well as the driveway and sidewalk.

First you will create the appropriate Layers.

1. *Layer Name*

		Color	*Linetype*
a.	C-ANNO-DIMS	Yellow	CONTINUOUS
b.	C-BLDG	WHITE	CONTINUOUS
c.	C-BLDG-PATT	254	CONTINUOUS
d.	C-BLDG-PRCH	YELLOW	CONTINUOUS
e.	C-WALK	RED	CONTINUOUS
f.	C-ROAD	RED	CONTINUOUS

Now you will temporarily Xref in your first floor plan so you can draw an outline of your building and see where the doors are.

2. **Xref** your first floor plan (flr1.dwg) into the site drawing.

3. Move the Xref'ed floor plan so it is in the proper position, as shown in Figure 8-2.1.

4. **Freeze** the *Dimension* layer in the floor plan Xref:

    a. When you Xref a drawing, all the visible *Layers* in that drawing are also visible in the Xref; you can Freeze some *Layers* in the Xref if you wish.

    b. Each *Layer* in the Xref'ed drawing shows up in the *Layer Properties Manager*, each with the Xref's filename as a prefix.

    c. So, to Freeze the Xref's dimension layer, you will Freeze the *Layer* named ***Flr1|A-Anno-Dims***.

Next you will draw a polyline around the perimeter of the building.

5. On the ***C-BLDG*** layer, draw a **Pline** around the perimeter of your building.

    a. Do not draw the outline around the porch, just the building.

    b. Use AutoCAD's *OSNAPs* to accurately draw the outline.

FIGURE 8-2.1
Site Plan; Xref positioned in proper location

6. Draw a **Polyline** along the exterior side of the porch;on layer C-Bldg-PRCH.

7. Add the dimensions shown in Figure 8 2.1; on layer C Anno Dims.

    TIP: *Make sure your Annotation Scale is set to 1″ = 20′-0″.*

8. Draw a 22′-0″ wide driveway centered on the garage doors; on *Layer C-Road*.

    TIP: *Draw a line from the Midpoint of the wall between the two garage doors and then Offset the line 11′-0″ each way.*

9. Now draw a 5′-0″ wide sidewalk as shown in Figure 8-2.3 on layer *C-Walk*.

    TIP: *Draw one side of the sidewalk, using Fillet and then Offset the lines 5′-0″ to create the other side of the sidewalk.*

Next you will *Unload* (not detach) the Xref. By Unloading the Xref, you can quickly Reload it without having to browse for it, position it and adjust the *Layers*. This is handy for verifying, occasionally, that your building outline is still up to date.

10. In the *External References Palette*, right-click and select **Unload** the Flr1 drawing (Figure 8-2.2).

    TIP: *Select the Xref name and right-click, then select the Unload button on the menu.*

11. Click **X** to close the *External References Palette*.

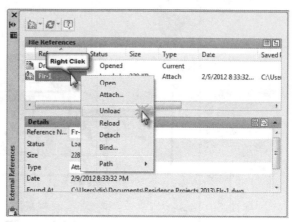

FIGURE 8-2.2
External References Palette; Flr1 drawing unloaded

Your drawing should now look like Figure 8-2.3.

FIGURE 8-2.3
Site Plan; building outline and paved areas added

Next you will fill the building footprint with a solid shade to help it stand out.

12. Using the **Hatch** command, add a *Solid* hatch pattern to the building footprint on layer *C-Bldg-Patt*.

13. Draw a 20'-0" x 16'-0" patio on the back inside corner of the residence (see Figure 8-2.4).

14. Use the *Hatch* pattern "**GRAVEL**" at a scale of **48** as a symbol for stone pavers in the patio.

15. From the *Landscaping* sample drawing (discussed in the previous exercise), **Insert** the picnic table; Rotate as shown in Figure 8-2.4.

16. Save your drawing as **ex8-2.dwg**.

FIGURE 8-2.4
Site Plan; building fill and patio added

Exercise 8-3:
Layout New Contours

Introduction:

In this lesson you will add new contours and take a quick look at drawing a cross section of the grade along a line.

The finished grade of the site needs to be modified primarily to handle site drainage. The drainage, as currently shown in Figure 8-2.4, would dump quite a bit of surface runoff (i.e., rainwater) into the back inside corner of the residence.

To indicate modified grading, new contours are added to the site plan. These contours show the contractor the final finished grade and intended drainage for the site.

New contours are shown with solid (i.e., continuous) lines:

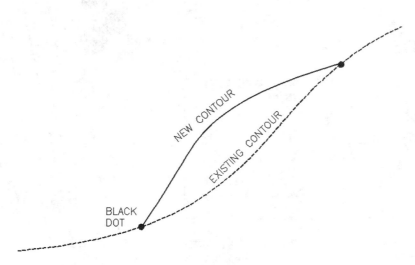

FIGURE 8-3.1
New Contour; new contour solid, existing contour dashed

As a contour with a smaller number (i.e., lower elevation) gets closer to a contour with a larger number (i.e., higher elevation), the contractor has to remove earth:

FIGURE 8-3.2 Earth Cut Example
Imagine the new contour extending straight into the existing hillside and coming back out to reconnect with the existing contour. All the earth above that line needs to be removed!

Conversely, when a higher contour is moved closer to a lower contour, the contractor has to add earth:

FIGURE 8-3.3 Earth Fill Example
Now imagine the new contour extending straight out into the air above the existing hillside and coming back to reconnect with the existing contour. Earth needs to be added below the line to support it!

Now you will draw new contours on your site plan.

1. Create a *Layer* named **C-Topo-Neww**.

    a. Linetype: **Continuous**

    b. Color: **Green**

    FYI: *It looks like a mistake, but the strict National CAD Standards require four characters in their standard Layer naming conventions.*

You do not need to be extremely accurate when drawing the new contours in the next step; just try to get it as close as possible.

2. Draw the **new contours** shown in Figure 8-3.4.

    a. Use the Polyline (aka, Pline) command to draw the lines.

    b. Use Pedit→*Spline* to smooth out the contours (or right-click menu).

    c. Use the *Nearest Snap* to accurately attach your new contour with the existing contour.

3. Use the **Donut** command to create the black dots at the start and end points of each new contour line (Figure 8-3.4).

    a. Set the inside diameter to **0″**.

    b. Set the outside diameter to **24″**.

    c. Draw the Donut on layer **C-Topo-Neww**.

    FYI: *To the right is a donut with its inside diameter set to something other than zero.*

4. Use the **MultiLeader** command to draw the "drainage flow" lines (Figure 8-3.4).

    a. Create a new *MultiLeader* style

        i.   Named *Drainage*

        ii. Select *Spline*

        iii. Max. leader points = 10

        iv. Multileader type = none

        v.   Linetype to **Center2**.

    b. Place the *MultiLeader* on the **C-Anno-Text** layer.

    FYI: *You will be drawing two multileaders.*

5. Add the text "DRAINAGE FLOW" (as shown in Figure 8-3.4).

FIGURE 8-3.4
New contours added; Plines drawn and smoothed out with the Pedit command

Notice in the image above that the contour line 1040′ cuts into the earth near each end of the new contour line and requires fill to be added in between.

The new contour lines reach up toward the higher contour where it intersects the drainage flow line. This creates a swale (not unlike a river, but more subtle of course) that "directs" water around the building.

A spot elevation should be called out in the back inside corner. The elevation should be high enough to allow any rainwater that falls in that area to flow away from the building.

Drawing a Grade Profile:

Now you will take a look at drawing a grade profile. A grade profile is analogous to drawing a building section; you are showing what the land looks like in a section view.

The profile in this example will show both the new and existing profiles. This could then be used to calculate the amount of cut and fill required on the site. It can also be used to determine the floor elevation of the building relative to the finished grade.

In this example you will draw a line generally perpendicular to the slope of the site. The first thing you will do is draw a line on the site plan that indicates where the profile is to be cut.

6. Draw a line on your site plan, approximately perpendicular to the contour lines as shown in Figure 8-3.5.

7. At this point you may want to temporarily copy your entire site plan off to one side so you can rotate it, making the section line aligned with the drawing window (Figure 8-3.5).

   *TIP: The most accurate way to rotate the drawing is to use Rotate and then the Reference sub-command. First you pick your base point, then R for reference. Next you pick one end of the section line and then the other end. Finally, you type 0 (or 180) and press **Enter**. See AutoCAD's **Help** system for more information on this feature.*

8. In the closest available empty drawing area below the section line, draw 6 horizontal lines spaced 2'-0" apart (Figure 8-3.5).

   FYI: This spacing corresponds to the vertical distance between the contours.

9. Project a vertical line down from the location where each contour intersects the section line (Figure 8-3.5).

FIGURE 8-3.5
Reference lines for profile; copy of site plan rotated so section line is orthogonal

Now you simply play connect-the-dots to create the grade profile (Figure 8-3.6).

10. Draw a **Pline,** picking the points where the vertical projection lines intersect the horizontal reference lines.

11. Use the **Fit** feature of *Pedit* to smooth out the line (Figure 8-3.6).

FIGURE 8-3.6
Grade Profile; property lines also added for context

12. You can now **Erase** the vertical projection lines.

13. Use the same technique just covered to draw the new grade profile; then overlay the two to see the variation.

> ***FYI:*** *This section does not show a significant amount of cut and fill.*

The sample image shown below indicates how a profile looks with both new and existing profiles. This image can be used to estimate the amount of cut and fill required for the project. The ideal situation is to have equal amounts of each to avoid buying fill or paying to haul extra fill away.

FIGURE 8-3.7
Sample Grade Profile; sample profile with both new and existing shown (existing shown dashed)

14. **Save** your drawing.

> ***TIP:*** *Civil Engineers sometimes exaggerate the vertical scale of sections so they are easier to read.*

Defining your location on Earth:

It is possible to specify the location of your project on the Earth. This is done from the *Insert* tab, using the **Set Location** tool. The first time you click **Set Location → From Map** you are prompted to use **Live Map Data**. This will allow you to see satellite photometry in AutoCAD; this feature requires you to log into **Autodesk 360** first (see chapter 1 for more on this). When the *Geographic Location* window appears, simply type in the city or project address to define a location. To refine your location, right-click on the map and select **Drop Pin Here**.

Once the image is displayed in AutoCAD you will have a **Geolocation** tab on the *Ribbon*, which gives you several tools to adjust the location or remove it.

Self-Exam:

The following questions can be used as a way to check your knowledge of this lesson. The answers can be found at the bottom of this page.

1. You can use the Donut command to draw solid dots. (T/F)

2. You can "unload" an Xref and then quickly "reload" it later. (T/F)

3. You typically have to scale a survey drawing (drawn with Decimal units) down 12 times to work with Architectural units. (T/F)

4. You draw new contours on this *Layer*: _____

5. New contour lines are "continuous" and existing lines are "dashed".(T/F)

Review Questions:

The following questions may be assigned by your instructor as a way to assess your knowledge of this section. Your instructor has the answers to the review questions.

1. A grade profile can help to calculate the amount of cut and fill required. (T/F)

2. Scaling and rotating the tree blocks as they are inserted helps to make the drawing look more natural (less like a cookie-cutter). (T/F)

3. A swale helps to direct the flow of surface runoff on a site. (T/F)

4. With the Pedit command, the _____ sub command makes a smoothed-out polyline that maintains the points you picked to draw the

   contour; whereas the _____ sub-command allows the polyline to deviate from your original points.

5. Layers associated with an Xref have what as a name prefix? _____

6. You need to set which property of a polyline to "enabled" to make the dashes

   consistent: _____

7. When a "lower" (e.g., 1060′) contour is rerouted to move closer to a "high"

   (e.g., 1065′) contour, the contractor would have _____ earth.

8. After picking your first point, type the *Command* window instructions to draw a line 321.125′ long with an angle of 43°12′ (ccw off the horizontal):
   @_____<_____.

9. To draw a solid black dot with a 24″ diameter you would use the Donut command with the "inside radius" set to 0″ and the "outside radius" set to 12. (T/F)

10. What *Layer* does the building outline go on? _____

SELF-EXAM ANSWERS:
1– T, 2– T, 3– F, 4 – c-topo-neww, 5 – T

Additional Tasks:

Task 8-1: Add Items to the Site Plan

Add additional items to the site plan, such as new trees and landscaping (labeling them as such). You can search the internet for pre-drawn blocks. Also add notes for the new road and sidewalk (e.g., blacktop driveway; concrete sidewalk).

Task 8-2: Draw another Grade Profile

Draw a grade profile that generally follows one of the swales; this will be a more dramatic cut and fill profile.

Task 8-3: Update the Grade Profile for Each Exterior Elevation

You can draw a grade profile at each side of the building and then superimpose that profile on your exterior elevations to accurately describe how the grade engages the building's perimeter.

Lesson 9
Residential Project: SCHEDULES & SHEET SETUP::

In this lesson you will learn to use the new Table feature to create schedules in AutoCAD. You will also explore how drawings are setup on sheets so they can be plotted with a professional look and fashion.

Exercise 9-1:
Room Finish Schedule

Introduction:

A *Room Finish Schedule* indicates what finish the walls, ceiling and floors get in each room. This information is typically organized in a grid of rows and columns, where each row represents a room and each column represents a surface to be finished. AutoCAD has a feature, called *Tables*, that is designed to accommodate this type of data (i.e., schedules).

Most rooms have both a name and a number to facilitate accurate identification on plans and schedules. Numbers are not always required on residential projects; however, it is typically done for consistency. Using a number is necessary when you have multiple rooms with the same name. In your plan, for example, you have multiple bathrooms and bedrooms. On large commercial projects, a floor plan might have 30-40 rooms all labeled "office", so it is easy to see how important numbers are.

The first step is to add the room numbers to your floor plans.

1. **Open** your **Flr-1** drawing.

2. Add the room numbers:

   a. Double-click on each room name.

   b. Click the cursor at the end of the room name.

   c. Press **Enter** to start a new line.

   d. Type the room numbers shown in Figure 9-1.1.

   FYI: Having the room name and number in the same Mtext object helps to keep them aligned. It also makes moving them easier as you only have to worry about selecting one object, not two.

FIGURE 9-1.1
First floor plan; room numbers added

3. **Open** your **Flr-2** drawing.

4. Add the room numbers per Figure 9-1.2.

5. **Open** your **Flr-B** drawing.

6. Add the number **001** below the room name (i.e., UNFINISHED BASEMENT).

7. **Save** your floor plan drawings.

FIGURE 9-1.2
Second floor plan; room numbers added

Creating a Table:

8. Create a new drawing using **Architectural Imperial.dwt** as your template file.

9. Switch to *Model Space* and then click the **Table** icon from the *Home* panel (or type *Table* and press Enter).

You are now in the *Insert Table* dialog box (Figure 9-1.3). At this point you could create a table using the *Standard* table style; if other styles existed, you could select one of them as well. You will create a *Table* using the *Standard* style.

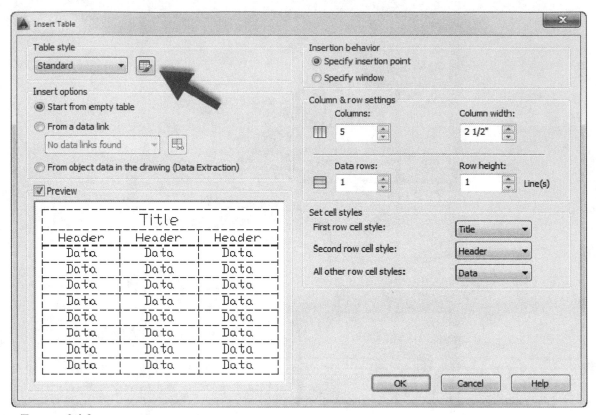

FIGURE 9-1.3
Insert Table dialog; initial view

Adjusting the Table Style Settings:

The first thing you will do is adjust the *Standard* table style. You will adjust the *Text Height* to a smaller size as well as change the *Text Style*.

10. Click on the **Table Style Settings** button (Figure 9-1.3).

11. Click the **Modify...** button to modify the *Standard* table style.

12. Make changes shown in **Figure 9-1.4** to the **Data** *Cell styles*.

13. Make changes shown in **Figure 9-1.5** to the **Header** *Cell styles*.

> **FYI:** *Only the* Text *tab has changes to it (typically).*

14. Make changes shown in **Figure 9-1.6** to the **Title** *Cell styles*.

FIGURE 9-1.4
Modify Table Style dialog; Data tab

FIGURE 9-1.5
Modify Table Style dialog; Column Heads tab

FIGURE 9-1.6
Modify Table Style dialog; Title tab

15. Click **OK** to close the *Modify Table Style* dialog.

16. Click **Close** to exit the *Table Style Manager* and return to the *Insert Table* dialog.

At this point you need to have an idea how many rows and columns you need. You can sketch out what information you will need to display in the schedule (see Figure9-1.7 for an example). You also need to specify the row height and the column width; this will be the size for the standard row/column. You will be able to adjust the size of individual columns/rows once the *Table* has been created. You can also add rows and/or columns after creating the *Table*. Therefore, you do not need to be too concerned about forgetting a row or column at this point as it can easily be added later.

FIGURE 9-1.7
Preliminary Room Finish Schedule Sketch

Based on the sketch above, you will create a quick *Table* that has 11 columns and six rows. You will make additional adjustments later.

17. Make the following adjustments to the *Insert Table* dialog:

a. <u>Columns</u>: **11**

b. <u>Column Width</u>: **1″**

c. <u>Data Rows</u>: **6**

d. *Leave everything else at the default* (Figure9-1.3).

18. Click **OK** to insert the *Table.*

At this point you will see the specified *Table* attached to your cross-hairs so you can visually place it.

19. Move your cursor so the entire *Table* is visible and centered on the screen and click the mouse to place it.

You are now automatically prompted for the title of the table.

20. For the *Table* title, type "**ROOM FINISH SCHEDULE**" (Figure 9-1.8).

TIP: Just start typing; no need to click anywhere.

FIGURE 9-1.8
Inserted Table; entering table title text

21. Click **Close Text Editor** on the *Text Editor* tab/ribbon.

You now have a *Table* created in your drawing. Next you will adjust the width of the columns to match the sketch.

22. Select a column to adjust its width per the following:

    a. Click and drag the mouse from the lowest cell to the highest cell (or vice versa).

    b. See Figure 9-1.9.

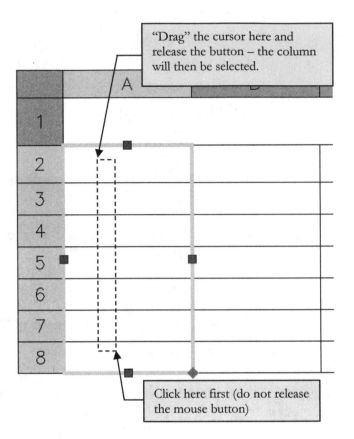

"Drag" the cursor here and release the button – the column will then be selected.

Click here first (do not release the mouse button)

FIGURE 9-1.9
Table and its Properties; column selected
(selected cells properties displayed)

23. In the *Properties Palette*, change the *Cell width* to **.5″** (for the selected column, column A) and then press **Enter**.

The *Table* column has now been updated to display the *column width* per your specifications (Figure 9-1.10).

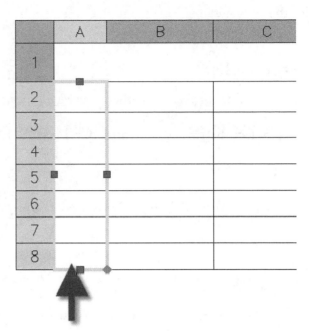

FIGURE 9-1.10
Table and its Properties; column width adjusted

24. Press **Esc** to deselect the column.

25. Adjust the remaining column widths per the following information (Figure 9-1.11):

    a.   Column B (room name): **2″**

    b.   Columns C – J: **1″**

    c.   Column K (remarks): **2″**

FIGURE 9-1.11
Table; all column widths adjusted

As you will recall, you specified 11 columns and six rows. In addition to that, a *Table* automatically has a *Title* row and a *Header* row. Compare the image above (Figure 9-1.11) with the preview image in Figure 9-1.3.

Merge Cells:

Next you will merge cells together to create larger cells within the *Table*.

26. Select the two cells identified in Figure 9-1.12.

> *FYI: This is where the room number label goes.*

27. Select **Merge Cells → Merge All** icon from the *Ribbon* (Figure9-1.13).

FIGURE 9-1.12
Table; two cells merged together

You now have a merged cell in your *Table*! Take a moment to notice the other commands on the *Ribbon* in Figure 9-1.13. (Hover your cursor over each icon for a tooltip of the command name.

FIGURE 9-1.13
Merge Cells; two cells selected and then right-click

28. Use the **Merge Cells** feature to make your table look like the one in Figure 9-1.14.

ROOM FINISH SCHEDULE					
①	②	③		④	⑤	⑥

FIGURE 9-1.14
Merge Cells; several cells merged

Inserting Additional Rows:

Before adding data to the table, you will insert additional rows. A few too many will be added so you can learn to delete rows later.

29. Click in any *Data* cell and then click and select the **Insert Row Below** icon from the *Ribbon* (Figure 9-1.15).

30. Repeat the previous step until you have **20** *Data* rows.

FIGURE 9-1.15
Insert rows; creates extra data lines

Now you can see why it is good to calculate the approximate number of rows you will need when creating the *Table*; you can type in the number of rows versus right-clicking for each row added later.

Adding Column Header Labels:

Now you will add the labels that indicate what information is in each column within the schedule (table).

31. Click to select the cell and then double-click within each *Header* cell and type the label per the sketch in Figure 9-1.7; see Figure 9-1.16 for the finished product.

    TIP: Once in "cell edit mode" you can arrow-key between cells.

Adding Data to Cells:

It is very easy to add data to your *Table*; you simply double click in a cell and type. Next you will add the data to your table.

32. Looking at Figure 9-1.16, enter the data into your Table.

    TIP: After you double-click in a cell, you can use the Tab and Arrow keys to move between cells.

    TIP: You can Copy/Paste multiple cells. Click and drag to select the cells to Copy, and then press Ctrl+C (copy to Windows Clipboard). Next click and drag to select the cells to Paste to, and then press Ctrl+V (paste from Windows Clipboard).

| RM NO | ROOM NAME | FLOOR | | WALLS | | | | CEILING | | REMARKS |
		FINISH	BASE	NORTH	EAST	SOUTH	WEST	MAT'L	HEGIHT	
001	BASEMENT	SEALED	N/A	CMU	CMU	CMU	CMU	EXP.	—	
100	FOYER	Q.T.	Q.T.	WOOD PNL	WOOD PNL	WOOD PNL	WOOD PNL	GYP BD	8'-6"	
101	LIVING ROOM	WOOD	WOOD	GYP BD	GYP BD	GYP BD	GYP BD	GYP BD	8'-6"	
102	FORMAL DINING	WOOD	WOOD	GYP BD	GYP BD	GYP BD	GYP BD	GYP BD	8'-6"	
103	KITCHEN	Q.T.	Q.T.	GYP BD	GYP BD	GYP BD	GYP BD	GYP BD	8'-6"	
104	FAMILY DINING	CARPET	WOOD	GYP BD	GYP BD	GYP BD	GYP BD	GYP BD	8'-6"	
105	FAMILY ROOM	VINYL	WOOD	GYP BD	GYP BD	GYP BD	GYP BD	GYP BD	8'-6"	
106	BATH	MARBLE	MARBLE	C.T.	C.T.	C.T.	C.T.	GYP. BD.	8'-6"	
107	MUD ROOM	Q.T.	Q.T.	GYP BD	GYP BD	GYP BD	GYP BD	GYP BD	8'-6"	
108	GARAGE	SEALED	—	GYP. BD.	GYP BD	GYP BD	GYP BD	GYP BD	8'-6"	
200	HALLWAY	WOOD	WOOD	GYP BD	GYP BD	GYP BD	GYP BD	GYP BD	8'-0"	
201	MASTER BEDROOM	WOOD	WOOD	GYP BD	GYP BD	GYP BD	GYP BD	GYP BD	8'-0"	
202	CLOSET	WOOD	WOOD	GYP BD	GYP BD	GYP BD	GYP BD	GYP BD	8'-0"	
203	MASTER BATH	MARBLE	MARBLE	C.T.	C.T.	C.T.	C.T.	GYP. BD.	8'-0"	
204	BATH	C.T.	C.T.	C.T.	C.T.	C.T.	C.T.	GYP. BD.	8'-0"	
205	STORAGE	WOOD	—	GYP BD	GYP BD	GYP BD	GYP BD	GYP BD	8'-0"	
206	BEDROOM #1	CARPET	WOOD	GYP BD	GYP BD	GYP BD	GYP BD	GYP BD	8'-0"	
207	BEDROOM #2	CARPET	WOOD	GYP BD	GYP BD	GYP BD	GYP BD	GYP BD	8'-0"	

ROOM FINISH SCHEDULE

FIGURE 9-1.16
Room Finish Schedule; with data entered

Deleting Rows:

Next you will delete one of the extra rows. The following technique works the same way for columns as well.

33. Click within the cell <u>directly below</u> BEDROOM #2.

34. Select **Delete Rows** from the *Ribbon* (Figure 9-1.17).

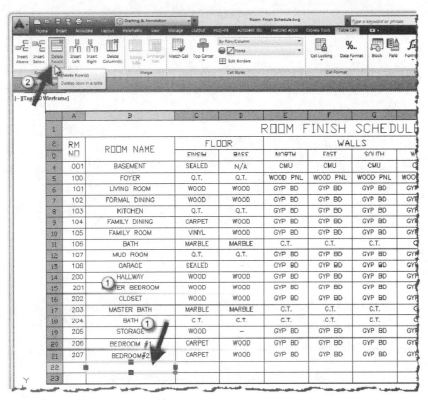

FIGURE 9-1.17
Room Finish Schedule; deleting a row

Making the Table Title Text Bold:

Finally, you will change the font for the *Table Title* (i.e., Room Finish Schedule) to Arial Black, which is a distinctive bold font. To do this you will need to create a new AutoCAD *Font Style* and then modify the *Table Style* to use the new *Text Style*.

35. Press the Esc key to unselect the table, and then click the **Text Style...** link, *Annotate* tab, *Text* panel.

You are now in the *Text Style* dialog where you manage AutoCAD *Text Styles*.

FYI: AutoCAD Text Styles allow you to predefine several settings for a particular type of note or label. Additionally, like other "styles" in AutoCAD, if you change a style setting (e.g., the Width Factor), all the text of that style will update automatically.

FIGURE 9-1.18
Text Style dialog; initial view

Notice, in the image above, the settings for the "Roman" *Text Style*. The *Font Name* is "Romans.shx"; the *Style Name* is similar but can be anything. The *Height* is set to 0′-0″, which means you can adjust the height for each instance in your drawing.

36. Notice under *Styles* that only two exist in the current drawing (*Standard* and *Roman*).

Now you will create a new *Text Style* named *Bold*.

37. Click the **New** button.

You are now prompted for a name (Figure 9-1.19).

FIGURE 9-1.19
New Text Style dialog; style name Bold entered

38. Type the new *Style Name* **Bold** and then click **OK**.

39. Make the following adjustments (Figure 9-1.20):

    a. Font Name: **Arial Black**

    b. Width Factor: **0.9**

FIGURE 9-1.20
Text Style dialog; setting for text style named "*Bold*"

40. Click **Apply** to finalize your new *Text Style* settings.

41. Click **Close**.

The new *Text Style* is now available for use in the current drawing. If you want regular access to the *Bold* text style, you would add it to your *Drawing Template* file. Now you will modify the *Table Style* title text.

42. On the *Table* panel, in the *Annotate* tab, select the **Table Style** link *(see image to the right)*.

43. Click the **Modify...** button *(to Modify the Standard Table Style)*.

44. Under the **Title** *Cell styles*, change the following:

    a. *Text* tab: *Text style* to **Bold** and *Color* to **250** (Figure 9-1.21B).

    b. *General* tab: *Fill color* to **Color 255** (Figure 9-1.21A).

    FYI: Another option is to select the Title cell and adjust these settings in the Properties Palette.

FIGURE 9-1.21A
Modify Table Style; Title – General tab

FIGURE 9-1.21B
Modify Table Style; Title – Text tab

45. Click **OK** and then **Close** to close the dialog boxes.

You should notice the text for the *Title* is now *Bold* and the cell is filled with color 255 (a grey shade) in your *Room Finish Schedule* (Figure 9-1.22). Similarly, if you had additional tables inserted into the current drawing (and using the *Standard* style), they would all be updated to use the *Bold* font as well.

RM NO	ROOM NAME	FLOOR		WALLS				CEILING		REMARKS
		FINSIH	BASE	NORTH	EAST	SOUTH	WEST	MAT'L	HEIGHT	
001	BASEMENT	SEALED	N/A	CMU	CMU	CMU	CMU	GYP BD	8'-6"	
100	FOYER	Q.T.	Q.T.	WOOD PNL	WOOD PNL	WOOD PNL	WOOD PNL	GYP BD	8'-6"	
101	LIVING ROOM	WOOD	WOOD	GYP BD	GYP BD	GYP BD	GYP BD	GYP BD	8'-6"	
102	FORMAL DINING	WOOD	WOOD	GYP BD	GYP BD	GYP BD	GYP BD	GYP BD	8'-6"	
103	KITCHEN	Q.T.	Q.T.	GYP BD	GYP BD	GYP BD	GYP BD	GYP BD	8'-6"	
104	FAMILY DINING	CARPET	WOOD	GYP BD	GYP BD	GYP BD	GYP BD	GYP BD	8'-6"	
105	FAMILY ROOM	VINYL	WOOD	GYP BD	GYP BD	GYP BD	GYP BD	GYP BD	8'-6"	
106	BATH	MARBLE	MARBLE	C.T.	C.T.	C.T.	C.T.	GYP BD	8'-6"	
107	MUD ROOM	Q.T.	Q.T.	GYP BD	GYP BD	GYP BD	GYP BD	GYP BD	8'-6"	
108	GARAGE	SEALED	–	GYP BD	GYP BD	GYP BD	GYP BD	GYP BD	8'-0"	
200	HALLWAY	WOOD	WOOD	GYP BD	GYP BD	GYP BD	GYP BD	GYP BD	8'-0"	
201	MASTER BEDROOM	WOOD	WOOD	GYP BD	GYP BD	GYP BD	GYP BD	GYP BD	8'-0"	
202	CLOSET	WOOD	WOOD	GYP BD	GYP BD	GYP BD	GYP BD	GYP BD	8'-0"	
203	MASTER BATH	MARBLE	MARBLE	C.T.	C.T.	C.T.	C.T.	GYP BD	8'-0"	
204	BATH	C.T.	C.T.	C.T.	C.T.	C.T.	C.T.	GYP BD	8'-0"	
205	STORAGE	WOOD	–	GYP BD	GYP BD	GYP BD	GYP BD	GYP BD	8'-0"	
206	BEDROOM #1	CARPET	WOOD	GYP BD	GYP BD	GYP BD	GYP BD	GYP BD	8'-0"	
207	BEDROOM #2	CARPET	WOOD	GYP BD	GYP BD	GYP BD	GYP BD	GYP BD	8'-0"	

ROOM FINISH SCHEDULE

FIGURE 9-1.22
Modify Table Style; Text style for title set to "Bold"

46. **Save** your drawing as **ROOM FINISH SCHEDULE.DWG**.

Exercise 9-2:
Sheet Setup and Management (Sheet Sets)

Introduction:

This exercise covers an AutoCAD feature called *Sheet Sets*, which represents a very powerful feature previously found only in more advanced, architecture specific, programs like Autodesk Revit.

The *Sheet Set Manager* allows one or more drafters to see a list that represents all the sheets in the project set. Each sheet can be opened by double-clicking on the sheet label in the list. Once a sheet is open, you can place drawings on it. Reference bubbles can be placed on sheets which are automatically updated when the drawing numbers or sheet numbers are changed.

When you have completed this section you will have created several sheets with title blocks and will have placed your drawings on them using the *Sheet Set Manager*.

Procedural and Organizational Overview:

The following information outlines the basic procedure and organization of a *Sheet Set*. This will give you a good understanding of this feature before you actually try it.

Sheet Sets pivot around three types of files:

- ♦ Resource Drawings (Model Views)
- ♦ Sheet Files (Sheet Views)
- ♦ A Sheet Set Data File

In addition to the three types of files listed above, other files are used as well (e.g., callout blocks and template files). Next you will take a closer look at the three file types listed above and what role they play in the *Sheet Set* feature.

Resource Drawings:

- o Drawing files (DWG's)

  - – Each floor plan, elevation, detail, etc., in a drawing file, has a *Named View* associated with it.

  - – These files are the files you have created thus far in this book.

  - – You will cover *Named Views* later in this exercise.

- o Any text or dimensions drawn in a *Resource Drawing* need to be scaled appropriately based on the scale at which that drawing will ultimately be plotted.

Sheet Files:

- o Drawing files (DWG's)

    - Each of these files represents a sheet in a set of drawings (e.g., 24″x36″ sheet)

- o *Named Views*, from various *Resource Drawings*, are placed on these sheets.

- o *Named Views* can be placed at various scales at the time of insertion. A drawing title tag is automatically inserted below the drawing view; the tag is even automatically filled out with the view's number (if/when one is provided in the *Sheet Set Manager*), and scale (i.e., the scale you selected when the view was placed on the sheet). The image below describes the default drawing tag:

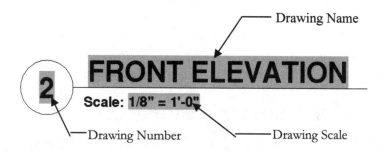

- o Once a *View* has been placed on a sheet, you can specify a *Drawing Number*, you can also change the *Drawing* (view) *Name*. This must be done in the *Sheet Set Manager* to insure all sheets and views are correctly cross-referenced.

- o *Callout Bubbles* (elevation and detail) can be placed on sheets. The bubbles reference a *Named View* from a *Resource Drawing*. The reference bubble is automatically filled out with the view's number and the sheet number the view is placed on (all of which is stored in the *Sheet Set Data* file). The image below describes the basic components of a callout bubble:

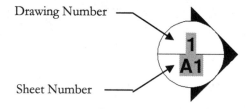

- o The shaded rectangle behind the text lets you know that the text is updated automatically and should not be modified manually. Specifically, they are called *fields*, and are updated at key points while working on a drawing (e.g., Open, Save, Plot, Regen). These are similar to the *fields* in *MS Word*, the *Date* field is shaded and automatically updated.

<u>A Sheet Set Data File:</u>

o File name and extension: *filename*.dst.

o This file is a database that maintains information about the *Sheet Set* and detail/sheet numbering and cross-references.

o The file can be located anywhere on your system (including a network drive). This file should be stored in your project folder for easy backup.

Creating Named Views in Your Resource Drawings:

As mentioned above, each of the various plans, elevations, sections and details you wish to place on a sheet needs to be identified by a *Named View*, which is simply defined by an imaginary rectangular area within a drawing file. If you move a door detail, for example, to another part of *Model Space*, the *Named View* does NOT move and would be "looking" at an empty portion of the drawing at that point.

You will start with the exterior elevations.

1. Open your **Exterior Elevations** drawing created in Lesson 5.

If created per the tutorial outlined in Lesson5, you have all four elevations in one drawing. You will create one *Named View* for each elevation in the *Exterior Elevation* drawing.

2. **Zoom In** to the South elevation.

3. Select **View Manager** from the *View* tab.

   TIP: You can also type V and Enter to load View Manager.

South elevation

You are now in the *View Manager* dialog (Figure 9-2.1).

FIGURE 9-2.1
View Manager dialog box; click "New…" to create a named view

4.   Click **New** to create a new *Named View*.

You are now in the *New View* dialog (Figure 9-2.2), where you can create a *Named View*.

5.   Enter **South Elevation** for the *View* name (Figure 9-2.2).

> *TIP: The name entered here is the default name used in the drawing title tag when the view is placed on a sheet.*

6.   Click **Define window** in the *Boundary* area (Figure 9-2.2).

FIGURE 9-2.2
New View dialog; create a view named "South Elevation"

Immediately after clicking *Define window* you are temporarily brought back to the drawing to select a boundary window around your South elevation.

7. <u>Select a window</u> (rectangular area) around your South elevation (Figure 9-2.3) and then <u>right-click to finish</u>.

    TIP: Note the following regarding your boundary window selection:

    ****You should try to pick a window as tight to the drawing as possible, leaving room for any anticipated additions to the drawing (e.g., more building or notes).*

    ****By default, the drawing title tag is placed just below the lower left corner of the view when it is placed on a sheet, so too much extra space to the left of the drawing would position the title tag so that it is not under any of the drawing.*

    ****If your drawing does grow larger than the Named View's specified boundary, you can use the Edit Boundaries feature (see Figure9-2.1) to resize the boundary.*

FIGURE 9-2.3
South Elevation; select window as shown to define view

8. Click **OK** to close the *New View* dialog and create the view.

9. Repeat the previous steps to create a *Named View* for the **North**, **East** and **West** elevations in your *Exterior Elevations* drawing.

When finished, you will see each *Named View* listed in the *View* dialog box (Figure 9-2.4).

FIGURE 9-2.4
View dialog; a named view created for each elevation in the Exterior Elevations drawing

10. **Open** your other drawings and create *Named Views* per the chart below.

Drawing name	Named View to create
Flr-B.dwg	Basement Floor Plan
Flr-1.dwg	First Floor Plan
Flr-2.dwg	Second Floor Drawing
Building Section.dwg	Building Section
Wall Section.dwg	Wall Section
Bathroom Elevation.dwg	Bathroom Elevation
Room Schedule.dwg	Room Finish Schedule
Site.dwg	Site Plan
Additional Task dwg's	*Name views appropriately*

> **FYI:** *Remember, these drawings will be referred to as the Resource Drawings in the Sheet Set Manager (on the Model Views tab).*

11. **Save** your drawings.

Next you will create the *Sheet Set Data* file via the *Sheet Set Manager*.

Setting Up a Sheet Set:

You will look at one of the methods provided to set up a *Sheet Set*. This involves using the *Create Sheet Set Wizard*.

12. Make sure a drawing is open. You must have at least one drawing open to get started; it can be a blank drawing or one of your project files.

13. **Open** the **Sheet Set Manager** by clicking its icon on the *View* tab, *Palettes* panel.

Sheet Set Manager

14. At the top of the *Sheet Set Manager* palette, click the down-arrow and then select **New Sheet Set...** from the menu (Figure 9-2.5).

FIGURE 9-2.5
Sheet Set Manager; click the Down-Arrow and select "New Sheet Set..." to start a new Sheet Set

This starts the *Sheet Set Manager Wizard* (Figure 9-2.6).

15. Click **Next**.

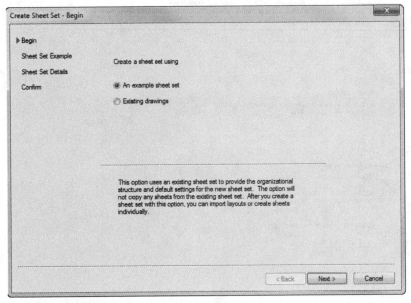

FIGURE 9-2.6
Create Sheet Set Wizard; Begin screen

16. Next, make sure **Architectural Imperial Sheet Set** is selected and then click **Next** (Figure 9-2.7).

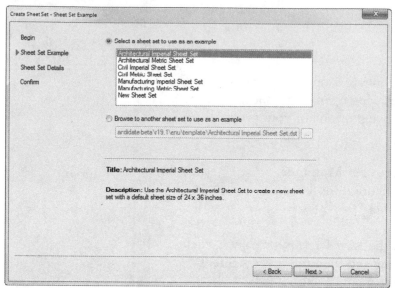

Create Sheet Set Wizard; Sheet Set Example screen

17. Enter the name of new *Sheet Set*; use your last name (e.g., *last name* Residence). See Figure 9-2.8.

18. Click the " 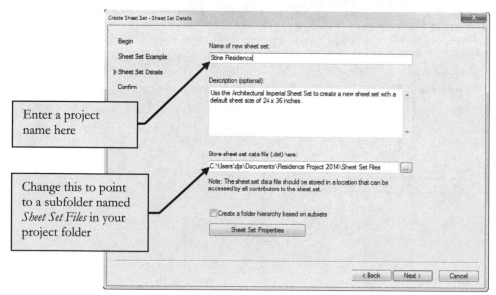 ton to change the location where the *Sheet Set Data* file will be stored; **a**.) Create a subfolder named <u>Sheet Set Files</u> in the folder that contains the files you created in this book, or **b**.) Select the new folder.

FIGURE 9-2.8
Create Sheet Set Wizard; Sheet Set Details screen

TIP: *To insure the remainder of this lesson proceeds smoothly, you should make sure all your project files are located in one folder. Only include the current files, not backup DWG (i.e., .BAK) files or old copies.*

You are now at the final screen of the wizard. You are given detailed information on the "what and where" for the new *Sheet Set* about to be created.

Click **Next** and then select **Finish** to create the new *Sheet Set* (Figure 9-2.9).

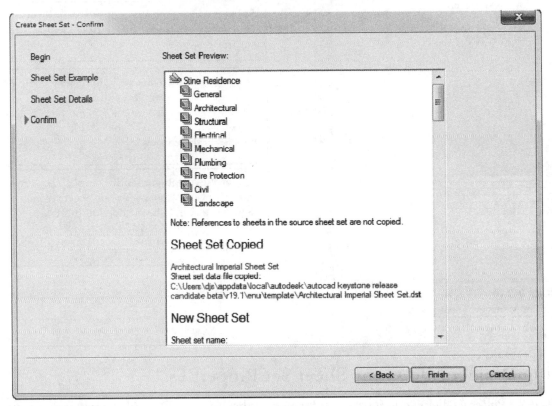

FIGURE 9-2.9
Create Sheet Set Wizard; Confirm screen

The wizard closes and the *Sheet Set Manager* is populated with the specified information. If you use *MS Windows Explorer* to browse to your *Sheet Set Files* folder, you will see a new file named "*Last name* Residence.dst"; this is the *Sheet Set Data* file previously discussed.

The *Sheet Set Example* file used contained several *Subsets* (e.g., Architectural, Structural, etc.), which are seen on the *Sheet List* tab (Figure 9-2.10). *Subsets* allow *Sheets* to be organized, by discipline in this example. The right-click menu allows you to easily add, rename or remove a *Subset* at anytime.

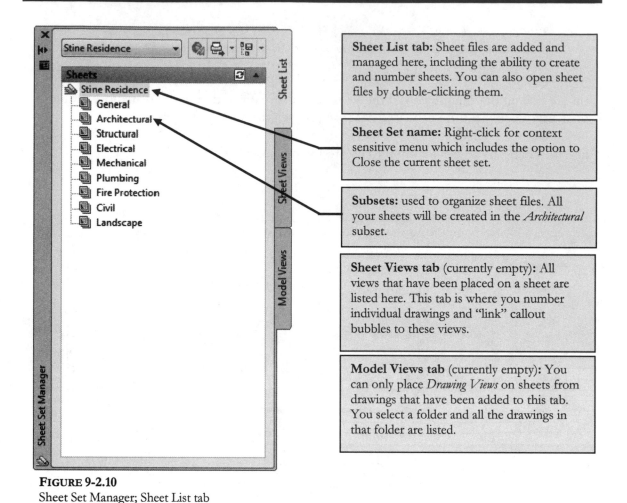

FIGURE 9-2.10
Sheet Set Manager; Sheet List tab

The following text boxes appear in the figure:

Sheet List tab: Sheet files are added and managed here, including the ability to create and number sheets. You can also open sheet files by double-clicking them.

Sheet Set name: Right-click for context sensitive menu which includes the option to Close the current sheet set.

Subsets: used to organize sheet files. All your sheets will be created in the *Architectural* subset.

Sheet Views tab (currently empty): All views that have been placed on a sheet are listed here. This tab is where you number individual drawings and "link" callout bubbles to these views.

Model Views tab (currently empty): You can only place *Drawing Views* on sheets from drawings that have been added to this tab. You select a folder and all the drawings in that folder are listed.

Adding Project Info to the Sheet Set Properties:

The *Sheet Set Properties* dialog contains key information that AutoCAD needs to properly manage and control the *Sheet Set*. Next you will enter the project name and address, which is automatically placed in the title block of each sheet in the set!

> **NOTE:** *For the remainder of this lesson, substitute your last name for Stine when referring to the sheet set/project name.*

19. In the *Sheet Set Manager*, on the *Sheet List* tab, right click on the sheet set name (*Stine Residence*) at the top of the list – under the *Sheets* label – and select **Properties** from the pop-up menu.

20. In the *Sheet Set Custom Properties* section, add information similar to that shown in **Figure 9-2.11**.

FIGURE 9-2.11
Create Sheet Set Properties; partial view of dialog

TIP: If you do not need one field, such as the "Project Address 3" line above, make it blank; otherwise any text entered will show up on the drawings.

21. Click **OK** to complete the changes.

Creating Sheets for Placing Named Views:

Creating a sheet with a title block, a number and client information has NEVER been easier in AutoCAD! In just minutes you will have all the empty sheets setup and ready for *Named Views* to be placed on them.

As you create sheets in the *Sheet Set Manager*, AutoCAD creates a drawing file in the specified folder (*Sheet Set Files* sub-folder in this example). This file IS the sheet. If the file is erased or corrupt, that sheet will no longer be available. Therefore, you should backup the files in the *Sheet Set Files* sub-folder, just as you would your *Resource Drawings* or any important files on your computer.

Next you will setup the entire set of sheets, starting with the project *Title* sheet.

22. On the *Sheet List* tab, in the *Sheet Set Manager*, right-click on the *Architectural* subset, and then click **New Sheet...** from the pop-up menu (Figure 9-2.12).

You are now in the *New Sheet* dialog box where you enter the sheet title and number, as well as specify the name of the drawing file that will be created.

23. Enter the following:

    a. Number: **A0**

    b. Sheet title: **Title Sheet**

    c. File name: *default*

    d. See **Figure 9-2.13**.

FIGURE 9-2.12
Sheet Set Manager; create new sheet

24. Click **OK** to create the sheet.

FIGURE 9-2.13
New Sheet dialog; enter sheet number, title and file name

You have just created your first sheet! You now see the sheet listed under the *Architectural* subset in the *Sheet Set Manager* (Figure9-2.14).

25. Per the steps above, create new sheets so that you have all the sheets listed in the table below.

FIGURE 9-2.14
Sheet Set Manager

Sheet name	Sheet number
Title Sheet	A0
Basement Floor Plan	A1
First Floor Plan	A2
Second Floor Plan	A3
Exterior Elevations	A4
Exterior Elevations	A5
Building Sections	A6
Wall Sections	A7
Interior Elevations	A8
Schedules	A9

Once finished, all the sheets will be listed in the *Sheet Set Manager* as shown in Figure 9-2.15.

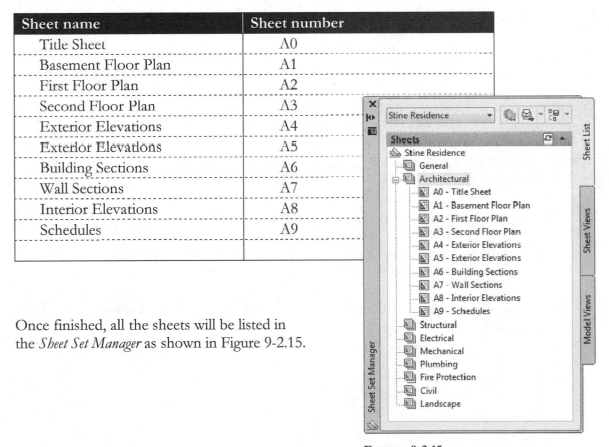

FIGURE 9-2.15
Sheet Manager; all sheets created in Architectural subset

A0 Title Sheet
AutoCAD Drawing
48.6 KB

A1 Basement Floor Plan
AutoCAD Drawing
48.7 KB

A2 First Floor Plan
AutoCAD Drawing
48.7 KB

A3 Second Floor Plan
AutoCAD Drawing
48.7 KB

A4 Exterior Elevations
AutoCAD Drawing
48.8 KB

A5 Exterior Elevations
AutoCAD Drawing
48.8 KB

A6 Building Sections
AutoCAD Drawing
48.7 KB

A7 Wall Sections
AutoCAD Drawing
48.7 KB

A8 Interior Elevations
AutoCAD Drawing
48.8 KB

A9 Schedules
AutoCAD Drawing
48.7 KB

Stine Residence
AutoCAD Sheet Set
35.1 KB

Take a minute to browse to the *Sheet Set* files folder you previously created and notice an AutoCAD file has been created for each sheet (Figure 9-2.16).

These files can be opened here, by double-clicking, or from *Open* on the *QAT* within AutoCAD.

Next you will see how the *Sheet Set Manager* allows you to do this.

FIGURE 9-2.16
Windows Explorer view of your *Sheet Set Files* sub-folder you created in your project folder; files automatically created with the Sheet Set Manager. Be sure to backup these files.

Opening Sheets from the Sheet Set Manager:

In the *Sheet Set Manager* you can double-click on a sheet title (on the *Sheet List* tab) to open the drawing file that represents that sheet. Once the drawing is open you can save and close it just like any other drawing file.

Next you will open the exterior elevation sheet A4 to place one of your drawings on it.

26. On the *Sheet List* tab, in *Sheet Set Manager*, double-click on the sheet title
A4 – Exterior Elevations.

The drawing **A4 -Exterior Elevations** (located in your *SheetSet Files* sub-folder) is now open.

27. **Zoom In** to the lower right corner of the sheet to see the information that was automatically entered in the title block (Figure 9-2.17).

28. Notice that the sheet number, project name and date have been automatically added to the title block.

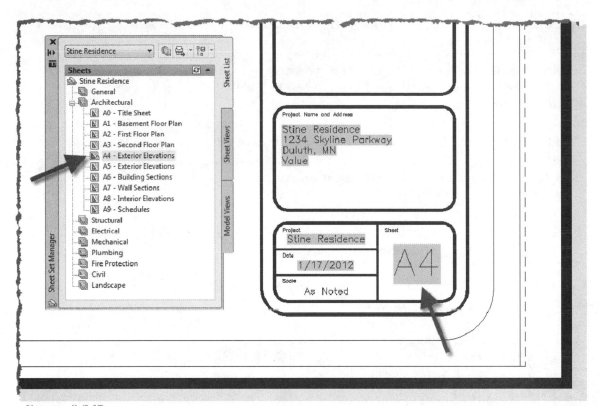

FIGURE 9-2.17
Sheet A4 – Exterior Elevations; Shaded text are fields which are modified/updated using the Sheet Set Manager

29. **Zoom Previous** so you see the entire sheet.

Contos Residence

*Image courtesy of Anderson Architects
Alan H. Anderson, Architect, Duluth, MN*

Specifying *Resource Drawing* Locations:

You are just about ready to start placing drawings on sheets. But first you need to tell the *Sheet Set Manager* where to look for your drawing files that contain the *Named Views*. You will do this next.

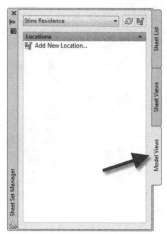

30. Click on the *Model Views* tab in the *Sheet Set Manager*.

31. Double-click the **Add New Location...** icon (Figure 9-2.18).

32. Browse to the folder where all your drawings, created in the book, are stored and then click **OK**.

FIGURE 9-2.18
Model Views tab;
no folder listed yet

Notice in Figure 9-2.19 that the folder you selected is now listed in the *Locations* pane (on the *Model Views* tab).

Notice, like other palettes, you are able to adjust the size of the palette. This is useful when the information runs past the current width of the palette. Simply place your cursor near one of the edges and drag the palette wider or narrower.

The *Refresh* button, in the upper right, will scan your hard drive to see if any files have been added or changed, and update the listing.

FIGURE 9-2.19
Model Views tab;
Residence Project 2014 folder and contents now listed

The "plus" symbol next to the new *Locations* folder allows you to expand the view to show the drawings listed in that folder. After clicking the plus symbol, the drawings and folders are displayed and the "plus" changes to a "minus" symbol (Figure 9-2.20).

Adding Named Views to Sheets:

You are now to the point where you can start placing drawings (*Named Views*) on your *Sheets*. Basically, you drag on a *Named View* from the *Model Views* tab onto your *Sheet*.

FIGURE 9-2.20
Model Views tab; Named Views in
Exterior Elevations.dwg

Similar to the previous discussion on how the "plus" symbol expands the *Locations* folder, the "plus" symbol next to the drawings (listed in the *Locations* folder) expands that drawing's view to display its *Named Views*.

First you will open a sheet to place a drawing (*Named View*) on.

33. On the *Sheet List* tab, double-click the **A4 – Exterior Elevations** sheet to open it (if not already open).

34. Click the *Model Views* tab to make it current.

35. Click the "**plus**" symbol next to the **Exterior Elevations** drawing to view that drawing's *Named Views*.

You can now see the four *Named Views* you created in the "Exterior Elevations" drawing (Figure 9-2.20).

36. Click and drag the **South Elevation** from the *Sheet Set Manager* onto your **A4 – Exterior Elevations** sheet (Figure 9-2.21).

Move your cursor about the screen to see how the view is attached to your cursor and AutoCAD is prompting for the location at which to place the drawing. Before you click to place the drawing, you need to specify the scale at which you want the drawing printed.

37. **Right-click** to display the *Insertion Scale* pop-up menu (Figure 9-2.20).

38. Select **¼″ = 1′-0″** from the list.

Notice how the size of the drawing changes to correspond to the selected scale. Displaying the drawing at the correct scale helps you to correctly position the drawing on the sheet. You should also notice that a drawing title tag is positioned below and to the left of your view which you will look at closer after the view is placed.

FIGURE 9-2.21
A4 - Exterior Elevations; placing the South Elevation view and right-clicking to see scale options

39. Position your mouse so the elevation is centered on the sheet and then click to place the view on the sheet.

You have placed your first drawing on a sheet (Figure 9-2.22)! In just minutes you could have all the *Named Views* placed, but first you will explore a few other options and see how they are affected when you change a few sheet numbers.

FIGURE 9-2.22
A4 - Exterior Elevations; South Elevation placed at ¼″=1′-0″

40. **Zoom In** on the *Drawing Title* tag (Figure9-2.23).

Click this arrow *Grip* to adjust the length of the horizontal line.

FIGURE 9-2.23
A4 - Exterior Elevations; zoomed in on drawing title tag

Notice that the drawing name has been automatically filled in using the name you provided when you created the *Named View* in the *Resource Drawing* (exterior elevations.dwg).

Also notice that the drawing scale has been added and, of course, corresponds to the scale you selected when you placed the view.

The only field not filled in yet is the drawing number. You enter the drawing number for a view, once it is placed on a sheet, in the *Sheet Set Manager.* Next you will provide the sheet number via the *Sheet Set Manager.*

TIP: If the fields are not visible, delete the symbol and then right-click on the view name in Figure 9-2.24 and select "place view label block."

WARNING: Do not change the number in the drawing as it will be overwritten by the Sheet Set Manager.

41. Select **Sheet Views** tab.

Notice that the *South Elevation* view is listed. Eventually all your *Named Views* will be listed here once they are all placed on sheets (Figure 9-2.24).

42. Right-click on the *South Elevation* view and select **Rename & Renumber...** from the pop-up menu.

43. Enter number **1** in the *Number* textbox (Figure 9-2.25).

44. Click **OK** to apply the change.

FIGURE 9-2.24
Sheet Set Manager; View List tab

FIGURE 9-2.25
Rename and Renumber View; enter number 1

You will notice that your drawing has not updated yet. The following step will cause the drawing title tag to update.

45. Type **Regen** and then press **Enter**.

The drawing title tag now has the number 1 in the circle (Figure 9-2.26). A few other key events cause AutoCAD to update the tags, for example, opening or plotting a drawing.

FIGURE 9-2.26
A4- Exterior Elevations; field updated automatically

Placing Callout Tags:

Another powerful feature related to *Sheet Sets* is the ability to place *Callout* tags that are automatically cross-referenced with a sheet and drawing number. Next you will place an elevation *Callout* tag (that references the South Elevation) on the floor plan.

First, though, you will need to place the first floor plan on the appropriate sheet.

46. Per the steps previously outlined, place the **First Floor Plan** view at ¼″ = 1′-0″ (from the Flr-1.dwg resource drawing) onto sheet **A2 – First Floor Plan** (Figure9-2.27).

> *TIP: Open the sheet from the Sheet List tab and then drag the view from the Model Views tab.*

FIGURE 9-2.27
A2- First Floor Plan; First floor plan view placed on sheet at 1/4″

47. **Zoom In** to the bottom center of the floor plan sheet.

48. On the *Sheet Views* tab, right-click on the *South Elevation* view, and then select **Place Callout Block → Callout** (Figure 9-2.28).

FIGURE 9-2.28
View List tab; right click on '1 – South Elevation'

49. Click to place the elevation tag approximately as shown in Figure 9-2.29 (it will be pointing to the right).

Notice that the *Elev. Indicator* has been automatically filled out. It references both the sheet and drawing number where the elevation (i.e., the elevation the tag is pointing at) can be found.

The *Callout* symbol is a *Dynamic Block* that is setup to allow easy rotation of the pointer arrow (without rotating the text). The default orientation is pointing to the right, so you will adjust the arrow so it points north. The next numbered steps will walk you through this process. As you recall, selecting a *Dynamic Block* causes its special control *Grips* to display. One of these controls the rotation of the arrow (which has been setup to snap to certain angles).

50. Click to select the symbol.

51. Click the round *Grip*.

52. Move the cursor so the arrow is pointing north and then click.

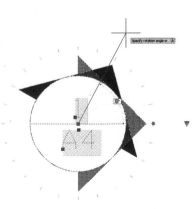

That's it; the callout has been modified.

Place the *Callout Block* approximately as shown, just below the dimensions and centered on the building.

FIGURE 9-2.29
First Floor Plan sheet; elevation callout placed

53. **Save** both your elevation and plan sheet (*Save* on *QAT*); don't forget to save often so you don't lose any work.

Changing Sheet Numbers:

Looking at Figure 9-2.22, you realize that you will need two more exterior elevation sheets because one elevation takes up most of the sheet at ¼″ = 1'-0″. Next you will increment all the sheets that come after the exterior elevation sheets by 2 and then add two more exterior elevations sheets; all this is done in the *Sheet Set Manager*.

54. On the *Sheet List* tab, right click on sheet **A9 – Schedules** and select **Rename & Renumber**.

55. Make the following changes in the dialog box:
    a. Change the *Number* to **A11**
    b. Check <u>all</u> boxes under **Rename options**
       TIP: If the rename file options are not checkable, the file is probably open and needs to be closed first.
    c. Click **OK** (Figure 9-2.30)

This is similar to renumbering and renaming a view on the *View List* tab (look back at Figure 9-2.24).

FIGURE 9-2.30
Rename & Renumber Sheet; change sheet A9 to A11

FIGURE 9-2.31
Sheet View tab; last six sheets renumbered, making room to insert two sheets

56. **Renumber** all the sheets after sheet *A3 – Second Floor* to make room to insert two new sheets numbered *A4* and *A5* (you will add the new sheets later). (See Figure 9-2.31.)

   TIP: *When renumbering, use the* Previous *button to step back through the sheets.*

   FYI: *Files (i.e., sheets) must be closed before renaming can be done. Opened files cannot be renamed.*

Normally, changing sheet numbers is not a good idea because, no matter how hard you look, you will usually miss one reference bubble, leaving the bubble pointing to the wrong sheet. This leads to confusion and possible loss of time and money.

AutoCAD has provided a solution to this problem. The callout bubbles, drawing titles and sheet borders are all linked to the information in the *Sheet Set Manager*. So once you changed the sheet numbers in the *Sheet Set Manager*, all the sheets were (or will be) updated automatically. You will verify this next.

57. In the **A6 – Exterior Elevations** sheet, zoom into the lower right corner to see the sheet number (Figure 9-2.32).

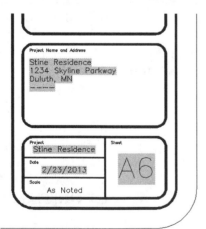

FIGURE 9-2.32
A6 – Exterior Elevations sheet; sheet number in title block has been updated automatically

TIP: You may need to Regen the drawing to see the change.

As you can see, the sheet number has been updated automatically!

What about the elevation tag you placed on the floor plan sheet?

58. On the **A2 – First Floor Plan** sheet, **Zoom In** on the callout bubble (elev indicator). See Figure 9-2.33.

> *TIP: You may need to Regen the drawing to see the change. However, if the file is closed and reopened the update will be automatic.*

FIGURE 9-2.33
A2 – First Floor Plan sheet; sheet number in callout block has been updated automatically.

As you can see, the elevation callout tag has been updated automatically, thus eliminating the possibility of cross-reference errors when this system is used.

59. Add the following sheets to complete the set:

> *TIP: You can drag the sheet labels (on the Sheet List tab) to change the listed order.*

Sheet name	Sheet number
Exterior Elevations *Filename: A4 Exterior Elevations*	A4
Exterior Elevations *Filename: A5 Exterior Elevations*	A5

60. Place the remaining views (see step 36) on the appropriate sheets.

> *FYI: The room schedule view should be placed at a scale of 1:1.*

61. On the *Sheet Views* tab, give each view a number (see the *TIP* on the next page).

TIP:

Drawings are typically numbered in the direction indicated below. The first drawings are placed in the upper right, and fill in the sheet toward the left. The main reason for starting on the right is this: if a sheet is only half full (for example); you would not have to open the set all the way to see the drawings on that sheet.

Also, it is usually a good idea to wait until the sheet is mostly full before numbering drawings. That way you can organize the drawings neatly on the sheet and avoid a situation where the drawing numbers are not in sequence.

62. Place **Callout** blocks on your floor plan sheets to reference all your elevations (interior and exterior). See Figure 9-2.34.

FIGURE 9-2.34

A3 – Second Floor Plan sheet, callout bubble added

> *TIP:* The rectangle surrounding your drawings when placed on a sheet (cf. Figure
> 9-2.34) is called a viewport. This line cannot be erased, but it can be moved to its own Layer
> (e.g., Viewport) and then that layer can be Frozen; the drawing will still be visible but the rectangle
> (viewport) will not.

63. **Save** and close all your open drawing files.

64. **Close** the *Sheet Set Data* file via the *Sheet Set Manager;* right-click on the *Sheet Set* project name (i.e., *Stine Residence*) and select **Close Sheet Set**.

    a.   Any drawings opened with the *Sheet Set Manager* can be closed similar to any other AutoCAD drawing file. They can later be opened again via the *Sheet Set Manager* or using the normal *Open* command.

This concludes the study on *Sheet Sets.*

Manually Setting up a Sheet:

On occasion you will want to know how to setup a sheet without using the *Sheet Set Manager*. This will help you better understand what the *Sheet Set Manager* is automatically doing for you every time you add a view to a sheet.

You will use the *Layout View* existing in your Flr-1 drawing. This tab came from the template which you started. Every drawing must have a *Model Space* tab and at least one *Layout View* (paper space) tab. If you recall, after creating each new drawing you had to switch to *Model Space* because the *Layout View* tab was current.

As previously stated, *Model Space* is where all the drawing is done and *Layout View* is where the plot sheet is setup. On the plot sheet you draw a special rectangle, called a *Viewport*, what looks into *Model Space*. You can set the scale for the *Viewport*. Also, you can have several *Viewports* in the *Layout View*. They can each have a different scale if you need it, and they can look at the same drawing. That is, you can have one Viewport looking at the overall floor plan at ⅛″ = 1′-0″ and another looking at the toilet rooms only, at ¼″ = 1′-0″.

65. Open your **Flr-1** drawing file. You do not need to have the *Sheet Set Manager* open for this.

66. Switch to the **Arch D** *Layout View* tab (a.k.a., *Paper Space*).

67. Type **MV** to activate the *Make Viewport* command.

68. Pick two points on the screen to define the extents of the *Viewport* (Figure 9-2.35).

    You now see everything in *Model Space*, which is zoomed to fit the *Viewport*.

FIGURE 9-2.35 Manually adding a viewport

69. Select the *Viewport*, and set the scale to **¼″ = 1′-0″** via the *Status Bar* (Figure 9-2.36)

The scale is now set correctly. Sometimes it is necessary to pan the drawing within the *Viewport*. This can be done by double-clicking within the *Viewport* and using the *Pan* command. Be careful not to zoom as this willmess up the scale. When finished, double-click outside of the *Viewport* or

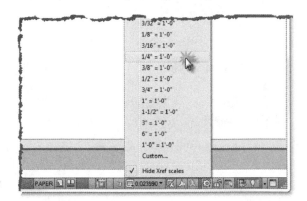

FIGURE 9-2.36 Setting the scale for the selected viewport

select the Model button on the Status Bar (which says Paper when you are not in the Viewport).

When the *Viewport* is selected you may also click the **Lock** icon on the Status Bar to lock the scale for the selected *Viewport* so it does not accidentally change (see image below).

FIGURE 9-2.37 Locking the scale of a manually created viewport

70. Create another *Viewport* as shown in the image below (a smaller rectangle within the larger one), zoom in on the toilet room and set the scale to **1/2″ = 1′-0″**.

   TIP: Press Ctrl+R *to toggle between Viewports once one is active.*

71. Create a *Layer* called **Viewport**, move the two *Viewports* to this *Layer* and turn its visibility off.

   FYI: It is not possible to place items on a layer coming from an xref (even though they are listed in the Layer Manager). You must create a Viewport layer if one does not already exist in your drawing.

72. **Save** your Flr-1 drawing file.

FIGURE 9-2.38 Two viewports created

Exercise 9-3:
Sheet Index

Introduction:

In this exercise you will take a look at the *Sheet Index* feature that takes advantage of both *Sheet Sets* and *Tables*. The *Sheet Index* feature extracts information stored in the *Sheet Set Data* file (sheet name and number) and then generates a *Table* to be placed on one of your sheets in the *Sheet Set*.

The *Sheet Index* has hyperlinks embedded in each listing; thus, you can "Ctrl+click" on a sheet name or number to open that sheet. As you will see in the next *Lesson*, these hyperlinks transfer to the electronic set (DWF file) which allows a client or consultant to easily navigate the set of drawings.

Opening an existing Sheet Set; via *Recent* flyout or *Open...* and browse

1. **Open** your *Sheet Set Data* file (*your name* Residence.dst).

    FYI: *The DST file can also be opened from the Application Menu → Recent Files.*

2. Open **A0 – Title Sheet** from the *Sheet List* tab.

3. Using **Mtext**, add large, bold text as shown in Figure 9-3.1.

    a. *Font:*   **Arial Black**

    b. *Height:*   **1″**

FIGURE 9-3.1
A0 – Title Sheet; text added to sheet

FYI: A Title sheet usually has the project title as its focal point. Additionally, you will typically find the following information:

- ◆ *Rendering or picture of a model of the project*
- ◆ *Sheet Index*
- ◆ *Abbreviation Legend (e.g., TYP. means TYPICAL)*
- ◆ *Symbol Legend (e.g., show a swatch of AR-CONC hatch pattern and identify it as the symbol for concrete)*
- ◆ *Building Code/Zoning Summary*
- ◆ *Site Plan (typically on smaller projects)*

The *Legends*, which are used over and over, without modification, can be created in a separate drawing and inserted as a block on the *Title* sheet.

Next you will insert a *Sheet Index*.

4. Right click on the *Sheet Set* project title (at the top of the list on the *Sheet List* tab).

5. Select **Insert Sheet List Table...** from the pop-up menu (Figure 9-3.2).

You are now in the *Insert Sheet List Table* dialog (Figure 9-3.3).

6. Click **OK** to accept the defaults and close the dialog.

7. Click anywhere on your *A0 - Title Sheet* to place the *Sheet List* table on the sheet.

The table is now placed on your *Title* sheet (Figure 9-3.4).

FIGURE 9-3.2
Sheet Set Manager; right click on project title (Stine Residence in this example)

FIGURE 9-3.3
Insert Sheet List Table dialog

Sheet List Table	
Sheet Number	Sheet Title
A0	Title Sheet
A1	Basement Floor Plan
A2	First Floor Plan
A3	Second Floor Plan
A4	Exterior Elevations
A5	Exterior Elevations
A6	Exterior Elevations
A7	Exterior Elevations
A8	Building Section
A9	Wall Sections
A10	Interior Elevations
A11	Schedules

FIGURE 9-3.4
A0 – Title Sheet; inserted sheet list table

After inserting the *Sheet List*, you decide to change the justification of the data cell so that everything is left-justified. You will make this change now...

8. From the *Annotate* tab, select the **Table Style** link (the small arrow in lower-right of the *Table* panel).

9. Select the ***Standard*** style and click the **Modify** button in the *Table Style Manager*.

10. On the *General* tab (for the **Data** *Cell styles*), set the *Alignment* to **Top Left**.

11. Click **OK** and **Close** to close all the open dialog boxes.

As you can see, this is the same process previously described in the *Room Finish Schedule* exercise, because the *Sheet List* is a table!

Sheet List Table	
Sheet Number	Sheet Title
A0	Title Sheet
A1	Basement Floor Plan
A2	First Floor Plan
A3	Second Floor Plan
A4	Exterior Elevations
A5	Exterior Elevations
A6	Exterior Elevations
A7	Exterior Elevations
A8	Building Section
A9	Wall Sections
A10	Interior Elevations
A11	Schedules

FIGURE 9-3.5
A0 – Title Sheet; modified sheet list table

If you add a sheet or change a sheet number via the *Sheet Set Manager*, the *Sheet List* can be updated by selecting the edge of the table, right-clicking and then selecting *Update Table Data Links.*

Inserting Raster Images into a Drawing:

While you still have your *Title* sheet open, you will take a quick look at inserting a raster image into a drawing. This can be done in any drawing file. The process is similar to Xref-ing a drawing.

This example will involve adding a raster image to the *Title* sheet. Ideally, you would be adding a raster image that contains a rendering of the exterior of your building. However, because you do not have one at the moment, you will insert an image that is installed with AutoCAD 2014.

12. From the *Insert* tab, select the **Attach** icon.

13. Browse to the following folder: **C:\Program Files\Autodesk\AutoCAD 2014 - English\Sample\VBA**

14. Select the file **WorldMap.TIF** and click **Open** (Figure 9-3.6).

FIGURE 9-3.6 Select Reference File dialog

You are now in a dialog which is similar to inserting external references (Xref's).

15. Accept the default settings and click **OK** (Figure 9-3.7).

TIP:
Click the Show Details button to view size and resolution information for the selected image file.

FIGURE 9-3.7 Image dialog

You now see the image outline near your cursor for insertion.

16. Click to place the image approximately centered below your large text.

17. At this point you can visually move the mouse to adjust the image size or type a value (you will accept the default value of 1).

18. Press **Enter** to accept the default scale of 1.

> *FYI: The image can be moved, rotated, scaled, or erased at any time (after insertion) using the standard AutoCAD commands.*

> *TIP: If you don't want the rectangle around the image, you can turn it off using the **image frame** variable. The default value is **1**, which makes the outline show and plot; **0** makes the outline invisible and the image is not selectable (i.e., you cannot move, scale, etc.); **2** makes the outline show but not plot.*

19. **Move** the *Sheet Index* to center it under the image.

The *Title* sheet should now look like Figure 9-3.8.

> *FYI: You can detach or unload images via the External References Palette... (see the next page).*

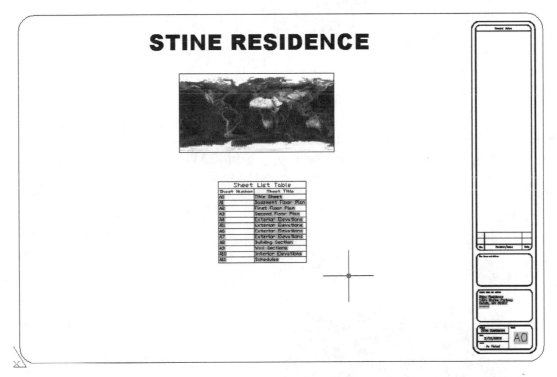

FIGURE 9-3.8

If you select the image and then right-click you will see a few options for editing the selected image also, selecting External References... from the *Insert* tab loads a *Palette* that shows all referenced files. Notice the Ribbon has several settings related to the image when it is selected (see images at the top of the next page).

Ribbon; image selected

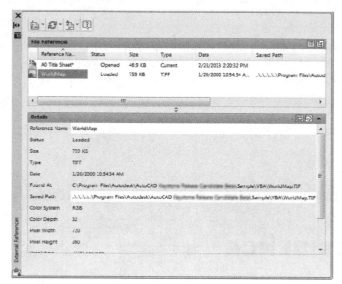

External References Palette

You can also scan a blueprint of a floor plan (or anything else) and use the scanned file to trace over with AutoCAD lines. You need to use Scale and its subcommand Reference to accurately adjust the size of the image before tracing.

You can also place photos of existing conditions on a sheet and add (AutoCAD) notes and leaders on top of the photo. For example, point out an entry roof to be removed on the front of a building (see example image below from an AutoCAD drawing).

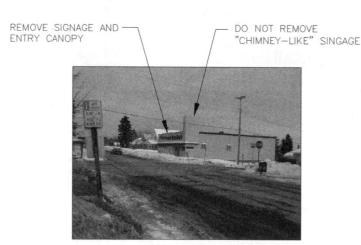

For more advanced raster placement and editing tools check out **Autodesk Raster Design**. This is an add-in to AutoCAD which allows you to select, move, delete and erase portions of an image and much more. It is often used to manipulate scanned hand drawn sheets.

20. **Save** your **A0 – Title Sheet** drawing.

That completes the introduction to *Sheet List* tables and raster images.

Self-Exam:

The following questions can be used as a way to check your knowledge of this lesson. The answers can be found at the bottom of this page.

1. The *Table Manager* is where you change a table's text height. (T/F)

2. You need to create *Named Views* for each drawing/detail that you want to place on a sheet. (T/F)

3. Once a *Sheet List* table is placed you have to manually update it if you add or remove any sheets. (T/F)

4. When dragging a view, from the *Sheet Set Manager* onto a sheet, you _____ to get a listing of scales to insert the view at.

5. In the *Named Views* dialog, you can change the view's boundary.(T/F)

Review Questions:

The following questions may be assigned by your instructor as a way to assess your knowledge of this section. Your instructor has the answers to the review questions.

1. Once a *Table* is created, you cannot add rows or columns. (T/F)

2. It is not possible to combine two or more table cells into one. (T/F)

3. AutoCAD creates a drawing file each time you create a new sheet in the *Sheet Set Manager.* (T/F)

4. Views are placed on sheets by dragging the view name from the _____ tab; views are numbered (and renamed) on the _____ tab in the *Sheet Set Manager*.

5. You cannot specify where the *Sheet Set Data* file is stored. (T/F)

6. The bottom number, in an elevation callout bubble, indicates the _____ number the elevation is located on.

7. This icon (⊞) allows you to insert a _____.

8. In a *Sheet Set*, sheets can be organized using _____.

9. You should not move or rename the files created by the *Sheet Set Manager* (except what you are able to do in the *Manager* itself). (T/F)

10. You right-click on the _____ to see the *Insert Sheet List* option.

Additional Tasks:

Task 9-1: Create a Door Schedule

Using the techniques learned in Lesson 9-1, create a door schedule and place it on the *Schedules* sheet. You will need to number the doors in your plans. Typically, a door has the same number as the room it swings into. If a door has more than one door (like the *Master Bedroom*), you add letters to the number (i.e., 201A and 201B). Include the following columns in your schedule: Door Number, Door Size, Door Material, Door Type, Frame Material, Frame Type, Jamb Detail, Head Detail, Sill Detail, Fire Rating, Remarks.

Task 9-2: Place All Your Views on Sheets

If you have been creating the drawings suggested in the previous "additional tasks", you can place them on the appropriate sheets; adding sheets if necessary.

Task 9-3: Place Callout Blocks to Reference Your Drawings

You can add additional callout blocks:

- ♦ Any other interior elevations you may have drawn.
- ♦ Building Section: you can draw a line through your floor plan, where your building section is cut, and place an elevation callout block at one end of the line to reference the building section.
- ♦ You can add a note to your floor plan that says "For room finish schedule see" and place the "basic" callout block next to the note.
- ♦ Wall Section: draw a rectangle (Fillet its corners and change the linetype to dashed) around a portion of your building section that represents the extents of your wall section and then place a "basic" callout bubble with a line drawn from the bubble to the rectangle.

Task 9-4: Add Additional Raster Images to Your Drawings

Add additional images to your drawings. If you have a scanner, you may try sketching a perspective of your building, scan it to a raster file and then place it on your *Title* sheet.

Lesson 10
Residential Project: LINEWEIGHTS & PLOTTING::

In this final lesson you will look at how lineweights work in AutoCAD. Finally, you will take another look at plotting; this time plotting to scale from the *Sheet Set Manager*.

When finished with this chapter you will have a formidable part of a set of residential working drawings.

Exercise 10-1:
Lineweights

Introduction:

As previously discussed, lineweights are an important part of a set of architectural drawings. They help to differentiate between the many lines contained in a drawing; more specifically, lineweights show what part of the drawing is in section versus elevation.

Hand drafters would create different line thicknesses as they drew, whereas CAD drawings typically don't show the actually lineweight until the drawing is printed.

AutoCAD has three primary ways to handle lineweights. This book will describe all three and give an overview of two methods. Then, you will use one method on your floor plan drawings.

Three Methods Described:

Color Dependent Plot Style:
With this method, the thickness of the plotted line is based on the color of the line whether the color is set ByLayer or ByEntity. This used to be the only method available in AutoCAD and is probably still the most used.

Named Plot Style:
With this method you assign a Named Plot Style to each Layer (and even ByEntity – not recommended). A Named Plot Style has a name, like Heavy, and has several settings assigned to it (i.e., line thickness, screened, etc.). A group of Named Plot Styles are stored in a file called a "Named Plot Style Table".

Lineweight ByLayer:
With this method, a Plot Style Table is not used (neither color nor named). Rather, the lineweight is set by the Lineweight column in the Layer Manager (or ByEntity in the Properties Dialog – not recommended). Note that the Lineweight column only applies when a Plot Style Table is not selected in Page Setup (Page Setup will be covered shortly).

Example of the "Lineweight ByLayer" Method:

Here you will take a look at a sample drawing, located on the Autodesk website, which uses this method. Because of the nature of this sample drawing, it has the lineweights set *ByEntity* rather than the preferred *ByLayer* method. However, we will use this drawing to understand this method of applying lineweights and why the *ByLayer* method is more preferable.

1. In your web browser (e.g. MS Internet Explorer), go to **http://www.autodesk.com/autocad-samples**, right-click **Line Weights**, and then click **Save Target As**. Save the file to your desktop and then open it.

By default, you should be on the layout titled "**Letter Size**" and see the image shown in Figure 10-1.1. However, you may not see the actual line thickness of each line yet; if not, you will set this next.

2. To toggle the *Lineweight* on-screen visibility on or off, click the **Show/Hide Lineweight** (LWT) button on the *Status Bar* (Figure 10-1.2).

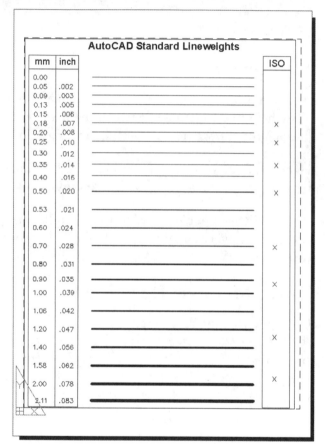

AutoCAD Standard Lineweights

mm	inch		ISO
0.00			
0.05	.002		
0.09	.003		
0.13	.005		
0.15	.006		
0.18	.007		x
0.20	.008		
0.25	.010		x
0.30	.012		
0.35	.014		x
0.40	.016		
0.50	.020		x
0.53	.021		
0.60	.024		
0.70	.028		x
0.80	.031		
0.90	.035		x
1.00	.039		
1.06	.042		
1.20	.047		
1.40	.056		x
1.58	.062		
2.00	.078		x
2.11	.083		

FIGURE 10-1.1
Sample Drawing; Lineweights.dwg

FIGURE 10-1.2
Status Bar; LWT stands for Lineweights

The **LWT** button works for any of the methods of defining lineweights discussed.

3.   Switch to *Model Space*.

The line thicknesses in *Model Space* are exaggerated. Most users do not typically have the lineweight visibility turned on when doing day-to-day drafting.

4.   Click the **Show/Hide Lineweight** button on the *Status Bar* to turn **off** the onscreen lineweight visibility.

The Lineweight column in the *Layer Properties Manager* controls the lineweight for each *Layer*. So anything drawn on a *Layer*, which has its lineweight property set to 0.13mm, will always print at 0.13mm (unless the lineweight has been changed for one or more lines in the *Properties* dialog; this overrides the *Layer* setting).

5.   **Open** the ***Layer Properties Manager*** (Figure 10-1.3).

FIGURE 10-1.3
Lineweights Sample Drawing; Lineweight column used when a Plot Style Table is not used.

The highlighted area in Figure 10-1.3 is the *Lineweight* column that you would adjust to various lineweights. So if you want everything drawn on layer *Lines* to be 0.70mm, you would adjust the *Lineweight* setting for the *Lines* layer to 0.70mm. This drawing actually has an override set for each line via the *Properties Palette*; you will look at these values in a moment.

As mentioned earlier, for AutoCAD to use these settings you need to make sure that a *Plot Style Table* is not selected in *Page Setup*. You will verify this next.

6. Right-click on the *Model Space* tab and then select **Page Setup Manager...** from the menu.

7. Click **Modify...** to adjust the default settings for the *Model* tab (Figure 10-1.4).

Notice, in the image below (Figure10-1.5) that a *Plot Style Table* is not specified; that is, it is set to *None*.

8. **Close** the open dialogs.

FIGURE 10-1.4 Page Setup Manager

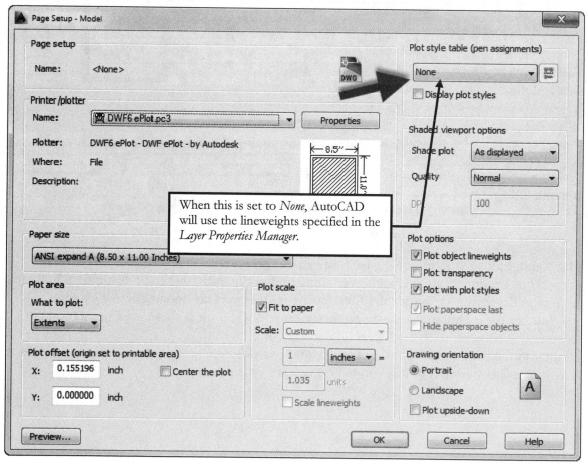

When this is set to *None*, AutoCAD will use the lineweights specified in the *Layer Properties Manager*.

FIGURE 10-1.5 Lineweights Sample Drawing; Page Setup

The last variation on this method is setting the lineweight *ByEntity*, which overrides the setting in the *Layer Manager*. It is generally recommended that you do <u>not</u> change settings (such as color, lineweight, etc.) *ByEntity*. The reason for this is that it is difficult to change the settings of several lines that have been changed *ByEntity*. Whereas, when you want to change the color of all the lines on layer *A-Wall*, all you have to do is change the color one time in the *Layer Manager*. Finally, having all the settings for an entity set to *ByLayer* allows for more control over *Externally Referenced* drawings.

Even though changing settings *ByEntity* is not recommended, the sample drawing is setup this way. Next you will look at this *ByEntity* type of modification to better understand what has been described.

9. Select the **0.35mm** line (i.e., the horizontal line to the right of the 0.35mm label). (See Figure 10-1.1.)

10. Right-click and select **Properties** (Figure 10-1.6).

Notice that the *Lineweight* setting for the selected line is set to 0.35mm, so no matter which *Layer* this line is on, it will always print 0.35mm thick.

The lineweight for the selected entity could be changed via the *Properties* dialog shown in Figure10-1.6. In addition to several other lineweights, you can select *ByLayer*; this setting uses the lineweight assigned to the *Layer* and is generally the preferred method of assigning lineweights (i.e., *ByLayer*).

11. Select a few other lines and look at their properties; notice that each line has its *Lineweight* setting changed (to match its corresponding label in the case of this drawing).

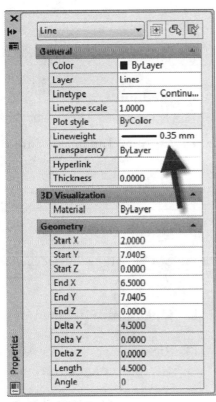

FIGURE 10-1.6
Properties; 0.35mm line selected

TIP: You may want to print the Lineweight.dwg sample drawing so you have a reference sheet showing what each line thickness really looks like printed on paper. Switching to the Letter Size Layout, you should be all set to print to an 8½″ x 11″ paper; you should only have to select the printer.

12. **Close** the Lineweight.dwg drawing file <u>without</u> saving.

Applying the "Color Dependent Plot Style" Method to Your Drawings:

Now you will apply lineweights to your floor plans. Below, you will take a minute to study lineweight theory; that is, what should be drawn with a heavy line and what should be drawn with a light line.

For floor plans:

- **Heaviest Lines**:   Wall lines and openings in floor; any major building component in section (e.g., column) **0.60mm**.

- **Medium Lines**:   Objects like cabinets, doors and windows should be the next heaviest **0.30mm**.

- **Lightest Lines**:   Any lines on the floor (e.g., furniture) and window sill lines should be the lightest lines **0.05mm**.

- **Light Gray Lines**:   Hatch patterns, such as ceramic tile or a recessed slab area, should be a light gray line so it is not too intense (use one of the screened plot styles) **0.10mm**.

For interior elevations lineweight descriptions, see page 7-20.

13. **Open** your **Flr-2** drawing.

14. Right-click on the *Model* tab and select **Page Setup Manager...** from the pop-up menu.

15. Click the **Modify...** button.

16. From the *Plot Style Table* drop-down list, select **New...** (Figure 10-1.7).

FIGURE 10-1.7
Page Setup; creating a new Plot Style Table

TIP: *If you only see tables that end with. STB, you started your drawing with the wrong template.*
You need to copy/paste your drawing into the correct template file per Lesson 3 – page 3-1.

You are now in the *Add Color-Dependent Plot Style Table Wizard*, which will walk you through the steps and information necessary to create a *Plot Style Table*.

17. Select **Start from scratch** and then click **Next >**.

18. Type **your last name** for the *Plot Style Table* file name and then click **Next >**.

19. Accept the default settings and click **Finish**.

Your new *Plot Style Table* is now selected as current in *Page Setup*. Next you will modify your new table so that each of the first seven AutoCAD colors equals a particular lineweight.

20. Click the **Edit Plot Style Table** icon.

21. Click on the *Form View* tab.

22. Modify each of the first seven *Plot Styles* (i.e., Color 1 thru Color 7) so the *Color Property* is set to *Black*.

23. Assign each of the first seven colors a lineweight (ranging from 0.1000mm to 1.0000mm). See Figure 10-1.8 for an example; also see the *TIPS* below:

     TIP #1: *Divide 1mm by seven and pick the closest lineweight available in the list for each of the 7 colors.*

     TIP #2: *On a separate piece of paper, write down the color number and then the lineweight you assigned to that color; this list will be useful shortly.*

     TIP #3: *If you prefer, you can use the color/lineweight settings shown in Figure 10-1.9 rather than coming up with your own. This is not the "standard" by any means, but is arranged so the "brighter" lines are heavier lineweights and the "dimmer" lines are lighter lineweights (based on a black drawing area background).*

24. Assign each of the last six colors (250-255) the lineweight **0.1500mm**; leave the *Color* property set to **Use Object Color**.

TIP: When you set a Layer's color to 250-255, the objects on those Layers will print in five shades of gray (depending on which of the five colors are used). This is used for building lines that are very far back in the elevation/ or existing. Another use would be for a patch pattern that represents brick coursing (which are lines that are close together and can be overpowering if not printed with grayscale lines). One more use might be for a solid hatch that might indicate circulation (i.e., hallways) or sidewalks and driveways.

FIGURE 10-1.8
Plot Style Table Editor; plot style "Color 5" selected

25. Click **Save & Close** to apply these changes to your *Plot Style Table* (Figure 10-1.8).

26. Click **OK** to close *Page Setup* and then **Close** to exit the *Page Setup Manager*.

Now in any drawing file, when your *Plot Style Table* is selected in *Page Setup*, any entity that is Color 5 (*Blue*) will print as a fairly light line (0.1000mm) using the example in Figure 10-1.8.

Once you create a standard, and use it for a while, you will instinctively know what color equals which lineweight.

27. **Open** the ***Layer Properties*** palette.

28. Adjust the **Color** for each *Layer* (Figure 10-1.9).

> ***TIP:*** *Based on your Plot Style Table, each color now corresponds to a particular lineweight.*

When you are finished, every *Layer* should be assigned a color ranging from 1 to 7; you should never use any other colors (except the "shade" colors discussed above) as they will print with unexpected results.

29. **Save** your **Flr-2** drawing.

30. **Make the same changes to your other floor plans**.

AutoCAD's seven named colors:

FYI: *AutoCAD has 255 standard colors (AutoCAD Color Index – ACI), of which the first seven also have names (see the chart below).*

AutoCAD also has a *True Color* system which allows for millions of colors. *True Colors* are great for presentation drawings. They are not controlled by a *Plot Style Table*; they will always print in the color specified (only on a color printer, of course).

Color number	Color name
1	Red
2	Yellow
3	Green
4	Cyan
5	Blue
6	Magenta
7	White (or black when background is white)

Backup Your Plot Style Table:

You should backup your Plot Style Table to a CD or Thumb Drive because you will need it on each computer you print from to get accurate lineweights. You also need to send this file with the drawings, if providing consultants or owners with the drawing files.

31. Backup your Plot Style Table file; this file is located at (see *TIP* below, if you have problems here):

    Windows XP: C:\Documents and Settings*your_login_name*\Application Data\Autodesk\AutoCAD 2014 - English\R19.1\enu\Plotters\Plot Styles

    WindowsWindows 7:
    C:\Users*your_login_name*\AppData\Roaming\Autodesk\AutoCAD 2014 - English\R19.1\enu\Plotters\Plot Styles

    TIP: Substitute your login name for the "your_login_name" placeholder above. Also, the Application Data folder may be hidden; see your system administrator for help.

    TIP: If the Application Data folder is not visible, go to Windows Explorer, select Organize → Folder and search options → View (tab) and check Show hidden files, folders and drives.

    FYI: In an office environment, these files can be shared on a network. This ensures everyone is using the same lineweight standards.

    FYI: Windows Vista is not supported.

Create a Lineweight Reference Chart:

Until you learn which color equals which lineweight, you will benefit from using a reference chart. If you want a line to be thin, you look at the chart, find a thin line you like and then look at what color is associated with that lineweight; then you modify the line to that color (by changing or creating *Layers*).

32. In a new drawing named **Reference Chart.dwg**, create the drawing shown in **Figure 10-1.9**.

    a. Adjust drawing to match your color/lineweight settings.

    b. Make all the text set to one of your medium lineweights.

    c. Print the chart, making sure your *Plot Style Table* is selected in *Page Setup*.

    d. The lines should be arranged from heaviest to lightest.

    e. Draw everything within a 6"x6" square.

STANDARD LINEWEIGHT CHART

COLOR	EXAMPLE LINE WEIGHTS
magenta	——————————— 1.0000mm
white	——————————— 0.8000mm
green	——————————— 0.6000mm
cyan	——————————— 0.5000mm
yellow	——————————— 0,3500mm
red	——————————— 0.1800mm
blue	——————————— 0.1000mm

SOLID FILLS

250	251	252
253	254	255

FIGURE 10-1.9 Lineweight reference chart

33. **Save** and **Close** any open drawings.

Summary:

Most people still use the *Color Dependent Plot Style Tables* because, no matter what Drawing/Layer a line is in/on, if it is green (for example), it will always print the same lineweight. Whereas the *Named Plot Style Table* requires extra settings in the *Layer Properties Manager* and entities that are green (again, for example) could be different lineweights, even in the same drawing. The visual color/lineweight relationship is very useful, especially when multiple people (or multiple firms) are working on the same set of drawings.

Exercise 10-2:
Plotting: Digital Set

Introduction:

In this exercise you will learn how to quickly and easily publish your entire set of drawings to a single file that can be viewed by downloading a free viewer from Autodesk.

The file is referred to as a *Design Web Format* (DWF). A DWF is smaller than the drawing file because it is only for viewing and printing, not editing. It can even be password protected. In fact, one of the best things about DWF's is that they cannot be edited. Thus, you can share the DWF set with a client or contractor and not have to worry about them accidentally (or intentionally) changing the drawings. You can also create a PDF, which most everyone can open and view as Adobe Reader is a free download and used by many.

The first thing you need to do is adjust the *Page Setup* in each *Sheet* drawing, so the *Sheets* are ready to plot.

1. **Open** your sheet **A1 – Basement Floor Plan** from the *Sheet Set Manager*. (See Exercise 8-2 for instruction on this.)

2. Right-click on the **A1 Basement Floor Plan** layout tab (Figure 10-2.1).

FIGURE 10-2.1 A1 – Basement Floor Plan; right-click on layout tab

3. Select **Page Setup Manager...** from the pop-up menu.

4. With ***A1 Basement Floor Plan*** selected, click the **Modify...** button (Figure 10-2.2).

FIGURE 10-2.2
Page Setup Manager; modify the default layout settings

5.   Select your *Plot Style Table* (created in Exercise 10-1): *yourname*.ctb (Figure 10-2.3).

6.   **Check** the "*Display Plot Styles*" option just below the selected *Plot Style Table* (Figure 10-2.3).

> *TIP: Selecting "Display Plot Styles" will cause AutoCAD to display your Layout View in black and white rather than color. This is more of a "what you see is what you get" type of view – even more so when LWT is toggled on from the Status Bar.*

NOTE: The lines are only black if you are using colors 1-7.

FIGURE 10-2.3
Page Setup – Basement Floor Plan; select your plot style table

7. Click **OK** and then **Close** to exit the open dialog boxes.

8. **Save** and **Close** the *Basement Floor Plan* sheet drawing.

9. Now open each sheet in your *Sheet Set* and make the same modification; **Save** and **Close** each drawing when done.

Now you will look at the *Options* related to *Publishing* "sheets" from the *Sheet Set Manager*.

10. If not open, **Open** your *Sheet Set Data* file. (See Exercise 8-2.)

11. Right-click on the *Sheet Set* project title (*Stine Residence* in this example). (See Figure 10-2.4.)

12. Select **Publish** → **Sheet Set Publish Options…**(Figure 10-2.4).

FIGURE 10-2.4
Sheet Set Manager; right-click menu for sheet set label
(Stine Residence in this example)

Take a minute to notice the various options available for publishing sheets from the *Sheet Set Manager*; see Figure 10-2.5.

♦ **Default output directory (plot-to-file)**
Here you can specify a default location to save a file to.

♦ **General DWF/PDF options**
When **Single-sheet** is selected, each sheet is created as a separate DWF/PDF file. When **Multi-sheet** is selected, all sheets are published into one DWF/PDF file.

♦ **Naming**
Here you can specify the file name or have AutoCAD prompt you for the name each time you publish; this option is only available if **Multi-sheet** is selected above.

♦ **Password Protection**
Allows you to assign a password to the DWF file. When a password is assigned, you, and anyone you send the file to, will need to know the password to view the DWF file.

♦ **Layer information**
Allows you to include the AutoCAD layers in the DWF file. With this option selected, you can control *Layer* visibility in the DWF/PDF file viewer; example, turn off dimensions and notes to print a clean plan. *Adobe Reader* can control the visibility of Layers when they are present in a PDF.

♦ **3D DWF**
Controls settings related to 3D drawing information.

> *FYI: You are only drawing 2D information in this book.*

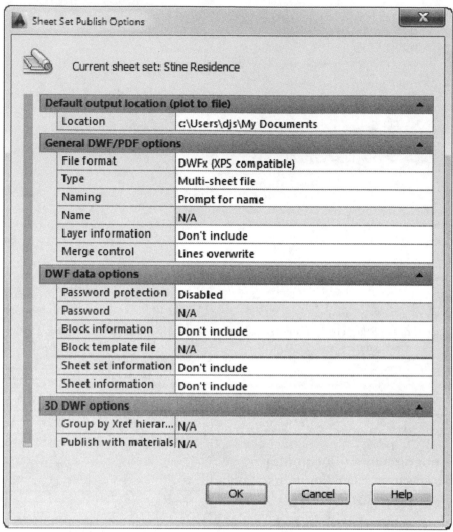

FIGURE 10-2.5
Sheet Set Publish Options – default settings shown

13. Accept the default options and click **OK**.

14. Right-click on the *Sheet Set* project title again (*Stine Residence* in this example). See Figure 10-2.4.

15. **Publish → Publish to DWFx** (Figure 10-2.4).

You are now prompted to specify the name and location for the DWF file. Notice, though, that the default location is "Documents", which is the specified folder in the *Publish Options* dialog.

AutoCAD suggests the *Sheet Set* project name for the file name; you will accept that name next.

16. Browse to your project folder and accept the suggested file name and click **Select** to start the publishing process (Figure 10-2.6).

FIGURE 10-2.6
Select DWF File dialog– specify DWF file name and location

AutoCAD now begins to Publish each drawing to the DWF file you specified. The *Publish* routine runs in the background so you can continue to work. Depending on your computer speed, a set this size might take 5 – 15 minutes. AutoCAD has to open each file and plot it.

AutoCAD provides a small "plotter" icon on the right-hand side of the *Status Bar*. You can hover your cursor over this icon to see a tooltip that displays the status of the background *Publish* project (Figure 10-2.7).

FIGURE 10-2.7
Plot and Publish Status Icon
Hover cursor over icon to display status tooltip.

When the publishing process is complete, a balloon message will be displayed indicating such (Figure 10-2.8), and also provides a link to a report. You will take a quick peek at the report before viewing the DWF file.

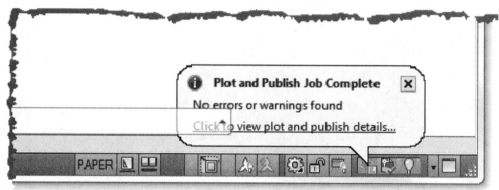

FIGURE 10-2.8
Plot and Publish Status Icon; Balloon notification that job is complete.

17. Click on the link "*Click to view plot and publish details…*" in the *Plot and Publish* balloon notification message (Figure10-2.8).

Notice the report lists the date, number of sheets, the location of each plotted file and the location of the DWF file (Figure 10-2.9).

18. Click **Close** to close the *Plot and Publish* window.

FIGURE 10-2.9
Plot and Publish Details; report on job just completed

Downloading the Autodesk DWF Viewer:

If you have a previous version of AutoCAD, such as 2012 or 2013, you will likely already have *Autodesk Design Review* installed on your computer. This software is no longer installed by default with AutoCAD. However, the software can still be installed separately.

If you will be sharing your DWF files with someone that does not have a *DWF Viewer* (**NOTE:** *AutoCAD cannot open DWF files directly*) installed on his or her computer, you can give them instructions on downloading the free program from Autodesk's website.

Using an internet browser, such as *Microsoft Internet Explorer*, go to **http://usa.autodesk.com/design-review**. Next, click on the **Downloads and Plug-ins** link.

As mentioned in chapter 1, Autodesk is developing many Clod-based tools. These include DWG and DWF viewers. You can view these files on your tablet or smart phone.

Viewing the DWF File:

Next you will view the DWF file using Autodesk *Design Review*. You can view this file by double-clicking the file in *Windows Explorer*, or you can access the file from the **Plot and Publish** icon.

19. The next several steps require *Autodesk Design Review* be installed on your computer. If you do not have it, download it and install it. If you are not able to install it, skip to the next exercise.

20. Right-click on the **Plot and Publish** icon on the right side of the *Status Bar*.

21. Select **View Plotted File...** from the pop-up menu (Figure 10-2.10).

FIGURE 10-2.10
Plot and Publish Icon Menu; right-click on icon to see menu

A totally separate program (*Autodesk Design Review*) now opens with the DWF project you just created (Figure 10-2.11); this program is typically installed with AutoCAD – it is also a free download.

The *Viewer* allows you to zoom, pan and print the sheets in the multi-sheet DWF file.

FIGURE 10-2.11
Autodesk DWF Viewer; your residential project loaded

You can view the various sheets in the DWF file by either clicking on one of the *Thumbnail* images on the left or by clicking the right/left arrows on the toolbar (at the bottom).

A DWF file is still a vector based file, so like the DWG file, you can zoom in really far and not see any pixilation of the image. These drawings also have all your lineweights assigned in them so your drawings will print accurately.

Next you will navigate to another sheet and zoom in to see the drawing's lineweights.

22. Scroll down in the *Thumbnails* pane until you see your **A6 Exterior Elevations** sheet.

23. Click on the **A6 Thumbnail** image to select it.

24. Using your wheel mouse (or the Zoom icon), **Zoom In** on the elevation as shown in Figure 10-2.12.

FIGURE 10-2.12
Autodesk DWF Viewer; sheet A6 – Exterior Elevations displayed

NOTE: In Figure 10-2.12, various lineweights can be seen in the elevation drawing.

Try repeating this process to create a PDF file.

Linking Feature in the Multi-Sheet DWF File:

Another great feature associated with *Sheet Sets* and *Multi-sheet DWF* files is the hyperlinking embedded in the *Sheet List* and *Callout Bubbles*.

25. In your DWF file, switch back to the *Title Sheet* and zoom in on the *Sheet List*.

26. Hover your cursor over the "A2 – First Floor Plan" text to see the pop-up tooltip (Figure 10-2.13).

The pop-up tooltip displayed in Figure 10-2.13 indicates you can follow a link by CTRL + clicking the text. You will try this next.

SHEET INDEX	
Sheet Number	Sheet Title
A0	Title Sheet
A1	Basement Floor Plan
A2	First Floor Plan
A3	Second Floor Plan
A4	Exterior Elevations
A5	Exterior
A6	EXTERIOR

A2 First Floor Plan, CTRL + click to follow link

Hover cursor over "First Floor Plan" text

FIGURE 10-2.13
Multi-sheet DWF file; hyper linked text in Sheet List

27. While pressing the Ctrl key, click the "**First Floor Plan**" text in the *Sheet List Table* location on the *Title Sheet*.

As you can see, this is an easy way for you or a client to navigate a set of drawings (Figure 10-2.14).

FIGURE 10-2.14
Multi-sheet DWF file; view displayed by clicking hyper-linked sheet index on title sheet

DWF files do not typically take up a lot of disk space. The DWF file just created should only be about 1MB; you can verify this with *Windows Explorer*. Given the file's small size, it can easily be emailed or loaded on a web site.

The *Viewer's Print* dialog (Figure 10-2.15) allows you to print one sheet of the entire set to *Scale* on 24″x36″ paper or *Fit to page* on 8½″ x 11″paper as you can see in Figure 10-2.15.

> **FYI:** *If you plan to create a DWF file on a project, you can print your hard copy set(s) from this DWF file, eliminating the need to complete the steps outlined in the next section (10-3), which shows how to print directly to the plotter rather than to a DWF file.*

FIGURE 10-2.15
Autodesk DWF Viewer; print dialog box

28. **Save** and **Close** all files and programs to complete this exercise.

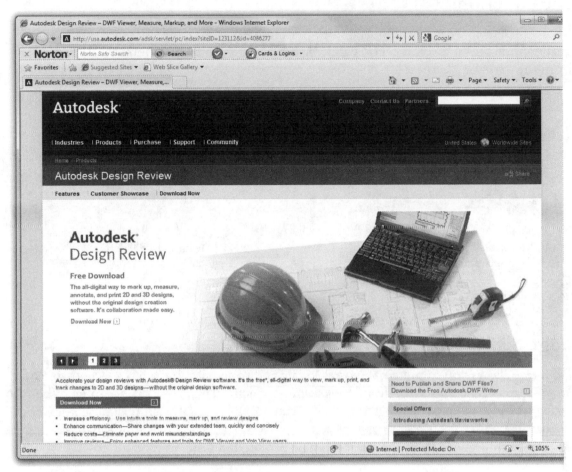

FIGURE 10-2.16
Autodesk Web Site; DWF Design Review page

Exercise 10-3:
Plotting: Hardcopy Set

Introduction:

In this final exercise you will look at a few settings that you should be aware of to create high quality print-outs (i.e., plots). You will look at plotting both from an individual sheet and from the *Sheet Set Manager*.

Xerox 8850 Digital Solution
High speed B/W plotter + scanner

HP Designjet 1000 series
High quality color and B/W plotter

Page Setup Settings for Your Layout View:

Page Setup allows you to pre-set things like scale and paper size. Each tab has its own *Page Setup* settings. The *Page Setup* dialog looks almost exactly like the *Plot* dialog. In fact, the *Plot* dialog box gets its initial settings from the current *Page Setup* settings. Again, each drawing file has its own *Page Setup* settings for each *Layout View* tab; this saves time when plotting because each drawing/*Layout View* tab can be pre-set and ready to plot.

1. **Open** your **A3 – Second Floor Plan**sheet from the *Sheet Set Manager. (This can be opened directly with the Open command as well.)*

2. Right-click on the *Layout View* tab and select **Page Setup Manager...**

You are now in the *Page Setup Manager*. Here you can create/modify named *Page Setups*, apply one to the current *Layout* and *Import Page Setups* from other drawings. You will modify an existing *Page Setup*.

3. Select **D Size – Full Scale** from the list and then select **Modify...** (Figure 10-3.1).

FIGURE 10-3.1
Page Setup Manager; Page Setup "D Size – Full Scale" selected

You are now in the *Page Setup* for "D Size – Full Scale".

4. Note and adjust the following settings (**Figure 10-3.2**):

    a. *Select your plotter.* In this case, select one that is capable of printing a large sheet like 24"x36".

    b. Make sure your *Plot Style Table* is selected, **Stine.ctb** in this example.

    c. Check the box next to **Display plot styles**.

    FYI: This setting will make the on-screen display look more like the plotted version of your drawing. (You can also click the LWT toggle on the Status Bar to see the lineweights on-screen as well.)

    d. Check the box next to **Scale Lineweights**.

    FYI: If the drawing is printed half-scale, for example, the lineweights are adjusted.

FIGURE 10-3.2
Page Setup; "D Size – Full Scale" modifications to be made

    e. Note these settings as well; they should be set already as they are the default (Figure 10-3.2).

        i. The paper size is set to **24″x36″**.

        FYI: This setting controls the size of paper you see on the screen in each Layout View.

        ii. The *Plot Area* is set to **Layout.**
            1. *Layout* = *the paper size selected*
            2. *Extents* = *all lines selected to print*
            3. *Display* = *only lines displayed on screen*
            4. *Window* = *user selected area to be plotted*

        iii. The *Plot Scale* is set to **1:1.**

        FYI: The 1:1 scale means the 24″x36″ sheet will print 24″x36″.

        iv. **Plot with plot styles** is checked.

    5. Select **OK** to close the *Page Setup* dialog box.

6. Click **Close** to exit the *Page Setup Manager*.

Next you will explore the *Plot* dialog box.

7. From the *Quick Access* toolbar, select **Plot...**

Notice the similarities between the *Plot* dialog and the *Page Setup* dialog (Figure 10-3.3). You should also notice that the settings previously set in *Page Setup* are NOT the defaults in the *Plot* dialog. Your modifications are not the default settings because you did not set the "D Size – Full Scale" page setup to be current (see Figure10-3.1). However, you can select this on the fly in the plot dialog.

Additional settings on the *Plot* dialog box (vs. *Page Setup*):

♦   **Plot to File**: Creates a "plot file" that can be copied to disk and brought to a print shop (if you don't have a large format or color printer). You need to call the print shop and ask which printer driver to use because the "plot file" is printer specific.

♦   **Number of copies**: You can specify the number of prints here.

FIGURE 10-3.3
Plot dialog; initial settings; no page setup selected

8. Select **D Size – Full Scale** from the *Page Setup* drop-down list near the top of the dialogbox (Figure 10-3.3).

Notice how all your settings change to correspond with the selected *Page Setup* (Figure 10-3.4 – fully expanded dialog view).

FIGURE 10-3.4
Plot dialog; page setup applied

If you click the arrow pointing to the right (see Figure 10-3.3) in the lower right corner, you will see additional plot settings. These settings are less used, so they are hidden so the user is not bothered by too much information (compare Figure 10-3.4).

Next you will print your floor plan sheet. If you do not have access to a large format plotter, you can skip ahead to the discussion on how to print sets via the *Sheet Set Manager*.

9.   Click **OK** to plot the floor plan drawing (if you have access to a large format plotter).

You should now have a 24″x36″ plotted sheet. You should also be able to see lineweights in your drawing.

10. Plot the basement and first floor plans per the previous steps.

Plotting Sets Using the Sheet Set Manager:

The previous steps are useful when printing one or two sheets. However, on large projects with 20-30 sheets it would take a lot of your time to open and plot each sheet. Large commercial projects can have hundreds of sheets.

The *Sheet Set Manager* allows you to print the entire set of drawings at one time. When printing large sets, it can still take quite a while. However, anytime the computer can do the work and save the user time is well worth the effort. Also, the plotting occurs in the "background", which means you can still work in AutoCAD during this process.

11. Open your *Sheet Set* via the *Sheet Set Manager* (see Exercise 8-2 for information on how to do this).

Similar to the first part of this exercise, the *Sheet Set* has a *Page Setup Manager*. Here you can prepare a *Page Setup* that can be used for all *Sheets* in your *Sheet Set*; this is called a *Page Setup Override*. The *Override* option ensures consistency and eliminates the need to open every drawing if a *Page Setup* change is required.

12. Right-click on the *Sheet Set* title (*Stine Residence* in the book example).

13. Select **Publish → Manage Page Setups...** from the pop-up menu (Figure 10-3.5).

FIGURE 10-3.5
Sheet Set Manager; Select Manage Page Setups...

You are now in the *Page Setup Manager* (Figure 10-3.6). This is almost identical to the one previously discussed (see Figure10-3.1). The difference is this *Page Setup Manager* applies to the current *Sheet Set* (*Stine Residence*) whereas the previous one applied to the *Layout View* (*Paper Space*) in that drawing. Notice one reads *"Current sheet set"* and the other *"Current layout"* at the top of the dialog box.

FIGURE 10-3.6
Page Setup Manager; D Size – Full Scale selected

14. Select the *Page Setup* named "**D Size – Full Scale**".

15. Click the **Modify...** button.

You are now able to adjust the settings for the named *Page Setup*. Again, this is identical to what you just did a few pages ago (the difference is the icon next to the page setup name).

16. Make the changes shown in **Figure 10-3.7**.

17. Click **OK** and **Close** to save the changes and exit the *Page Setup Manager*.

   TIP: Select a plotter you have access to.

FIGURE 10-3.7
Page Setup; adjust settings for the selected named page setup

Publishing the Sheet Set:

Looking back at Figure 10-3.5, notice two things: under the *Publish* fly-out menu, you have **Publish to Plotter** and **Publish using Page Setup Override**. The former uses the current *Page Setup* settings in the *Sheet* file, whereas the later uses the specified *Page Setup* from the *Sheet Set Manager*. You will try the **Override** option next.

18. Right-click on the sheet set title and select: **Publish → Publish using Page Setup Override** (Figure 10-3.5).

    FYI: *This step will actually print sheets if you have a plotter. From the Override fly-out, select **D Size – Full Scale**.*

The plotting process now begins in the background. You will notice the **Plot and Publish** icon on the right side of the *Status Bar*.

    FYI: *You can right-click on it to cancel the current print job at any time.*

Drawings should start printing shortly after the process begins!

Publishing a Small Review Set:

The last variation on plotting will be to print out a small, not to scale, review set. This time you will create a new *Page Setup* for use in the *Page Setup Manager*.

19. From the *Sheet Set's Page Setup Manager* select **New…** (Figure 10-3.6).

20. Enter "**A Size – Scaled to Fit**" for the name and select **D Size – Full Scale** from the *Start with* area (Figure 10-3.8).

FIGURE 10-3.8
New Page Setup; creating a new page setup

21. Select **OK** to continue.

22. Make the changes shown in Figure 10-3.9.

> *FYI: Notice the "What to plot" is set to Extents; this is a work-around necessary to plot a layout setup for 24x36 onto an 8½ x 11 piece of paper.*

> *TIP: If you have access to a printer that has 11″x17″ paper, you can select that paper size; sets are a little larger and easier to read. Also, one nice thing about using 22″ x 34″ sheets (rather than 24″x36″) is that 11″x17″ sets are half-scale which is better than scaled to fit.*

23. Select **Save** and then **Close** to complete the open dialog boxes.

FIGURE 10-3.9
New Page Setup; make changes shown

24. Now, simply *Publish* using a *Page Setup Override* as previously reviewed, selecting the new *Page Setup*: "A Size – Scaled to Fit".

Your drawing will begin to print in a moment.

25. **Save** your drawings and close your sheet set.

You have now completed this book (except for the *Additional Tasks*)! You should possess the fundamental skills required for most tasks necessary to complete a set of residential drawings.

With the solid foundation you have built using this book, you should be able to explore and develop additional commands and techniques on your own. Using the Help system, News Groups and a little "trial and error", you can draw just about anything. **Good luck with your CAD drafting endeavors!**

Self-Exam:

The following questions can be used as a way to check your knowledge of this lesson. The answers can be found at the bottom of this page.

1. You access *Plot Styles* to your plan *Layer Properties Manager*. (T/F)

2. You can specify "number of copies" via *Page Setup*. (T/F)

3. You access page setups via the *Page Setup Manager*. (T/F)

4. What type of *Plot Style Table* associates a lines color with its lineweight?

   _____

5. The *Layout* tab is real-word scale for the paper.(T/F)

Review Questions:

The following questions may be assigned by your instructor as a way to assess your knowledge of this section. Your instructor has the answers to the review questions.

1. The *Callout Bubbles* are placed in the *Resource Drawings*. (T/F)

2. A DWF file is a vector based file like AutoCAD files. (T/F)

3. The LWT button on the *Status Bar* toggles lineweight visibility. (T/F)

4. A DWF file is a little larger than a DWG file. (T/F)

5. You specify which *Plot Style Table* to use in the *Page Setup* dialog. (T/F)

6. In a *Layout* view's *Page Setup*, the plot scale should be set to _____.

7. Autodesk *Design Review* is a free download with which you can view and redline DWF files. (T/F)

8. Which lines should be light gray in a plan drawing?_____

9. You can plot an entire set of drawings from a *Multi-sheet* DWF file. (T/F)

10. You can organize *Sheets* in subsets within the *Sheet Set Manager*. (T/F)

Additional Tasks:

Task 10-1: Apply Lineweights to All Your Drawings
Using the techniques learned in Lesson 10-1, apply lineweights to all your other drawings (or per your instructor's direction), including the exterior elevations, sections and interior elevations.

Task 10-2: Plot All Your Drawings Full Size
Using the techniques learned in Lesson 10-3, plot each of your drawings that have been setup on a sheet. Plot them full size if your plotter supports large format paper.

Task 10-3: Email a DWF File
Create a *Multi-view* DWF file and email it to your instructor or friend and verify that they were able to open it and view the drawings.

Task 10-4: View your files in the Cloud
Log in to your Autodesk 360 account and view your files using the Cloud-based viwers.

Image courtesy of Anderson Architects
Alan H. Anderson, Architect, Duluth, MN

Interior Design, Steven W. Sanborn, A.I.A.,
Santa Rosa, CA

Notes:

Appendix A
Engineering Graphics:

This appendix is meant to compliment the lessons learned in this book. Several exercises are provided to help the student learn to make to most out of both digital and "analog" design techniques and develop a three-dimensional vocabulary.

Appendix A-1:
Introduction

What is Engineering Graphics?

Engineering Graphics is the philosophy and process of describing and documenting three-dimensional objects via 2D drawings. The academic study of this concept is often limited to mechanical parts (e.g., gears, bolts, nuts, etc.). Furthermore, within the mechanical engineering world, many specific standards have been developed to document these mechanical parts so they can be manufactured by machine shops. Many of these standards are not really applicable to architectural design and documentation so they will not be covered in this appendix; rather, just the applicable, fundamental concepts of engineering graphics (related to architecture) will be studied by the reader.

Appendix A-2:
Engineering graphics

The simple object below describes the standard views used to describe the 2D drawings that are created for a 3D object. Looking at the 2D elevations below and then at the 3D object above you should be able to visualize how each represents the object under consideration. Of course things can get more difficult with complex objects.

The exercises on the following pages are provided as a way to help you to think three-dimensionally; for some it just comes naturally and for others it takes a little practice. One thing you will find interesting with the exercises that follow is that totally different looking objects can have identical 2D views (i.e., the linework for the top elevation is exactly the same).

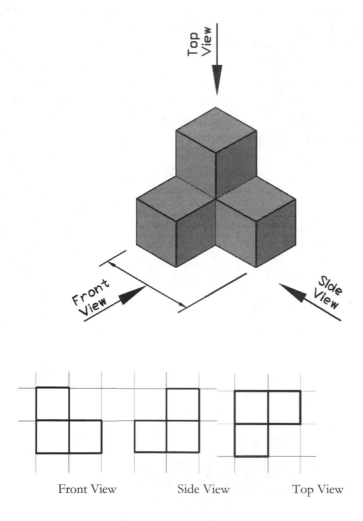

Front View   Side View   Top View

DIRECTIONS: Match the small top, front and side views with the proper isometric view (i.e., the two large views). Write the *view type* (top, front or side) and the *isometric name* that view corresponds to (one example shown on this page). Place a star on duplicate views for both isometric views.

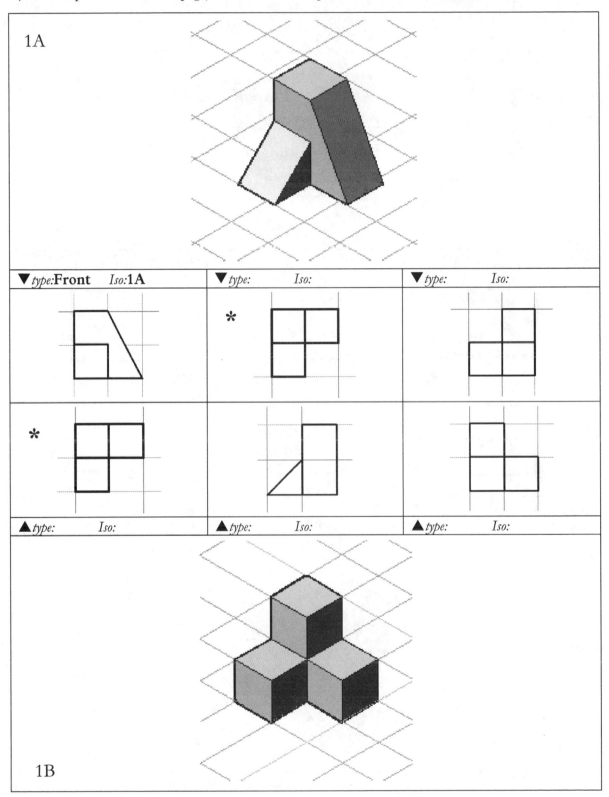

▼ *type:* **Front** *Iso:* **1A**	▼ *type:* *Iso:*	▼ *type:* *Iso:*
	*	
*		
▲ *type:* *Iso:*	▲ *type:* *Iso:*	▲ *type:* *Iso:*

DIRECTIONS: Match the small top, front and side views with the proper isometric view (i.e., the two large views). Write the *view type* (top, front or side) and the *isometric name* that view corresponds to.

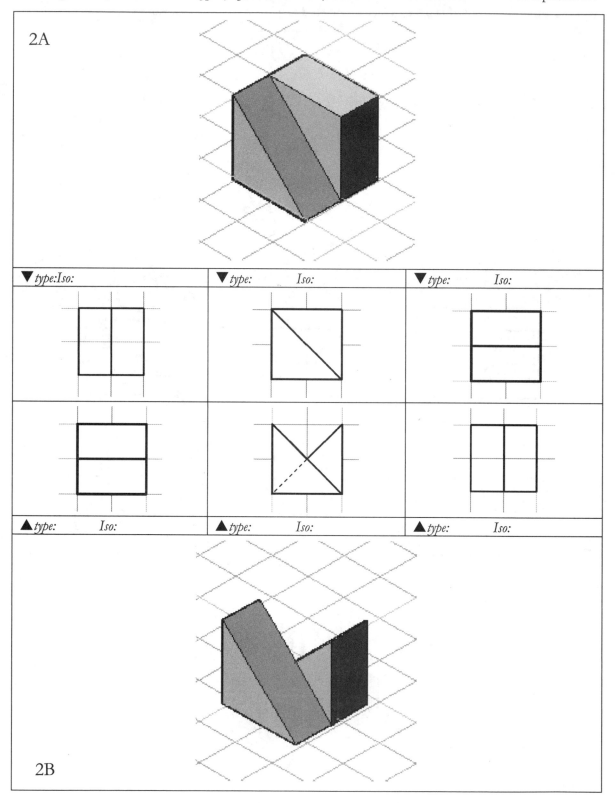

2A

▼ *type: Iso:*   ▼ *type:*   *Iso:*   ▼ *type:*   *Iso:*

▲ *type:*   *Iso:*   ▲ *type:*   *Iso:*   ▲ *type:*   *Iso:*

2B

DIRECTIONS: Match the small top, front and side views with the proper isometric view (i.e., the two large views). Write the *view type* (top, front or side) and the *isometric name* that view corresponds to.

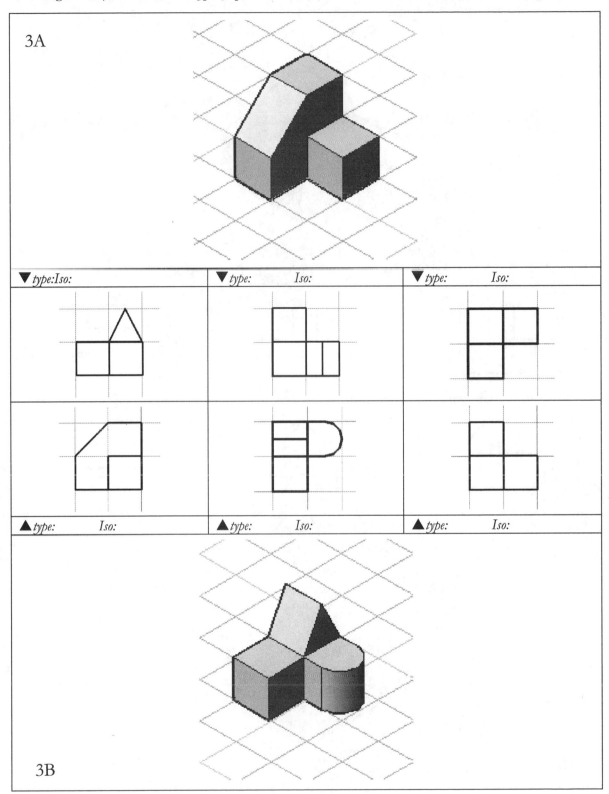

3A

▼ *type:* Iso: ▼ *type:* Iso: ▼ *type:* Iso:

▲ *type:* Iso: ▲ *type:* Iso: ▲ *type:* Iso:

3B

DIRECTIONS: Match the small top, front and side views with the proper isometric view (i.e., the two large views). Write the *view type* (top, front or side) and the *isometric name* that view corresponds to.

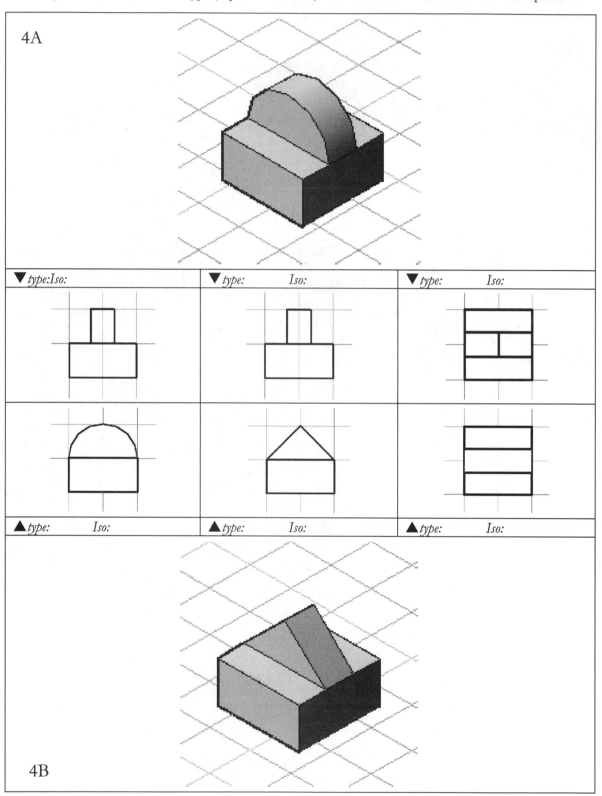

4A

▼ *type:* Iso: ▼ *type:* Iso: ▼ *type:* Iso:

▲ *type:* Iso: ▲ *type:* Iso: ▲ *type:* Iso:

4B

DIRECTIONS: Match the small top, front and side views with the proper isometric view (i.e., the two large views). Write the *view type* (top, front or side) and the *isometric name* that view corresponds to.

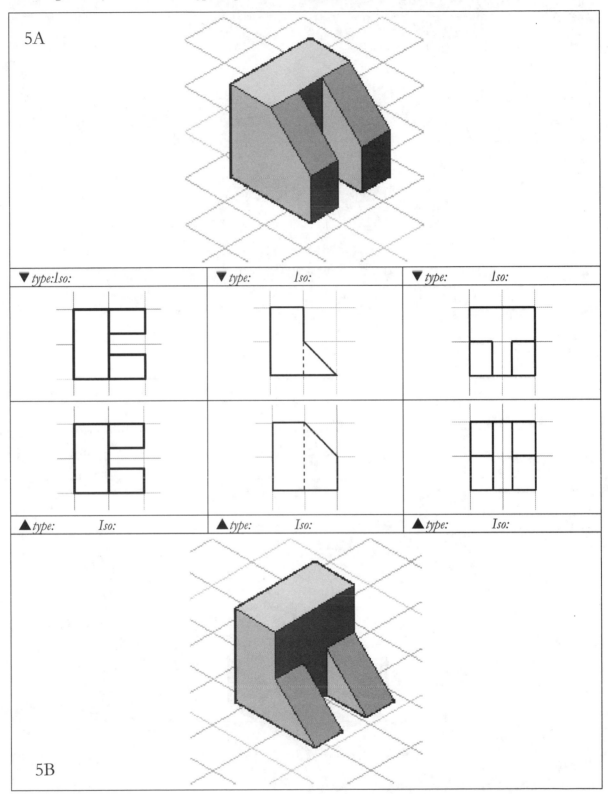

5A

▼ *type:* Iso: ▼ *type:*   Iso: ▼ *type:*   Iso:

▲ *type:*   Iso: ▲ *type:*   Iso: ▲ *type:*   Iso:

5B

DIRECTIONS: Match the small top, front and side views with the proper isometric view (i.e., the two large views). Write the *view type* (top, front or side) and the *isometric name* that view corresponds to.

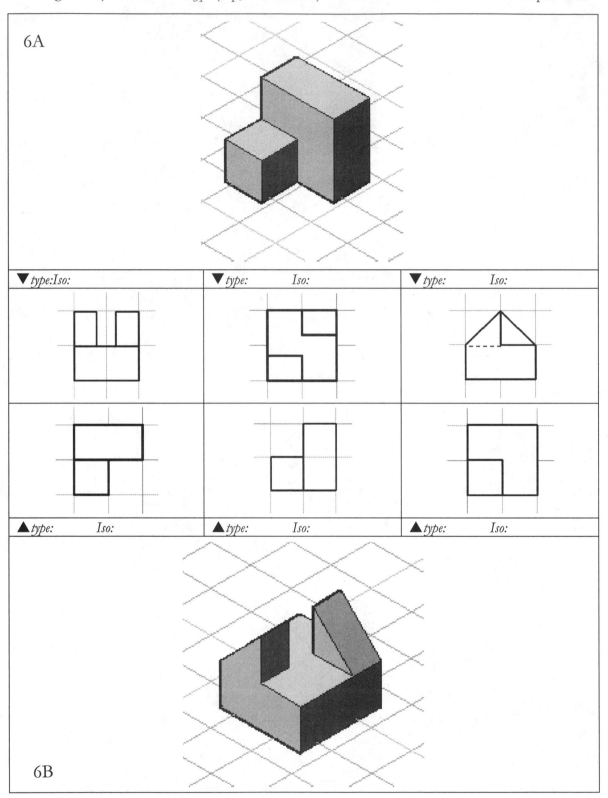

6A

▼ *type: Iso:*   ▼ *type: Iso:*   ▼ *type: Iso:*

▲ *type: Iso:*   ▲ *type: Iso:*   ▲ *type: Iso:*

6B

DIRECTIONS: Match the small top, front and side views with the proper isometric view (i.e., the two large views). Write the *view type* (top, front or side) and the *isometric name* that view corresponds to.

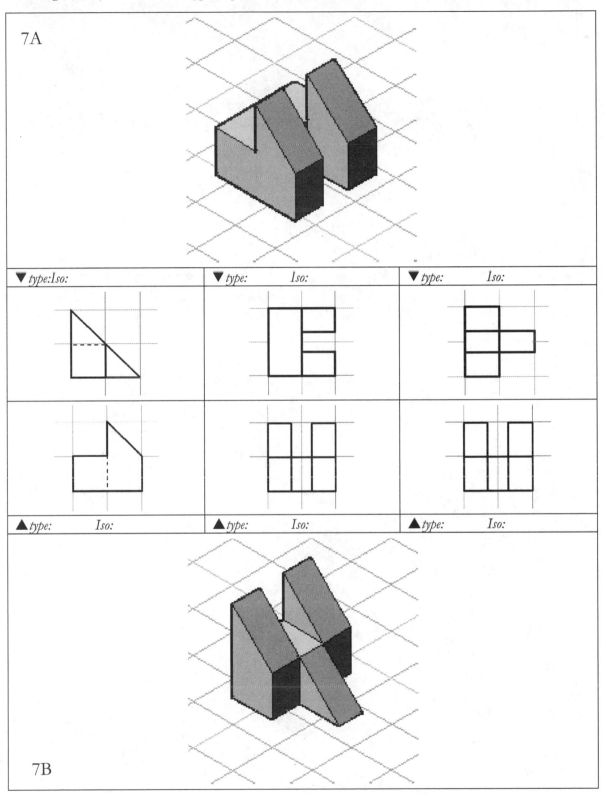

7A

▼ *type:* Iso: ▼ *type:*   Iso: ▼ *type:*   Iso:

▲ *type:*   Iso: ▲ *type:*   Iso: ▲ *type:*   Iso:

7B

DIRECTIONS: Match the small top, front and side views with the proper isometric view (i.e., the two large views). Write the *view type* (top, front or side) and the *isometric name* that view corresponds to.

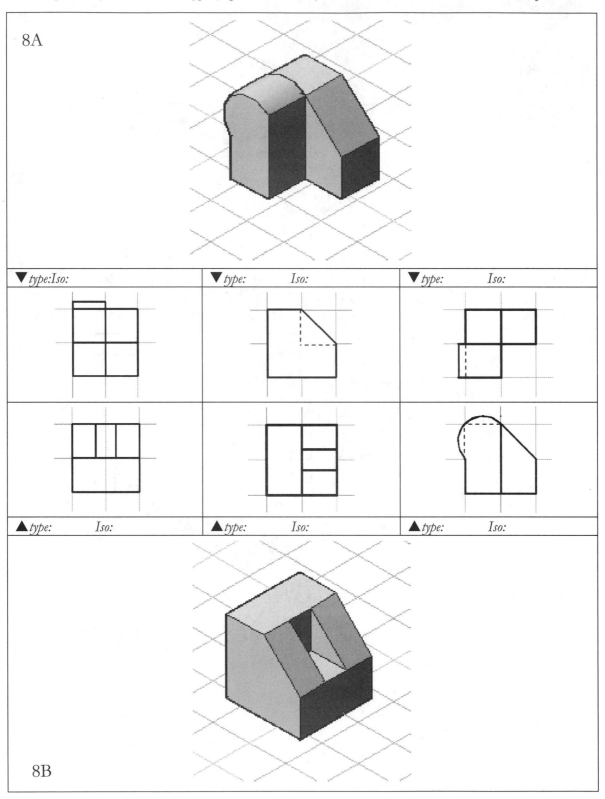

8A

▼ *type:Iso:*   ▼ *type: Iso:*   ▼ *type: Iso:*

▲ *type: Iso:*   ▲ *type: Iso:*   ▲ *type: Iso:*

8B

Appendix A-3:
Orthographic projection

Introduction

In this section of the appendix you will spend some time sketching various building forms. This will give you practice drawing various lines (i.e., weights and styles). The lines drawn will help convey the depth of the image.

Below is an example of a three-dimensional image that will be presented in the subsequent exercises in the chapter. The assignment will be to sketch two-dimensional views of the south and east elevations, plus the roof plan (examples of which can be found on the next page).

Using the Orthographic Projection Method

The most common way to draw two-dimensional views of a 3D object is by using the orthographic projection method. The image above shows an overview of how this method works. The dimensions shown represent the "given" information and the dashed lines show how information from one view can be projected onto another view. The 45 degree line simply represents the mirror plane utilized to project the line around a 90 degree corner. Finally, the dashed lines with arrows show information that can only be derived from another view (at least without having to do any math).

The image in the upper left represents the East Elevation and the one to its right is the south elevation. The lower right image represents the Roof Plan (roof plans are covered in the Roof Study Workbook found on the DVD).

The next page begins a short overview of the process for sketching this assignment.

The first step is to sketch the roof plan. You have all the information you need in the three-dimensional image provided. You should notice that the roof is a simple gable with a smaller cross-gable at the south elevation. Also, even if the dimensions where not provided, you could determine the cross-gable end is not as wide (in plan view) as the main gable end, which is because the ridgelines do not align.

Remember that the intersecting roof surfaces (which are the same slope) form a 45 degree line. Another thing to remember is that *north* should be upward for the roof plan. The last step would be to add the slope arrows.

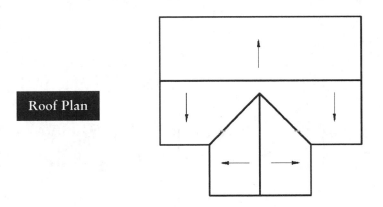

Next, one could begin to sketch either of the required elevations. You will start with the South elevation.

The image on the next page shows a step-by-step on how the South elevation might be drawn. This process is completely manual, but you can derive all the vertical lines by projecting lines up from the roof plan; all of the vertical lines can simply "connect the dots". The only exception is the ridgeline for the main roof; not enough information has been provided to draw that line. This is where Orthographic Projection comes into play. By sketching the East elevation you will establish the ridgeline and then be able to project it back to the South elevation (this requires the floor line of the two elevations to align with each other).

NOTE: Two additional pieces of information, which will be provided for the upcoming exercises, are that all the roof slopes are to be 12/12 (which is a 45 degree line) and the walls are 20'-0" tall.

Sketching the South Elevation
The image above shows a detailed example of how one might sketch the South elevation for the three-dimensional image previously provided. The process is simplified by projecting lines up from the roof plan and using the provided grid (which is 5'x5').

Below is one possible step-by-step example of how one might draw the East elevation. Again, many of these lines can be drawn by projecting lines for the roof plan and the South elevation.

Sketching the East Elevation
The image above shows a detailed example of how one might sketch the East elevation for the three-dimensional image previously provided. Again, one ridgeline is derived by projecting the roof up, at the correct pitch, until it intersects the opposite side. However, the other ridgeline is not possible to locate directly. Information from the South elevation is required to complete this elevation. The final steps are covered next.

Now that you have both the East and South elevations drawn you can use Orthographic Projection to complete both drawings.

It is now possible to project the known ridgeline from the East elevation to the previously unknown ridgeline in the South elevation (and visa versa).

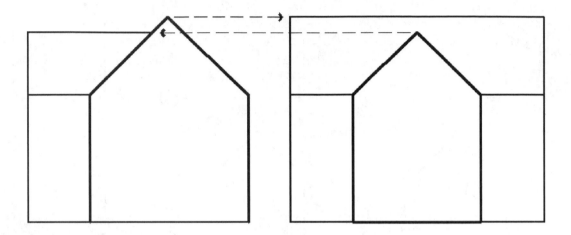

The concept just covered may seem overly simplistic, but the same simple principles are used to develop much more complicated designs!

The reader should take a moment and notice the lineweights in the image above. As previously covered in this workbook, the gable end in the East view has heavier lines so the fact that that part of the building is closer to the viewer is graphically clarified. The same is also true for the South elevation.

The Assignment:

Using the information learned in previous sections, sketch the two-dimensional elevations on the grid provided. Don't forget to add the slope arrows in the roof plan view.

Also, make sure you use the proper lineweights: heavy lines for the perimeter of masses that are closer and lighter lines for items that are "deeper" into the view.

Tear out each page, add your name and date in the space provided and turn them in to your instructor. You might want to make copies of the page for practice and then turn in the final version on the original page from the book.

The first exercise is shown completed so you know what is expected. You may have light reference lines, but must be distinct from the actual drawings being created.

This section will not incorporate any roof overhangs. Additionally, all roof slopes are to be 12/12, which is a 45 degree line in elevation.

Remember that the following is how the view names are related between architectural drawings and mechanical drawings:

> Roof plan = top view
> South elevation = front view
> East elevation = side view

Notes:

Exercise A3-1

Sketch the *roof plan* (top), *South elevation* (front) and *East elevation* (side) of the building shown. Use the provided 5′x5′ grid space. See pages A-12 and 13 for typical information needed to complete this problem. <u>This problem is completed as an example.</u>

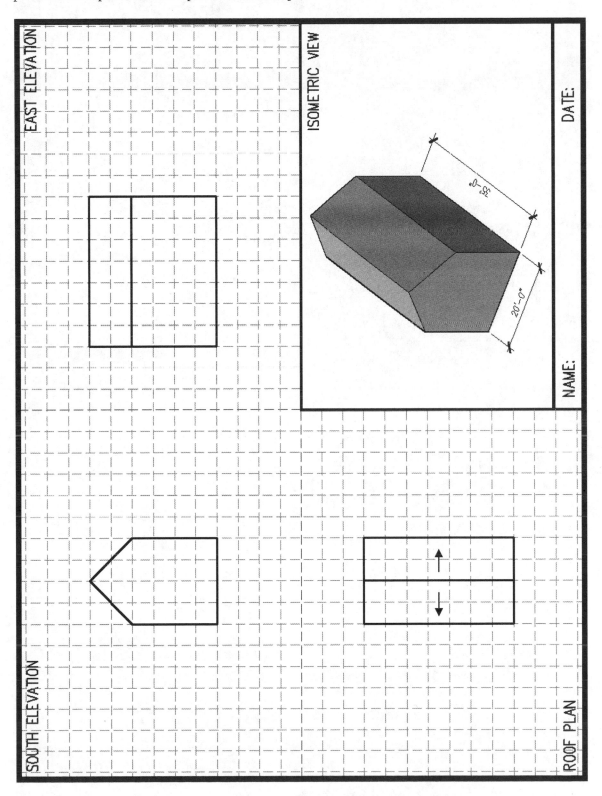

Notes:

Exercise A3-2

Sketch the *roof plan* (top), *South elevation* (front) and *East elevation* (side) of the building shown. Use the provided 5′x5′ grid space. See pages A-12 and 13 for typical information needed to complete this problem.

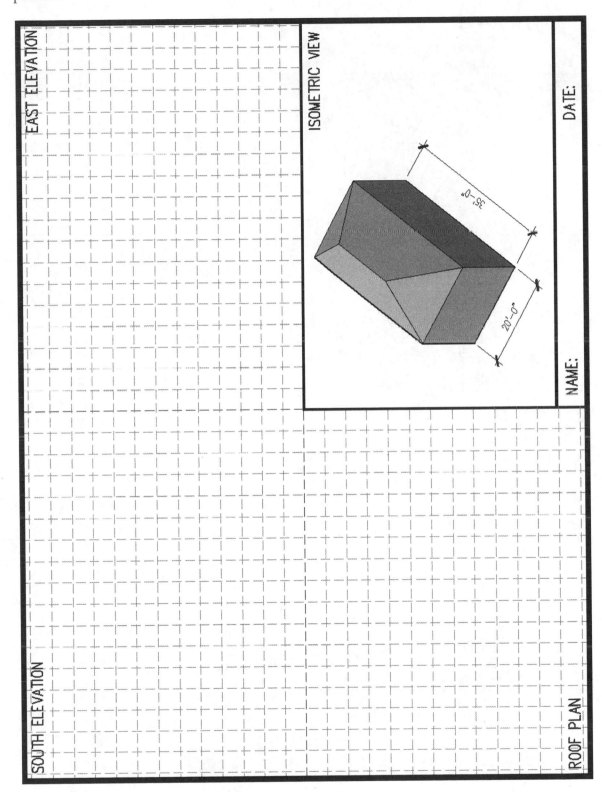

Notes:

Exercise A3-3

Sketch the *roof plan* (top), *South elevation* (front) and *East elevation* (side) of the building shown. Use the provided 5′x5′ grid space. See pages A-12 and 13 for typical information needed to complete this problem.

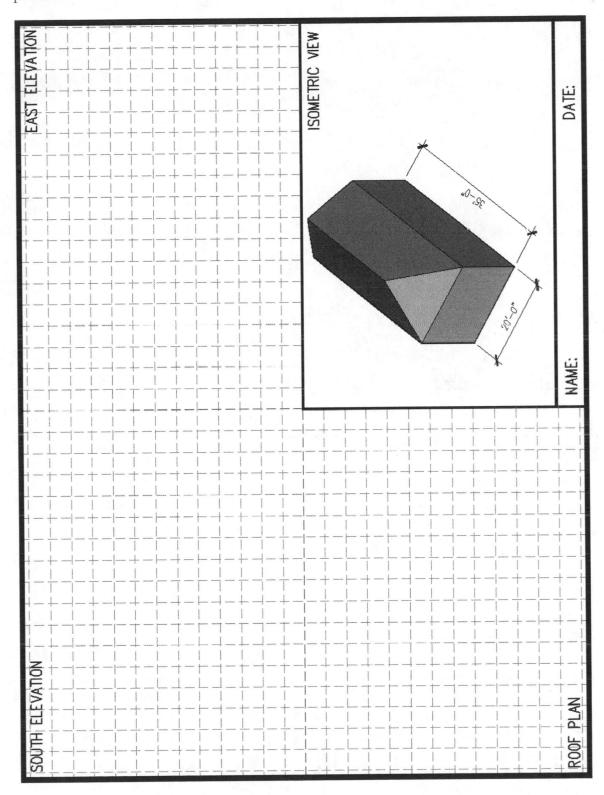

Notes:

Exercise A3-4

Sketch the *roof plan* (top), *South elevation* (front) and *East elevation* (side) of the building shown. Use the provided 5'x5' grid space. See pages A-12 and 13 for typical information needed to complete this problem.

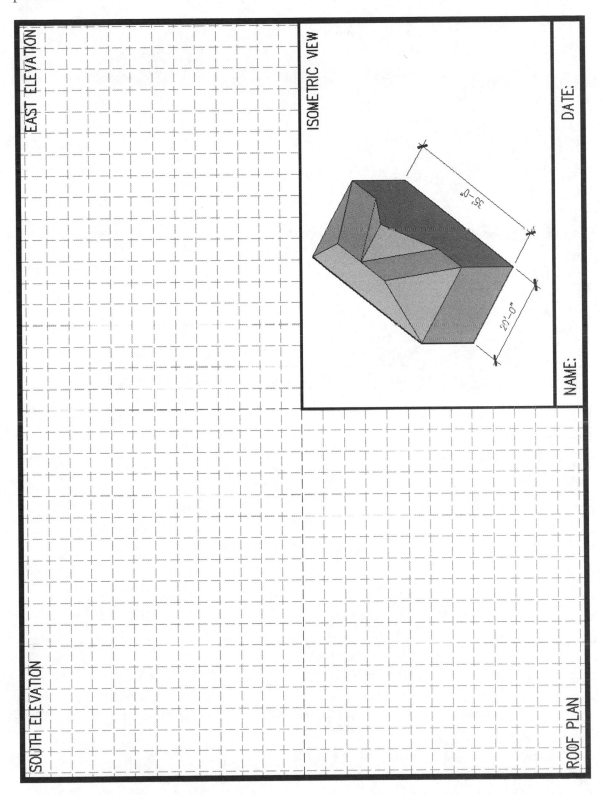

EAST ELEVATION

ISOMETRIC VIEW

SOUTH ELEVATION

ROOF PLAN

DATE:

NAME:

Notes:

Exercise A3-5

Sketch the *roof plan* (top), *South elevation* (front) and *East elevation* (side) of the building shown. Use the provided 5′x5′ grid space. See pages A-12 and 13 for typical information needed to complete this problem.

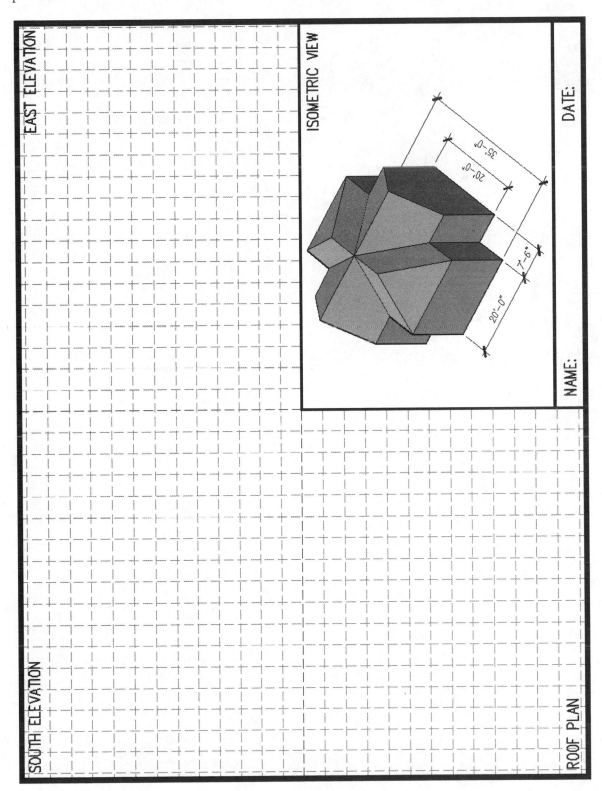

EAST ELEVATION

ISOMETRIC VIEW

DATE:

NAME:

SOUTH ELEVATION

ROOF PLAN

Notes:

Exercise A3-6

Sketch the *roof plan* (top), *South elevation* (front) and *East elevation* (side) of the building shown. Use the provided 5′x5′ grid space. See pages A-12 and 13 for typical information needed to complete this problem.

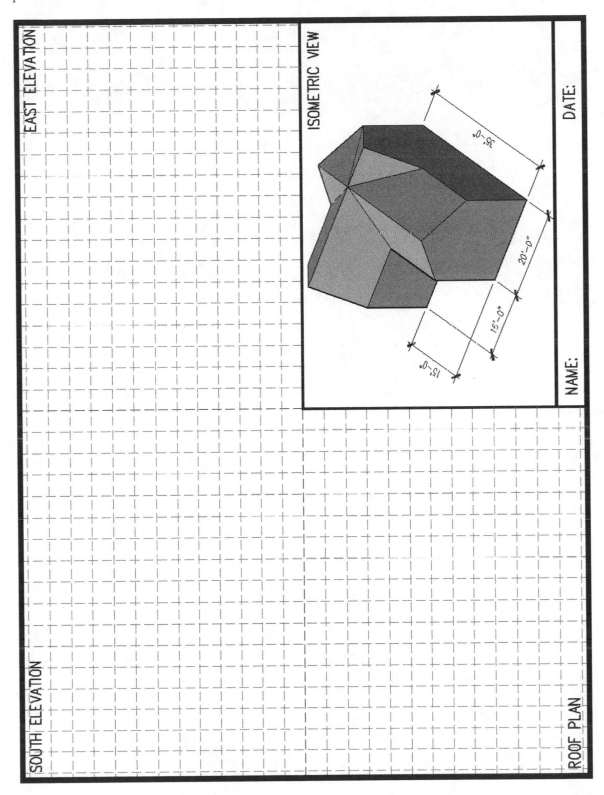

Notes:

Exercise A3-7

Sketch the *roof plan* (top), *South elevation* (front) and *East elevation* (side) of the building shown. Use the provided 5'x5' grid space. See pages A-12 and 13 for typical information needed to complete this problem.

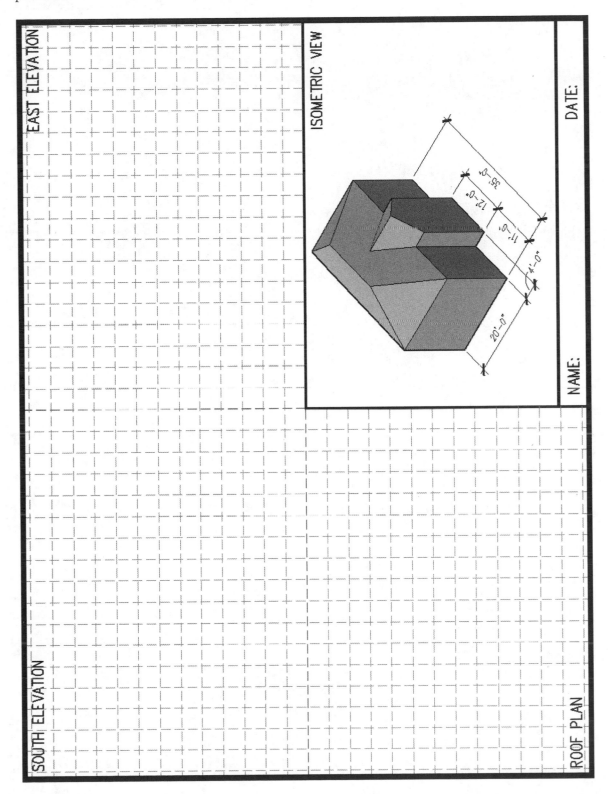

EAST ELEVATION

ISOMETRIC VIEW

SOUTH ELEVATION

ROOF PLAN

NAME:

DATE:

Notes:

Exercise A3-8

Sketch the *roof plan* (top), *South elevation* (front) and *East elevation* (side) of the building shown. Use the provided 5′x5′ grid space. See pages A-12 and 13 for typical information needed to complete this problem.

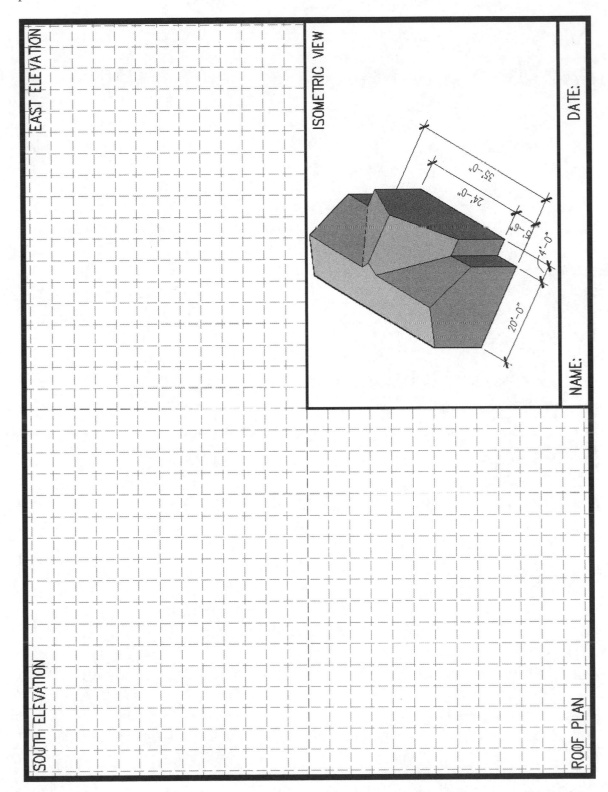

Notes:

Exercise A3-9

Sketch the *roof plan* (top), *South elevation* (front) and *East elevation* (side) of the building shown. Use the provided 5'x5' grid space. See pages A-12 and 13 for typical information needed to complete this problem.

Notes:

Exercise A3-10

Sketch the *roof plan* (top), *South elevation* (front) and *East elevation* (side) of the building shown. Use the provided 5′x5′ grid space. See pages A-12 and 13 for typical information needed to complete this problem.

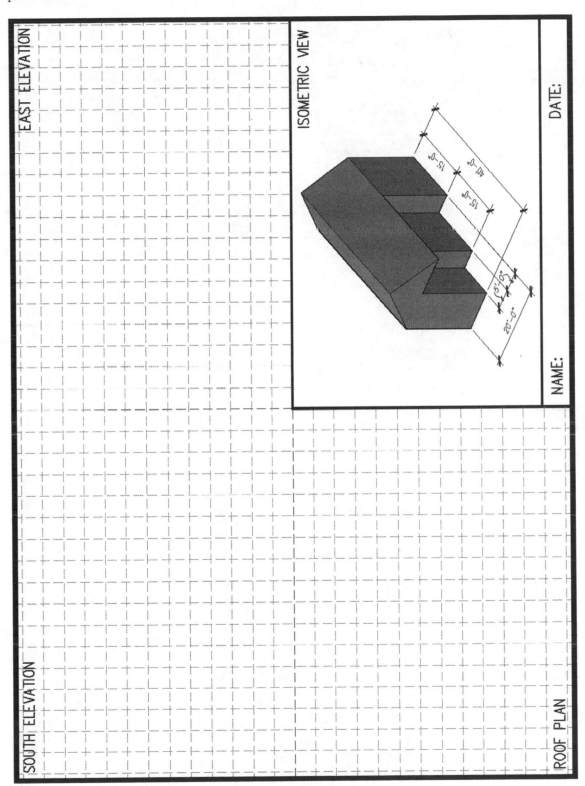

EAST ELEVATION

ISOMETRIC VIEW

DATE:

NAME:

SOUTH ELEVATION

ROOF PLAN

Notes:

Index

Interior elevation created while working through this textbook; see page 7-19. The floor plan is referenced in and clipped so lines could be projected onto the elevation (orthographic projection) and used to locate items…